MW01105407

BREAD FOR THE DAY

DAILY BIBLE READINGS AND PRAYERS

2013

 AUGSBURG FORTRESS

Minneapolis

BREAD FOR THE DAY 2013
Daily Bible Readings and Prayers

Editors: Dennis Bushkofsky, Suzanne Burke
Cover design: Laurie Ingram
Interior design: Jessica Hillstrom
Cover art: Nicholas Wilton
Interior art: Joel Nickel, Margaret Adams Parker, Robyn Sand Anderson, Margaret Bussey, M. Paula Wiggins

Contributors to the weekday prayers: Steve Loy, Las Cruces, New Mexico (January); Dennis Bushkofsky, Arlington Heights, Illinois (February); Benjamin Larzelere III, Santa Fe, New Mexico (March); Jim Drury, Price, Utah (April); Tanya Ferdinandusz, Colombo, Sri Lanka (May); Shelley Cunningham, Rochester, Minnesota (June); Joel Nau, Winterset, Iowa (July); Barb Larsen, Princeton, Minnesota (August); Robin McCullough-Bade, Baton Rouge, Louisiana (September); Melissa Bergstrom, Maple Grove, Minnesota (October); Luke Smetters, Wiota, Wisconsin (November); Kristin Berkey-Abbott, Hollywood, Florida (December)

ACKNOWLEDGMENTS
Scripture quotations are from the New Revised Standard Version Bible © 1989 Division of Christian Education of the National Council of the Churches of Christ in the United States of America. Used by permission.

Hymn suggestions and prayers of the day for Sundays and festivals are from *Evangelical Lutheran Worship*, copyright © 2006 Evangelical Lutheran Church in America.

Materials prepared by the Consultation on Common Texts (CCT), published in *Revised Common Lectionary* © 1992 and *Revised Common Lectionary Daily Readings* © 2005. Used by permission.

Materials prepared by the English Language Liturgical Consultation (ELLC), published in *Praying Together* © 1988: "Blessed are you, Lord" and "My soul proclaims the greatness of the Lord." Used by permission.

ISBN 978-1-4514-0257-5
Manufactured in the U.S.A.

CONTENTS

FOREWORD

Beloved of God,

For generations, the living word has sustained God's people. In times of prosperity and turmoil, joy and sorrow, the church has found hope and consolation in scripture.

The Evangelical Lutheran Church in America has embraced the initiative called Book of Faith. In it we have committed ourselves to deepening our fluency in the first language of faith, holy scripture. *Bread for the Day* is a wonderful resource for your daily encounter with the word. You will be nourished, encouraged, and sustained, as have the saints before you.

As the Conference of Bishops, we invite you to join us, and this whole church in persistent attentiveness to the word. Your faith will be deepened, your witness empowered, and your church enriched. God bless your journey in faith.

Conference of Bishops
Evangelical Lutheran Church in America

For more about Book of Faith, visit www.bookoffaith.org.

INTRODUCTION

Daily prayer is an essential practice for those who seek to hear God's voice and cultivate an inner life. Whether you pray alone or with others, with brevity or sustained meditation, the rhythm of daily prayer reveals the life-sustaining communion to which God invites all human beings. Such prayer is a serene power silently at work, drawing us into the ancient yet vital sources of faith, hope, and love.

The guiding principle of the selection of daily readings in *Bread for the Day* is their relationship to the Sunday readings as presented in the Revised Common Lectionary (a system of readings in widespread use across denominations). The readings are chosen so that the days leading up to Sunday (Thursday through Saturday) prepare for the Sunday readings. The days flowing out from Sunday (Monday through Wednesday) reflect upon the Sunday readings.

How this book is organized

- Each day's page is dated and named in relationship to the church's year. Lesser festivals are listed along with the date as part of the day heading. Commemorations are listed just below in smaller type. Notes on those commemorated can be found on pages 410–418.
- Several verses of one of the appointed scripture texts are printed. The full text citation is provided for those who would like to reflect on the entire text. In addition, two or three additional reading citations with short descriptions are provided.
- Two psalms are appointed for each week; one psalm for Monday through Wednesday and a second psalm for Thursday through Saturday. In this way the days leading up to Sunday or flowing out from Sunday have a distinct

relationship with one another in addition to their relationship with the Sunday readings.

- Following the printed scripture text is a hymn suggestion from *Evangelical Lutheran Worship* and a prayer that incorporates a theme present in one or more of the readings.
- Household prayers and blessings appropriate to the changing seasons are placed throughout the book. Simplified forms of morning and evening prayer, waking prayers, and bedtime prayers, including prayers with children, can be found on pages 424–431.

How to use this book

- Use the weekday readings to prepare for and reflect on the Sunday readings.
- Use the questions printed on page 432 to guide your reflection on the scripture texts.
- Use the resources for household prayer placed throughout the book. See the Contents on pages 3–4 for a complete list.
- Use the page at the beginning of each month to record prayer requests.
- In addition to being used to guide individual prayer, this book may also be used to guide family prayer, prayer in congregational or other settings during the week, prayer with those who are sick or homebound, or with other groups.

Even though Christians gather on the Lord's day, Sunday, for public worship, much of our time is spent in the home. We first learn the words, gestures, and songs of faith in the home. We discover our essential identity as a community of faith and mark significant transitions of life in the home. To surround and infuse the daily rhythm of sleeping and waking, working, resting, and eating with the words and gestures of Christian prayer is to discover the ancient truth of the gospel: the ordinary and the human can reveal the mystery of God and divine grace.

Like planets around the sun, our daily prayer draws us to the Sunday assembly where we gather for the word and the breaking of the bread in the changing seasons of the year. From the Sunday assembly, our daily prayer flows into the week.

PRAYER LIST FOR JANUARY

_____

_____

_____

_____

_____

_____

_____

_____

_____

_____

Blessing for the New Year

O God,
you have been our help in ages past,
our hope for years to come.
As we welcome this new year,
bless us with peace.
Fill our days with the light of Christ
and lead us on the path of life
until we see you in our heavenly home.
You live and reign forever and ever.
Amen.

Tuesday, January 1, 2013

Name of Jesus

Luke 2:15-21

The child is named Jesus

When the angels had left them and gone into heaven, the shepherds said to one another, "Let us go now to Bethlehem and see this thing that has taken place, which the Lord has made known to us." So they went with haste and found Mary and Joseph, and the child lying in the manger. When they saw this, they made known what had been told them about this child; and all who heard it were amazed at what the shepherds told them. But Mary treasured all these words and pondered them in her heart. The shepherds returned, glorifying and praising God for all they had heard and seen, as it had been told them.

After eight days had passed, it was time to circumcise the child; and he was called Jesus, the name given by the angel before he was conceived in the womb. (Luke 2:15-21)

Psalm	Additional Readings	
Psalm 8	Numbers 6:22-27	Galatians 4:4-7
How exalted is your name	*The Aaronic blessing*	*We are no longer slaves*

Hymn: All Hail the Power of Jesus' Name! ELW 634

Eternal Father, you gave your incarnate Son the holy name of Jesus to be a sign of our salvation. Plant in every heart the love of the Savior of the world, Jesus Christ our Lord, who lives and reigns with you and the Holy Spirit, one God, now and forever.

Wednesday, January 2, 2013

Johann Konrad Wilhelm Loehe, renewer of the church, died 1872

Proverbs 1:1-7

Grow in wisdom and knowledge

Let the wise also hear and gain in learning,
  and the discerning acquire skill,
to understand a proverb and a figure,
  the words of the wise and their riddles.

The fear of the LORD is the beginning of knowledge;
  fools despise wisdom and instruction. (Prov. 1:5-7)

Psalm

Psalm 147:12-20
Praising God in Zion

Additional Reading

James 3:13-18
The wisdom from above

Hymn: We Eat the Bread of Teaching, ELW 518

O God, you sent your Son to be our wisdom. Fill our minds with your teaching, shape our lives, and guide our wills that we may serve you in all we do.

Thursday, January 3, 2013

Week of Christmas 1

Psalm 72

Prayers for the king

Give the king your justice, O God,
    and your righteousness to a king's son.
May he judge your people with righteousness,
    and your poor with justice.

May the kings of Tarshish and of the isles
    render him tribute,
may the kings of Sheba and Seba
    bring gifts.
May all kings fall down before him,
    all nations give him service. (Ps. 72:1-2, 10-11)

Additional Readings

Job 42:10-17   Luke 8:16-21
Job's family   *Jesus' family*

Hymn: Angels, from the Realms of Glory, ELW 275

God of the nations, guide those who govern and all who are in positions of authority to work for the welfare of all your people. Let your way of justice and peace be known in all the earth, through Jesus Christ our Lord.

Friday, January 4, 2013

Week of Christmas 1

Isaiah 6:1-5

The Lord high and lofty

In the year that King Uzziah died, I saw the Lord sitting on a throne, high and lofty; and the hem of his robe filled the temple. Seraphs were in attendance above him; each had six wings: with two they covered their faces, and with two they covered their feet, and with two they flew. And one called to another and said:

"Holy, holy, holy is the LORD of hosts;
the whole earth is full of his glory."

The pivots on the thresholds shook at the voices of those who called, and the house filled with smoke. And I said: "Woe is me! I am lost, for I am a man of unclean lips, and I live among a people of unclean lips; yet my eyes have seen the King, the LORD of hosts!" (Isa. 6:1-5)

Psalm
Psalm 72
Prayers for the king

Additional Reading
Acts 7:44-53
Solomon's temple cannot contain God

Hymn: The Bells of Christmas, ELW 298

Holy One, the earth is full of your glory. Grant us vision to see your presence in all of life and to know the wonder and beauty of your majesty in ordinary moments.

Saturday, January 5, 2013

Week of Christmas 1

Jeremiah 31:7-14
Joy as God's scattered flock gathers

Hear the word of the LORD, O nations,
   and declare it in the coastlands far away;
say, "He who scattered Israel will gather him,
   and will keep him as a shepherd a flock."
For the LORD has ransomed Jacob,
   and has redeemed him from hands too strong for him.
They shall come and sing aloud on the height of Zion,
   and they shall be radiant over the goodness of the LORD,
over the grain, the wine, and the oil,
   and over the young of the flock and the herd;
their life shall become like a watered garden,
   and they shall never languish again. (Jer. 31:10-12)

Psalm
Psalm 72
Prayers for the king

Additional Reading
John 1:[1-9] 10-18
God with us

Hymn: The First Noel, ELW 300

God, when our lives are scattered and fragmented, you bring us to yourself and surround us with peace and mercy. We praise you for your goodness and cling to the promise that you will never leave us, through Jesus our Savior.

Blessing of the Home at Epiphany

Matthew writes that when the magi saw the shining star stop overhead, they were filled with joy. "On entering the house, they saw the child with Mary his mother" (Matt. 2:10-11). In the home, Christ is met in family and friends, in visitors and strangers. In the home, faith is shared, nurtured, and put into action. In the home, Christ is welcome.

Twelfth Night (January 5) or another day during the twelve days of Christmas or the time after Epiphany offers an occasion for gathering with friends and family members for a blessing of the home, using the following as a model. Someone may lead the greeting and blessing, while another person may read the scripture passage. Following an eastern European tradition, a visual blessing may be inscribed with white chalk above the main door; for example, 20 + CMB + 13. The numbers change with each new year. The three letters stand for either the ancient Latin blessing *Christe mansionem benedica,* which means "Christ, bless this house," or the legendary names of the magi (Caspar, Melchior, and Balthasar).

Gathering
Peace to this *house/dwelling/room* and to all who enter here.
A reading from Proverbs: By wisdom a house is built,
and through understanding it is established;
through knowledge its rooms are filled
with rare and beautiful treasures. *(Prov. 24:3-4)*

Reading
As we prepare to ask God's blessing on this household,
let us listen to the words of scripture.
A reading from John: In the beginning was the Word,
and the Word was with God, and the Word was God.
He was in the beginning with God.
All things came into being through him,
and without him not one thing came into being.

What has come into being in him was life,
and the life was the light of all people.
The Word became flesh and lived among us, and we have seen his glory,
the glory as of a father's only son, full of grace and truth.
From his fullness we have all received, grace upon grace.
(John 1:1-4, 14, 16)

Inscription

This inscription may be made with chalk above the entrance:

20 + C M B + 13

The magi of old, known as

C   Caspar,

M   Melchior, and

B   Balthasar,

followed the star of God's Son who came to dwell among us

20   two thousand

13   and thirteen years ago.

+   Christ, bless this house,

+   and remain with us throughout the new year.

Prayer of Blessing

O God,
you revealed your Son to all people by the shining light of a star.
We pray that you bless this home and all who live here
with your gracious presence.
May your love be our inspiration, your wisdom our guide,
your truth our light, and your peace our benediction;
through Christ our Lord. **Amen.**

Then everyone may walk from room to room, blessing the house with incense or by sprinkling with water, perhaps using a branch from the Christmas tree.

Sunday, January 6, 2013

Epiphany of Our Lord

Matthew 2:1-12
Christ revealed to the nations

In the time of King Herod, after Jesus was born in Bethlehem of Judea, wise men from the East came to Jerusalem, asking, "Where is the child who has been born king of the Jews? For we observed his star at its rising, and have come to pay him homage." When King Herod heard this, he was frightened, and all Jerusalem with him; and calling together all the chief priests and scribes of the people, he inquired of them where the Messiah was to be born. They told him, "In Bethlehem of Judea; for so it has been written by the prophet." (Matt. 2:1-5)

Psalm
Psalm 72:1-7, 10-14
All shall bow down

Additional Readings
Isaiah 60:1-6
Nations come to the light

Ephesians 3:1-12
The gospel's promise for all

Hymn: O Morning Star, How Fair and Bright! ELW 308

O God, on this day you revealed your Son to the nations by the leading of a star. Lead us now by faith to know your presence in our lives, and bring us at last to the full vision of your glory, through your Son, Jesus Christ our Lord, who lives and reigns with you and the Holy Spirit, one God, now and forever.

TIME AFTER EPIPHANY

On the Epiphany of Our Lord (January 6), the household joins the church throughout the world in celebrating the manifestation, the "epiphany," of Christ to the world. The festival of Christmas is thus set within the context of outreach to the larger community; it possesses an outward movement. The festival of the Epiphany asks the Christian household: How might our faith in Christ the Light be shared with friends and family, with our neighbors, with the poor and needy in our land, with those who live in other nations?

Table Prayer for Epiphany and the Time after Epiphany (January 6–February 12)

Generous God,
you have made yourself known in Jesus, the light of the world.
As this food and drink give us refreshment,
so strengthen us by your Spirit,
that as your baptized sons and daughters
we may share your light with all the world.
Grant this through Christ our Lord.
Amen.

Monday, January 7, 2013

Time after Epiphany

Ephesians 4:17—5:1

Life lived in Christ

Now this I affirm and insist on in the Lord: you must no longer live as the Gentiles live, in the futility of their minds. They are darkened in their understanding, alienated from the life of God because of their ignorance and hardness of heart. They have lost all sensitivity and have abandoned themselves to licentiousness, greedy to practice every kind of impurity. That is not the way you learned Christ! For surely you have heard about him and were taught in him, as truth is in Jesus. You were taught to put away your former way of life, your old self, corrupt and deluded by its lusts, and to be renewed in the spirit of your minds, and to clothe yourselves with the new self, created according to the likeness of God in true righteousness and holiness. (Eph. 4:17-24)

Psalm
Psalm 72
Prayers for the king

Additional Reading
Daniel 2:1-19
The king searches for wisdom

Hymn: Bright and Glorious Is the Sky, ELW 301

Saving God, you claim us as your own and clothe us in righteousness. By the power of your Spirit renew our minds, enliven our spirits, and form us into the image of your Son.

Tuesday, January 8, 2013

Time after Epiphany

Ephesians 5:15-20
Wise living in evil days

Be careful then how you live, not as unwise people but as wise, making the most of the time, because the days are evil. So do not be foolish, but understand what the will of the Lord is. Do not get drunk with wine, for that is debauchery; but be filled with the Spirit, as you sing psalms and hymns and spiritual songs among yourselves, singing and making melody to the Lord in your hearts, giving thanks to God the Father at all times and for everything in the name of our Lord Jesus Christ. (Eph. 5:15-20)

Psalm
Psalm 72
Prayers for the king

Additional Reading
Daniel 2:24-49
Daniel reveals the dream's meaning

Hymn: How Marvelous God's Greatness, ELW 830

O Lord, your faithfulness sustains us and your Spirit accompanies us. Guide our lives and fill us with courage to persevere on the path of faith for the sake of Jesus Christ our Lord.

Wednesday, January 9, 2013

Time after Epiphany

Luke 1:67-79

The Savior is seen

Then John's father Zechariah was filled with the Holy Spirit and spoke this prophecy...

"And you, child, will be called the prophet of the Most High;
    for you will go before the Lord to prepare his ways,
to give knowledge of salvation to his people
    by the forgiveness of their sins.
By the tender mercy of our God,
    the dawn from on high will break upon us,
to give light to those who sit in darkness and in the shadow of death,
    to guide our feet into the way of peace." (Luke 1:67, 76-79)

Psalm	Additional Reading
Psalm 72	Numbers 24:15-19
Prayers for the king	*A star coming out of Jacob*

Hymn: Blessed Be the God of Israel, ELW 552

We praise you, Lord, for those who in word, song, and prayer prepare the way for the coming of your reign. With Zechariah we join our voices in wonder and gratitude as your kingdom takes shape in us and around us.

Thursday, January 10, 2013

Time after Epiphany

Psalm 29
The voice of God upon the waters

Ascribe to the LORD, O heavenly beings,
   ascribe to the LORD glory and strength.
Ascribe to the LORD the glory of his name;
   worship the LORD in holy splendor.

The voice of the LORD is over the waters;
   the God of glory thunders,
      the LORD, over mighty waters.
The voice of the LORD is powerful;
   the voice of the LORD is full of majesty. (Ps. 29:1-4)

Additional Readings
Ecclesiastes 1:1-11   1 Corinthians 1:18-31
There is nothing new under the sun   *The power and wisdom of God*

Hymn: My God, How Wonderful Thou Art, ELW 863

*King of all creation and Lord of our lives, as the heavenly beings bow
before you and the mighty waters serve you, may all we do give glory
and majesty to your name now and forevermore.*

Friday, January 11, 2013

Time after Epiphany

1 Corinthians 2:1-10
The Spirit reveals the depths of God

But we speak God's wisdom, secret and hidden, which God decreed before the ages for our glory. None of the rulers of this age understood this; for if they had, they would not have crucified the Lord of glory. But, as it is written,

"What no eye has seen, nor ear heard,
   nor the human heart conceived,
what God has prepared for those who love him"—
these things God has revealed to us through the Spirit; for the Spirit searches everything, even the depths of God. (1 Cor. 2:7-10)

Psalm
Psalm 29
The voice of God upon the waters

Additional Reading
Ecclesiastes 2:1-11
Toil for pleasure is ultimately vanity

Hymn: Holy Spirit, Ever Dwelling, ELW 582

Wisdom of the ages, what we do not dare to imagine you reveal to us in Jesus. By your Spirit open our hearts to the depth of your love and the greatness of your mercy.

Saturday, January 12, 2013

Time after Epiphany

Ecclesiastes 3:1-15

All that is, is God's doing

What gain have the workers from their toil? I have seen the business that God has given to everyone to be busy with. He has made everything suitable for its time; moreover he has put a sense of past and future into their minds, yet they cannot find out what God has done from the beginning to the end. I know that there is nothing better for them than to be happy and enjoy themselves as long as they live; moreover, it is God's gift that all should eat and drink and take pleasure in all their toil. I know that whatever God does endures forever; nothing can be added to it, nor anything taken from it; God has done this, so that all should stand in awe before him. That which is, already has been; that which is to be, already is; and God seeks out what has gone by. (Eccles. 3:9-15)

Psalm
Psalm 29
The voice of God upon the waters

Additional Reading
1 Corinthians 2:11-16
God's wisdom taught by the Spirit

Hymn: How Small Our Span of Life, ELW 636

Our hours and days are in your hands, O God. With thankful hearts we embrace the present moment, and with eagerness we watch your will unfold in our lives. Guide our work, our rest, and our plans that all might serve you.

Sunday, January 13, 2013

Baptism of Our Lord

Luke 3:15-17, 21-22
The baptism of Jesus

As the people were filled with expectation, and all were questioning in their hearts concerning John, whether he might be the Messiah, John answered all of them by saying, "I baptize you with water; but one who is more powerful than I is coming; I am not worthy to untie the thong of his sandals. He will baptize you with the Holy Spirit and fire. His winnowing fork is in his hand, to clear his threshing floor and to gather the wheat into his granary; but the chaff he will burn with unquenchable fire."

Now when all the people were baptized, and when Jesus also had been baptized and was praying, the heaven was opened, and the Holy Spirit descended upon him in bodily form like a dove. And a voice came from heaven, "You are my Son, the Beloved; with you I am well pleased." (Luke 3:15-17, 21-22)

Psalm
Psalm 29
The voice of God upon the waters

Additional Readings
Isaiah 43:1-7
Passing through the waters

Acts 8:14-17
Prayer for the Holy Spirit

Hymn: Christ, When for Us You Were Baptized, ELW 304

Almighty God, you anointed Jesus at his baptism with the Holy Spirit and revealed him as your beloved Son. Keep all who are born of water and the Spirit faithful in your service, that we may rejoice to be called children of God, through Jesus Christ, our Savior and Lord, who lives and reigns with you and the Holy Spirit, one God, now and forever.

Monday, January 14, 2013

Time after Epiphany

Psalm 106:1-12
God saves through water

Praise the LORD!
  O give thanks to the LORD, for he is good;
  for his steadfast love endures forever.
Who can utter the mighty doings of the LORD,
  or declare all his praise?
Happy are those who observe justice,
  who do righteousness at all times. (Ps. 106:1-3)

Additional Readings
Judges 4:1-16   Ephesians 6:10-17
Israel's enemies drown   *The Christian's spiritual armor*

Hymn: Praise and Thanks and Adoration, ELW 783

Praise to you, mighty God, for your steadfast love and for your abundant grace. Praise to you, mighty God, for your justice that fills the earth and guides our deeds. Praise to you, mighty God, for your righteousness that makes us right with you.

Tuesday, January 15, 2013

Time after Epiphany

Martin Luther King Jr., renewer of society, martyr, died 1968

1 John 5:13-21
The life of those born of God

We know that those who are born of God do not sin, but the one who
was born of God protects them, and the evil one does not touch them.
We know that we are God's children, and that the whole world lies
under the power of the evil one. And we know that the Son of God
has come and has given us understanding so that we may know him
who is true; and we are in him who is true, in his Son Jesus Christ. He
is the true God and eternal life. (1 John 5:18-20)

Psalm
Psalm 106:1-12
God saves through water

Additional Reading
Judges 5:12-21
The song of Deborah

Hymn: Songs of Thankfulness and Praise, ELW 310

*Mothering God, you give us life, and then you give new life. You give
beyond our ability to comprehend. Turn us from habits of taking
without gratitude, and transform our hearts to know that all of life is a
gift from your generous hand.*

Wednesday, January 16, 2013

Time after Epiphany

Numbers 27:1-11

Daughters also promised inheritance

And the LORD spoke to Moses, saying: The daughters of Zelophehad are right in what they are saying; you shall indeed let them possess an inheritance among their father's brothers and pass the inheritance of their father on to them. You shall also say to the Israelites, "If a man dies, and has no son, then you shall pass his inheritance on to his daughter. If he has no daughter, then you shall give his inheritance to his brothers. If he has no brothers, then you shall give his inheritance to his father's brothers. And if his father has no brothers, then you shall give his inheritance to the nearest kinsman of his clan, and he shall possess it. It shall be for the Israelites a statute and ordinance, as the LORD commanded Moses." (Num. 27:6-11)

Psalm
Psalm 106:1-12
God saves through water

Additional Reading
Luke 11:33-36
Your body full of light

Hymn: Children of the Heavenly Father, ELW 781

O God, from your endless store of love you pass on to us an inheritance: the gift of your kingdom that comes now and continues on into eternal life.

Thursday, January 17, 2013

Time after Epiphany

Antony of Egypt, renewer of the church, died around 356
Pachomius, renewer of the church, died 346

Psalm 36:5-10
We feast on the abundance of God's house

Your steadfast love, O LORD, extends to the heavens,
 your faithfulness to the clouds.
Your righteousness is like the mighty mountains,
 your judgments are like the great deep;
 you save humans and animals alike, O LORD.

How precious is your steadfast love, O God!
 All people may take refuge in the shadow of your wings.
They feast on the abundance of your house,
 and you give them drink from the river of your delights.
For with you is the fountain of life;
 in your light we see light. (Ps. 36:5-9)

Additional Readings
Jeremiah 3:1-5   Acts 8:18-24
Unfaithful Israel   *God's gifts cannot be purchased*

Hymn: Hail to the Lord's Anointed, ELW 311

*God, when we are anxious your steadfast love calms us. When we are
impatient your steadfast love waits for us. When we feel helpless your
steadfast love supports us. When we hunger and thirst for meaning
your steadfast love fills us.*

Friday, January 18, 2013

Confession of Peter

Week of Prayer for Christian Unity begins

Matthew 16:13-19

Peter confesses: You are the Messiah

[Jesus] said to them, "But who do you say that I am?" Simon Peter answered, "You are the Messiah, the Son of the living God." And Jesus answered him, "Blessed are you, Simon son of Jonah! For flesh and blood has not revealed this to you, but my Father in heaven. And I tell you, you are Peter, and on this rock I will build my church, and the gates of Hades will not prevail against it. I will give you the keys of the kingdom of heaven, and whatever you bind on earth will be bound in heaven, and whatever you loose on earth will be loosed in heaven." (Matt. 16:15-19)

Psalm
Psalm 18:1-6, 16-19
My God, my rock, worthy of praise

Additional Readings
Acts 4:8-13
Salvation is in no one other than Jesus

1 Corinthians 10:1-5
Drinking from the spiritual rock of Christ

Hymn: Oh, Praise the Gracious Power, ELW 651

Almighty God, you inspired Simon Peter to confess Jesus as the Messiah and Son of the living God. Keep your church firm on the rock of this faith, so that in unity and peace it may proclaim one truth and follow one Lord, your Son, Jesus Christ our Savior, who lives and reigns with you and the Holy Spirit, one God, now and forever.

31

Saturday, January 19, 2013

Time after Epiphany

Henry, Bishop of Uppsala, martyr, died 1156

Jeremiah 4:1-4

A call to repentance

If you return, O Israel,

says the LORD,

   if you return to me,
if you remove your abominations from my presence,
   and do not waver,
and if you swear, "As the LORD lives!"
   in truth, in justice, and in uprightness,
then nations shall be blessed by him,
   and by him they shall boast.
For thus says the LORD to the people of Judah and to the inhabitants
of Jerusalem:
Break up your fallow ground,
   and do not sow among thorns.
Circumcise yourselves to the LORD,
   remove the foreskin of your hearts,
   O people of Judah and inhabitants of Jerusalem,
or else my wrath will go forth like fire,
   and burn with no one to quench it,
   because of the evil of your doings. (Jer. 4:1-4)

Psalm

Psalm 36:5-10

We feast on the abundance of God's house

Additional Reading

Luke 11:14-23

Looking for signs from heaven

Hymn: Great God, Your Love Has Called Us, ELW 358

Most holy God, when we chase after the gods of our own making or pursue our own desires without thought of your will for us, bring us back to yourself and guide us in the ways of holiness and righteousness.

32

Sunday, January 20, 2013

Second Sunday after Epiphany

John 2:1-11
The wedding at Cana

When the steward tasted the water that had become wine, and did not know where it came from (though the servants who had drawn the water knew), the steward called the bridegroom and said to him, "Everyone serves the good wine first, and then the inferior wine after the guests have become drunk. But you have kept the good wine until now." Jesus did this, the first of his signs, in Cana of Galilee, and revealed his glory; and his disciples believed in him. (John 2:9-11)

Psalm	Additional Readings	
Psalm 36:5-10	Isaiah 62:1-5	1 Corinthians 12:1-11
We feast on the abundance of God's house	*God like the bridegroom and the bride*	*A variety of gifts but one Spirit*

Hymn: Jesus, Come! For We Invite You, ELW 312

Lord God, source of every blessing, you showed forth your glory and led many to faith by the works of your Son, who brought gladness and salvation to his people. Transform us by the Spirit of his love, that we may find our life together in him, Jesus Christ, our Savior and Lord.

Monday, January 21, 2013

Time after Epiphany

Agnes, martyr, died around 304

Psalm 145
Praise God's faithfulness

I will extol you, my God and King,
   and bless your name forever and ever.
Every day I will bless you,
   and praise your name forever and ever.
Great is the Lord, and greatly to be praised;
   his greatness is unsearchable.

One generation shall laud your works to another,
   and shall declare your mighty acts.
On the glorious splendor of your majesty,
   and on your wondrous works, I will meditate. (Ps. 145:1-5)

Additional Readings
Isaiah 54:1-8   Romans 12:9-21
God is married to Israel   *Live in harmony with one another*

Hymn: All Creatures, Worship God Most High! ELW 835

King of all creation, we pause in a moment of quiet to offer praise, not with boisterous shout or bold song, but with a peace that flows from grateful hearts at the wonder in our lives.

Tuesday, January 22, 2013

Time after Epiphany

I Corinthians 1:3-17

Appeal for unity

Now I appeal to you, brothers and sisters, by the name of our Lord
Jesus Christ, that all of you be in agreement and that there be no
divisions among you, but that you be united in the same mind and
the same purpose. For it has been reported to me by Chloe's people
that there are quarrels among you, my brothers and sisters. What
I mean is that each of you says, "I belong to Paul," or "I belong to
Apollos," or "I belong to Cephas," or "I belong to Christ." Has Christ
been divided? Was Paul crucified for you? Or were you baptized in
the name of Paul? (1 Cor. 1:10-13)

Psalm

Psalm 145
Praise God's faithfulness

Additional Reading

Song of Solomon 4:1-8
The bride's beauty extolled

Hymn: We Are Baptized in Christ Jesus, ELW 451

*Great God, the divisions in your church continue. We gather at your
table of grace under many names. Heal your church, unite us in mission,
form us into the image of your Son, and free us from our allegiance to
anyone or anything other than Christ, that together we might give our
lives to the world as he gave himself for us.*

Wednesday, January 23, 2013

Time after Epiphany

Song of Solomon 4:9—5:1

A love song

You have ravished my heart, my sister, my bride,
  you have ravished my heart with a glance of your eyes,
  with one jewel of your necklace.
How sweet is your love, my sister, my bride!
  how much better is your love than wine,
  and the fragrance of your oils than any spice!
Your lips distill nectar, my bride;
  honey and milk are under your tongue;
  the scent of your garments is like the scent of Lebanon.
(Song of Sol. 4:9-11)

Psalm

Psalm 145
Praise God's faithfulness

Additional Reading

Luke 5:33-39
Christ the bridegroom

Hymn: Love Divine, All Loves Excelling, ELW 631

O God, you have loved us with an everlasting love. You have given us yourself, and you claim us as your own. May our lives sing of your love for the world.

Thursday, January 24, 2013

Time after Epiphany

Psalm 19
The law revives the soul

The law of the LORD is perfect,
 reviving the soul;
the decrees of the LORD are sure,
 making wise the simple;
the precepts of the LORD are right,
 rejoicing the heart;
the commandment of the LORD is clear,
 enlightening the eyes;
the fear of the LORD is pure,
 enduring forever;
the ordinances of the LORD are true
 and righteous altogether.
More to be desired are they than gold,
 even much fine gold;
sweeter also than honey,
 and drippings of the honeycomb. (Ps. 19:7-10)

Additional Readings
Isaiah 61:1-7
The spirit of God is upon me

Romans 7:1-6
The new life of the Spirit

Hymn: Let the Whole Creation Cry, ELW 876

O God, shape our hearts and minds by your righteousness. Write your law on our hearts that your ways will be our ways, and that our ways will proclaim your love and justice for all people.

Friday, January 25, 2013

Conversion of Paul

Week of Prayer for Christian Unity ends

Galatians 1:11-24

Paul receives a revelation of Christ

You have heard, no doubt, of my earlier life in Judaism. I was violently persecuting the church of God and was trying to destroy it. I advanced in Judaism beyond many among my people of the same age, for I was far more zealous for the traditions of my ancestors. But when God, who had set me apart before I was born and called me through his grace, was pleased to reveal his Son to me, so that I might proclaim him among the Gentiles, I did not confer with any human being, nor did I go up to Jerusalem to those who were already apostles before me, but I went away at once into Arabia, and afterwards I returned to Damascus. (Gal. 1:13-17)

Psalm

Psalm 67
Let all the peoples praise you, O God

Additional Readings

Acts 9:1-22
Saul is converted to Christ

Luke 21:10-19
The end times will require endurance

Hymn: For by Grace You Have Been Saved, ELW 598

O God, by the preaching of your apostle Paul you have caused the light of the gospel to shine throughout the world. Grant that we may follow his example and be witnesses to the truth of your Son, Jesus Christ, our Savior and Lord, who lives and reigns with you and the Holy Spirit, one God, now and forever.

Saturday, January 26, 2013

Time after Epiphany

Timothy, Titus, and Silas, missionaries

Luke 2:39-52
Jesus increases in wisdom

After three days they found [Jesus] in the temple, sitting among the teachers, listening to them and asking them questions. And all who heard him were amazed at his understanding and his answers. When his parents saw him they were astonished; and his mother said to him, "Child, why have you treated us like this? Look, your father and I have been searching for you in great anxiety." He said to them, "Why were you searching for me? Did you not know that I must be in my Father's house?" (Luke 2:46-49)

Psalm
Psalm 19
The law revives the soul

Additional Reading
Nehemiah 5:1-13
Nehemiah deals with oppression

Hymn: Dear Christians, One and All, Rejoice, ELW 594

Almighty God, your Son leads us to worship you, and we come with reverence to your throne of grace. Fill us with understanding and wisdom that we might serve you all our days.

Sunday, January 27, 2013

Third Sunday after Epiphany

Lydia, Dorcas, and Phoebe, witnesses to the faith

Luke 4:14-21

Jesus reads the prophet Isaiah

When [Jesus] came to Nazareth, where he had been brought up, he went to the synagogue on the sabbath day, as was his custom. He stood up to read, and the scroll of the prophet Isaiah was given to him. He unrolled the scroll and found the place where it was written:
"The Spirit of the Lord is upon me,
  because he has anointed me
    to bring good news to the poor.
He has sent me to proclaim release to the captives
  and recovery of sight to the blind,
    to let the oppressed go free,
  to proclaim the year of the Lord's favor." (Luke 4:16-19)

Psalm

Psalm 19
The law revives the soul

Additional Readings

Nehemiah 8:1-3, 5-6,
8-10
Ezra reads the law

1 Corinthians
12:12-31a
You are the body of Christ

Hymn: O Zion, Haste, ELW 668

Blessed Lord God, you have caused the holy scriptures to be written for the nourishment of your people. Grant that we may hear them, read, mark, learn, and inwardly digest them, that, comforted by your promises, we may embrace and forever hold fast to the hope of eternal life, through your Son, Jesus Christ our Lord.

40

Monday, January 28, 2013

Time after Epiphany

Thomas Aquinas, teacher, died 1274

Psalm 119:89-96
The law of God gives life

The LORD exists forever;
   your word is firmly fixed in heaven.
Your faithfulness endures to all generations;
   you have established the earth, and it stands fast.
By your appointment they stand today,
   for all things are your servants.
If your law had not been my delight,
   I would have perished in my misery.
I will never forget your precepts,
   for by them you have given me life. (Psalm 119:89-93)

Additional Readings
Jeremiah 36:1-10
The scroll is read in the temple

1 Corinthians 14:1-12
The assembly's gifts

Hymn: Oh, That the Lord Would Guide My Ways, ELW 772

*Great God, your word orders our days and enriches our lives. We hold
to your law, for in it we find life. So fill our hearts and minds to see the
rich abundance of your ways in our midst that we might work for justice
and equity for all your people.*

Tuesday, January 29, 2013

Time after Epiphany

Jeremiah 36:11-26

Jehoiakim burns the scroll

Then the king sent Jehudi to get the scroll, and he took it from the chamber of Elishama the secretary; and Jehudi read it to the king and all the officials who stood beside the king. Now the king was sitting in his winter apartment (it was the ninth month), and there was a fire burning in the brazier before him. As Jehudi read three or four columns, the king would cut them off with a penknife and throw them into the fire in the brazier, until the entire scroll was consumed in the fire that was in the brazier. Yet neither the king, nor any of his servants who heard all these words, was alarmed, nor did they tear their garments. Even when Elnathan and Delaiah and Gemariah urged the king not to burn the scroll, he would not listen to them. (Jer. 36:21-25)

Psalm
Psalm 119:89-96
The law of God gives life

Additional Reading
2 Corinthians 7:2-12
Grief leads to repentance

Hymn: Word of God, Come Down on Earth, ELW 510

Gracious God, the light of your word illumines our paths. Bring us light when our hope is dim. Speak truth when we are unsure. Raise us to newness in the face of death. And in all things sustain us by your word.

Wednesday, January 30, 2013

Time after Epiphany

Jeremiah 36:27-32
Jeremiah dictates a second scroll

Now, after the king had burned the scroll with the words that Baruch wrote at Jeremiah's dictation, the word of the LORD came to Jeremiah: Take another scroll and write on it all the former words that were in the first scroll, which King Jehoiakim of Judah has burned. And concerning King Jehoiakim of Judah you shall say: Thus says the LORD, You have dared to burn this scroll, saying, Why have you written in it that the king of Babylon will certainly come and destroy this land, and will cut off from it human beings and animals? Therefore thus says the LORD concerning King Jehoiakim of Judah: He shall have no one to sit upon the throne of David, and his dead body shall be cast out to the heat by day and the frost by night. And I will punish him and his offspring and his servants for their iniquity; I will bring on them, and on the inhabitants of Jerusalem, and on the people of Judah, all the disasters with which I have threatened them—but they would not listen. (Jer. 36:27-31)

Psalm
Psalm 119:89-96
The law of God gives life

Additional Reading
Luke 4:38-44
Jesus heals and preaches in synagogues

Hymn: O God of Love, O King of Peace, ELW 749

Holy God, when we are faithless you are faithful. When we are wayward you are steadfast. In our doubt you are certain. O source of strength, hold us in your love.

Thursday, January 31, 2013

Time after Epiphany

Psalm 71:1-6
You have been my strength

In you, O LORD, I take refuge;
　　let me never be put to shame.
In your righteousness deliver me and rescue me;
　　incline your ear to me and save me.
Be to me a rock of refuge,
　　a strong fortress, to save me,
　　for you are my rock and my fortress.

Rescue me, O my God, from the hand of the wicked,
　　from the grasp of the unjust and cruel.
For you, O Lord, are my hope,
　　my trust, O LORD, from my youth. (Ps. 71:1-5)

Additional Readings
2 Chronicles 34:1-7　　　　　　　**Acts 10:44-48**
Youthful Josiah inaugurates reform　　*Gentiles receive the Holy Spirit*

Hymn:　How Firm a Foundation, ELW 796

Heavenly God, when enemies attack, you are our fortress and our strength. Rescue us from adversity and deliver us from fear. For you, O Lord, are our hope and our trust.

_____

_____

_____

_____

_____

_____

_____

_____

_____

_____

_____

Friday, February 1, 2013

Time after Epiphany

2 Chronicles 35:20-27

Jeremiah laments the death of Josiah

The archers shot King Josiah; and the king said to his servants, "Take me away, for I am badly wounded." So his servants took him out of the chariot and carried him in his second chariot and brought him to Jerusalem. There he died, and was buried in the tombs of his ancestors. All Judah and Jerusalem mourned for Josiah. Jeremiah also uttered a lament for Josiah, and all the singing men and singing women have spoken of Josiah in their laments to this day. They made these a custom in Israel; they are recorded in the Laments. Now the rest of the acts of Josiah and his faithful deeds in accordance with what is written in the law of the Lord, and his acts, first and last, are written in the Book of the Kings of Israel and Judah. (2 Chron. 35:23-27)

Psalm
Psalm 71:1-6
You have been my strength

Additional Reading
Acts 19:1-10
Believers speak in tongues

Hymn: O God, Why Are You Silent, ELW 703

Comforting God, we mourn the senseless deaths of great leaders and ordinary citizens who have lived out your mission in our own day. Inspire us through their legacies so that their witness to your power and love will continue on through us.

Saturday, February 2, 2013

Presentation of Our Lord

Luke 2:22-40

The child is brought to the temple

Simeon took [the child Jesus] in his arms and praised God, saying,
    "Master, now you are dismissing your servant in peace,
        according to your word;
    for my eyes have seen your salvation,
        which you have prepared in the presence of all peoples,
    a light for revelation to the Gentiles
        and for glory to your people Israel." (Luke 2:28-32)

Psalm

Psalm 84

How dear to me is your dwelling, O LORD

Additional Readings

Malachi 3:1-4

My messenger, a refiner and purifier

Hebrews 2:14-18

Jesus shares human flesh and sufferings

Hymn: In His Temple Now Behold Him, ELW 417

Almighty and ever-living God, your only-begotten Son was presented this day in the temple. May we be presented to you with clean and pure hearts by the same Jesus Christ, our great high priest, who lives and reigns with you and the Holy Spirit, one God, now and forever.

Sunday, February 3, 2013

Fourth Sunday after Epiphany

Ansgar, Bishop of Hamburg, missionary to Denmark and Sweden, died 865

Luke 4:21-30
The prophet Jesus not accepted

Then [Jesus] began to say to them, "Today this scripture has been fulfilled in your hearing." All spoke well of him and were amazed at the gracious words that came from his mouth. They said, "Is not this Joseph's son?" He said to them, "Doubtless you will quote to me this proverb, 'Doctor, cure yourself!' And you will say, 'Do here also in your hometown the things that we have heard you did at Capernaum.' " And he said, "Truly I tell you, no prophet is accepted in the prophet's hometown." (Luke 4:21-24)

Psalm
Psalm 71:1-6
You have been my strength

Additional Readings
Jeremiah 1:4-10
A prophet to the nations

I Corinthians 13:1-13
Without love, a noisy gong

Hymn: He Comes to Us As One Unknown, ELW 737

Almighty and ever-living God, increase in us the gifts of faith, hope, and love; and that we may obtain what you promise, make us love what you command, through your Son, Jesus Christ, our Savior and Lord.

Monday, February 4, 2013

Time after Epiphany

Psalm 56
In God I trust

Be gracious to me, O God, for people trample on me;
    all day long foes oppress me;
my enemies trample on me all day long,
    for many fight against me.
O Most High, when I am afraid,
    I put my trust in you.
In God, whose word I praise,
    in God I trust; I am not afraid;
    what can flesh do to me? (Ps. 56:1-4)

Additional Readings
I Kings 17:8-16   I Corinthians 2:6-16
The widow of Zarephath fed   *Interpreting spiritual things*

Hymn: O Day of Peace, ELW 711

*O God, when others confront us and seek to destroy the good that we do,
help us to recognize your blessing and support in our lives. Encourage
us to be channels of your power working for peace and reconciliation in
our world.*

Tuesday, February 5, 2013

Time after Epiphany

The Martyrs of Japan, died 1597

2 Kings 5:1-14
Naaman the Syrian healed

So Naaman came with his horses and chariots, and halted at the entrance of Elisha's house. Elisha sent a messenger to him, saying, "Go, wash in the Jordan seven times, and your flesh shall be restored and you shall be clean." But Naaman became angry and went away, saying, "I thought that for me he would surely come out, and stand and call on the name of the LORD his God, and would wave his hand over the spot, and cure the leprosy! Are not Abana and Pharpar, the rivers of Damascus, better than all the waters of Israel? Could I not wash in them, and be clean?" He turned and went away in a rage. But his servants approached and said to him, "Father, if the prophet had commanded you to do something difficult, would you not have done it? How much more, when all he said to you was, 'Wash, and be clean'?" (2 Kings 5:9-13)

Psalm	Additional Reading
Psalm 56	1 Corinthians 14:13-25
In God I trust	*Interpreting tongues*

Hymn: Healer of Our Every Ill, ELW 612

Great God, your awesome power is often contained in the simplest of actions. Help us to recognize your extravagant blessings through people who are right in our midst and to see how much we are already beneficiaries of your grace.

Wednesday, February 6, 2013

Time after Epiphany

Jeremiah 1:11-19

Jeremiah warns of disaster

Then the LORD said to me: Out of the north disaster shall break out
on all the inhabitants of the land. For now I am calling all the tribes
of the kingdoms of the north, says the LORD; and they shall come
and all of them shall set their thrones at the entrance of the gates
of Jerusalem, against all its surrounding walls and against all the
cities of Judah. And I will utter my judgments against them, for all
their wickedness in forsaking me; they have made offerings to other
gods, and worshiped the works of their own hands. But you, gird up
your loins; stand up and tell them everything that I command you.
Do not break down before them, or I will break you before them.
(Jer. 1:14-17)

Psalm
Psalm 56
In God I trust

Additional Reading
Luke 19:41-44
Recognizing the works of God

Hymn: How Great Thou Art, ELW 856

*God of all, how often do we devote most of our time and energy to things
of our own making? Teach us to order our priorities so that the natural
world and all creatures in need may have a greater measure of our
devotion.*

Thursday, February 7, 2013

Time after Epiphany

Psalm 99

Worship upon God's holy hill

The LORD is king; let the peoples tremble!
    He sits enthroned upon the cherubim; let the earth quake!
The LORD is great in Zion;
    he is exalted over all the peoples.
Let them praise your great and awesome name.
    Holy is he!
Mighty King, lover of justice,
    you have established equity;
you have executed justice
    and righteousness in Jacob.

Extol the LORD our God,
    and worship at his holy mountain;
    for the LORD our God is holy. (Ps. 99:1-4, 9)

Additional Readings

Deuteronomy 9:1-5   **Acts 3:11-16**
God's oath to Abraham, Isaac, and Jacob   *Abraham, Isaac, and Jacob's God glorifies*
                                             Jesus

Hymn: Oh, Worship the King, ELW 842

God of majesty, you are worthy of our praise and thanksgiving. Help us to proclaim your greatness so that all peoples on earth might come to know your glory.

Friday, February 8, 2013

Time after Epiphany

Acts 10:1-8
The vision of Cornelius

In Caesarea there was a man named Cornelius, a centurion of the
Italian Cohort, as it was called. He was a devout man who feared
God with all his household; he gave alms generously to the people
and prayed constantly to God. One afternoon at about three o'clock
he had a vision in which he clearly saw an angel of God coming in
and saying to him, "Cornelius." He stared at him in terror and said,
"What is it, Lord?" He answered, "Your prayers and your alms have
ascended as a memorial before God." (Acts 10:1-4)

Psalm
Psalm 99
Worship upon God's holy hill

Additional Reading
Deuteronomy 9:6-14
Remember your rebellion in the wilderness

Hymn: Lord, Teach Us How to Pray Aright, ELW 745

*All-powerful God, you call all people everywhere to be a part of your
great community of faith. Help us to proclaim your vision to those in our
world who do not know you, that they may also join us in our witness.*

Saturday, February 9, 2013

Time after Epiphany

Deuteronomy 9:15-24

Moses on the blazing mountain

So I [Moses] turned and went down from the mountain, while the mountain was ablaze; the two tablets of the covenant were in my two hands. Then I saw that you had indeed sinned against the LORD your God, by casting for yourselves an image of a calf; you had been quick to turn from the way that the LORD had commanded you. So I took hold of the two tablets and flung them from my two hands, smashing them before your eyes. Then I lay prostrate before the LORD as before, forty days and forty nights; I neither ate bread nor drank water, because of all the sin you had committed, provoking the LORD by doing what was evil in his sight. For I was afraid that the anger that the LORD bore against you was so fierce that he would destroy you. But the LORD listened to me that time also. (Deut. 9:15-19)

Psalm
Psalm 99
Worship upon God's holy hill

Additional Reading
Luke 10:21-24
Blessed are the eyes that see what you see

Hymn: Oh, Wondrous Image, Vision Fair, ELW 316

All-knowing God, we deceive ourselves if we think that our sinful behaviors are hidden from you. Convert us again to your ways that we might grow in faithfulness to your everlasting covenant with us.

Sunday, February 10, 2013

Transfiguration of Our Lord

Luke 9:28-36 [37-43]

Jesus is transfigured on the mountain

Now about eight days after these sayings Jesus took with him Peter and John and James, and went up on the mountain to pray. And while he was praying, the appearance of his face changed, and his clothes became dazzling white. Suddenly they saw two men, Moses and Elijah, talking to him. They appeared in glory and were speaking of his departure, which he was about to accomplish at Jerusalem. Now Peter and his companions were weighed down with sleep; but since they had stayed awake, they saw his glory and the two men who stood with him. (Luke 9:28-32)

Psalm

Psalm 99
Worship upon God's holy hill

Additional Readings

Exodus 34:29-35
Moses' face shone

2 Corinthians 3:12—4:2
We will be transformed

Hymn: Jesus on the Mountain Peak, ELW 317

Holy God, mighty and immortal, you are beyond our knowing, yet we see your glory in the face of Jesus Christ. Transform us into the likeness of your Son, who renewed our humanity so that we may share in his divinity, Jesus Christ our Lord, who lives and reigns with you and the Holy Spirit, one God, now and forever.

Monday, February 11, 2013

Time after Epiphany

Psalm 35:11-28
Do not be far from me

You have seen, O LORD; do not be silent!
   O Lord, do not be far from me!
Wake up! Bestir yourself for my defense,
   for my cause, my God and my Lord!
Vindicate me, O LORD, my God,
   according to your righteousness,
   and do not let them rejoice over me.
Do not let them say to themselves,
   "Aha, we have our heart's desire."
Do not let them say, "We have swallowed you up."

Let all those who rejoice at my calamity
   be put to shame and confusion;
let those who exalt themselves against me
   be clothed with shame and dishonor. (Ps. 35:22-26)

Additional Readings

Exodus 35:1-29
Offerings for the tent of meeting

Acts 10:9-23a
Peter's vision of what God makes clean

Hymn: Jesus Lives, My Sure Defense, ELW 621

O God, enable us to hear your words even amid the despairing silence of our troubles and fears. Help us to be patient as we wait for a clear sign of your presence.

Tuesday, February 12, 2013

Time after Epiphany

Acts 10:23b-33
Cornelius and Peter

On Peter's arrival Cornelius met him, and falling at his feet, worshiped him. But Peter made him get up, saying, "Stand up; I am only a mortal." And as he talked with him, he went in and found that many had assembled; and he said to them, "You yourselves know that it is unlawful for a Jew to associate with or to visit a Gentile; but God has shown me that I should not call anyone profane or unclean." (Acts 10:25-28)

Psalm
Psalm 35:11-28
Do not be far from me

Additional Reading
Ezekiel 1:1—2:1
Ezekiel's vision of the chariot

Hymn: We Are Called, ELW 720

O God, as Jesus reached across divisions and barriers in his ministry, you reconcile people to one another today. Enable us to break from racial prejudices and closed systems in order to celebrate your all-inclusive love with the world.

LENT

Lent is a forty-day journey to Easter. Christians keep company with Noah and his family, who were in the ark for forty days; with the Hebrews, who journeyed through the desert for forty years; and with Moses, Elijah, and Jesus, who fasted for forty days before they embarked on the tasks God had prepared for them.

During Lent Christians journey with those who are making final preparations for baptism at Easter. Together, Christians struggle with the meaning of their baptismal promises: Do you reject evil? Do you believe in God the Father, the Son, and the Holy Spirit? Do you believe in the church, the forgiveness of sins, the resurrection of the dead?

The disciples of the Lord Jesus are called to contend against everything that leads them away from love of God and neighbor. Fasting, prayer, and works of love—the disciplines of Lent—help the household rejoice in the gifts of baptism: God's forgiveness and mercy.

Blessing for the Lenten Season

Use this blessing to begin your prayer time during the season of Lent.

God of mercy,
as we move through the journey of this season
incite us to truthful reflection, faithful action,
and quiet release of all that is false and fleeting.
Deliver us from every evil and protect us from all anxiety
as we wait in joyful hope for the great feast of Easter,
the passover of the Lord Jesus from death to life with you.
Amen.

Table Prayer for the Season of Lent

Blessed are you, O Lord our God, maker of all things.
Through your goodness you have blessed us
with the gifts of this table.
Turn our hearts toward you
and toward all those in need.
May our Lenten journey bring us to the rebirth of Easter,
through Christ our Lord.
Amen.

Table Prayer for Ash Wednesday (February 13)

Now, O Lord, is the day of salvation;
now, O Lord, you have given us life.
On this day of dust hear our praise
for all the life you grant us,
and hear our plea for all the world,
that you may have pity on the people
and gather them all into life,
through Christ our Lord.
Amen.

Wednesday, February 13, 2013

Ash Wednesday

Matthew 6:1-6, 16-21

The practice of faith

[Jesus said,] "And whenever you fast, do not look dismal, like the hypocrites, for they disfigure their faces so as to show others that they are fasting. Truly I tell you, they have received their reward. But when you fast, put oil on your head and wash your face, so that your fasting may be seen not by others but by your Father who is in secret; and your Father who sees in secret will reward you." (Matt. 6:16-18)

Psalm

Psalm 51:1-17
Plea for mercy

Additional Readings

Joel 2:1-2, 12-17
Return to God

2 Corinthians
5:20b—6:10
Now is the day of salvation

Hymn: Savior, When in Dust to You, ELW 601

Almighty and ever-living God, you hate nothing you have made, and you forgive the sins of all who are penitent. Create in us new and honest hearts, so that, truly repenting of our sins, we may receive from you, the God of all mercy, full pardon and forgiveness through your Son, Jesus Christ, our Savior and Lord, who lives and reigns with you and the Holy Spirit, one God, now and forever.

Thursday, February 14, 2013

Week before Lent 1

Cyril, monk, died 869; Methodius, bishop, died 885; missionaries to the Slavs

Psalm 91:1-2, 9-16
God shall keep you

You who live in the shelter of the Most High,
    who abide in the shadow of the Almighty,
will say to the LORD, "My refuge and my fortress;
    my God, in whom I trust."

Because you have made the LORD your refuge,
    the Most High your dwelling place,
no evil shall befall you,
    no scourge come near your tent.

For he will command his angels concerning you
    to guard you in all your ways. (Ps. 91:1-2, 9-11)

Additional Readings

Exodus 5:10-23
Israel labors in Egypt

Acts 7:30-34
Moses, called from the burning bush to the exodus

Hymn: On Eagle's Wings, ELW 787

God our refuge and fortress, you are the sure foundation of the church. With your strength beneath us, enable us to reach out to others who may be further away from this support and in need of your care.

Friday, February 15, 2013

Week before Lent 1

Exodus 6:1-13

God promises deliverance

Then the LORD spoke to Moses, "Go and tell Pharaoh king of Egypt to let the Israelites go out of his land." But Moses spoke to the LORD, "The Israelites have not listened to me; how then shall Pharaoh listen to me, poor speaker that I am?" Thus the LORD spoke to Moses and Aaron, and gave them orders regarding the Israelites and Pharaoh king of Egypt, charging them to free the Israelites from the land of Egypt. (Exod. 6:10-13)

Psalm
Psalm 91:1-2, 9-16
God shall keep you

Additional Reading
Acts 7:35-42
The people complain to Moses

Hymn: Lift Every Voice and Sing, ELW 841

God of freedom, as you once brought an enslaved people from oppression in Egypt to a new way of life in the promised land, so give voice to us today to proclaim your grace in the midst of distress.

Saturday, February 16, 2013

Week before Lent 1

Ecclesiastes 3:1-8
For everything a season

For everything there is a season, and a time for every matter under
heaven:
   a time to be born, and a time to die;
   a time to plant, and a time to pluck up what is planted;
   a time to kill, and a time to heal;
   a time to break down, and a time to build up. (Eccles. 3:1-3)

Psalm
Psalm 91:1-2, 9-16
God shall keep you

Additional Reading
John 12:27-36
Jesus announces his passion

Hymn: O Christ the Same, ELW 760

*Eternal God, in all seasons of our lives you remain faithful to your
everlasting promises. Help all who face the pain of death to know that
you bring together all our beginnings and endings with the promise of
your redeeming love.*

Sunday, February 17, 2013

First Sunday in Lent

Luke 4:1-13

The temptation of Jesus

Jesus, full of the Holy Spirit, returned from the Jordan and was led by the Spirit in the wilderness, where for forty days he was tempted by the devil. He ate nothing at all during those days, and when they were over, he was famished. The devil said to him, "If you are the Son of God, command this stone to become a loaf of bread." Jesus answered him, "It is written, 'One does not live by bread alone'." (Luke 4:1-4)

Psalm

Psalm 91:1-2, 9-16

God shall keep you

Additional Readings

Deuteronomy 26:1-11

Saved from Egypt

Romans 10:8b-13

You will be saved

Hymn: O Lord, throughout These Forty Days, ELW 319

O Lord God, you led your people through the wilderness and brought them to the promised land. Guide us now, so that, following your Son, we may walk safely through the wilderness of this world toward the life you alone can give, through Jesus Christ, our Savior and Lord, who lives and reigns with you and the Holy Spirit, one God, now and forever.

Monday, February 18, 2013

Week of Lent 1

Martin Luther, renewer of the church, died 1546

Psalm 17
Prayer for protection from evil ones

I call upon you, for you will answer me, O God;
  incline your ear to me, hear my words.
Wondrously show your steadfast love,
  O savior of those who seek refuge
  from their adversaries at your right hand.

Guard me as the apple of the eye;
  hide me in the shadow of your wings. (Ps. 17:6-8)

Additional Readings
1 Chronicles 21:1-17   1 John 2:1-6
Satan tempts David   *Obey God's commandments*

Hymn: Lord, Keep Us Steadfast in Your Word, ELW 517

God, strengthen us in keeping our Lenten disciplines of prayer, fasting, and giving alms. Hear the concerns of our hearts that we may be comforted in the shadow of your protective wings.

Tuesday, February 19, 2013

Week of Lent 1

Zechariah 3:1-10

Satan tempts Joshua

Then the angel of the LORD assured Joshua, saying "Thus says the LORD of hosts: If you will walk in my ways and keep my requirements, then you shall rule my house and have charge of my courts, and I will give you the right of access among those who are standing here. Now listen, Joshua, high priest, you and your colleagues who sit before you! For they are an omen of things to come: I am going to bring my servant the Branch. For on the stone that I have set before Joshua, on a single stone with seven facets, I will engrave its inscription, says the LORD of hosts, and I will remove the guilt of this land in a single day. On that day, says the LORD of hosts, you shall invite each other to come under your vine and fig tree." (Zech. 3:6-10)

Psalm
Psalm 17
Prayer for protection from evil ones

Additional Reading
2 Peter 2:4-21
Believers who fall into sin

Hymn: Let Us Ever Walk with Jesus, ELW 802

O God, we give thanks for brave women and men who have risked and given their lives for the sake of the gospel. Though we face temptations of many kinds, hold us firm in faith that we may boldly follow you, no matter the price.

Wednesday, February 20, 2013

Week of Lent I

Job 1:1-22
Satan tempts Job

Then Job arose, tore his robe, shaved his head, and fell on the ground and worshiped. He said, "Naked I came from my mother's womb, and naked shall I return there; the LORD gave, and the LORD has taken away; blessed be the name of the LORD."

In all this Job did not sin or charge God with wrongdoing. (Job 1:20-22)

Psalm
Psalm 17
Prayer for protection from evil ones

Additional Reading
Luke 21:34—22:6
Satan enters Judas

Hymn: By Gracious Powers, ELW 626

God of compassion, time and time again you have demonstrated your solidarity with all human suffering and pain. Encourage all who face adversities of their own to know that you will remain with them through all things.

Thursday, February 21, 2013

Week of Lent 1

Psalm 27
The Lord shall keep me safe

The LORD is my light and my salvation;
   whom shall I fear?
The LORD is the stronghold of my life;
   of whom shall I be afraid?
When evildoers assail me
   to devour my flesh—
my adversaries and foes—
   they shall stumble and fall.

Though an army encamp against me,
   my heart shall not fear;
though war rise up against me,
   yet I will be confident. (Ps. 27:1-3)

Additional Readings
Genesis 13:1-7, 14-18
Abram begins his pilgrimage

Philippians 3:2-12
Paul affirms the Abrahamic tradition

Hymn: If God My Lord Be for Me, ELW 788

O God, sometimes our fears overtake us and keep us awake. Though we know that you have not promised to remove us from every danger, help us to know that with your light before us we can indeed make our way through treacherous times.

Friday, February 22, 2013

Week of Lent 1

Philippians 3:17-20
Our citizenship is in heaven

Brothers and sisters, join in imitating me, and observe those who live according to the example you have in us. For many live as enemies of the cross of Christ; I have often told you of them, and now I tell you even with tears. Their end is destruction; their god is the belly; and their glory is in their shame; their minds are set on earthly things. But our citizenship is in heaven, and it is from there that we are expecting a Savior, the Lord Jesus Christ. (Phil. 3:17-20)

Psalm
Psalm 27
The Lord shall keep me safe

Additional Reading
Genesis 14:17-24
Abram is blessed by Melchizedek

Hymn: Come, We That Love the Lord, ELW 625

Eternal God, it is easy for us to be seduced by temporal matters, with many glittering promises and earthly comforts, yet none are as lasting as the realm you have secured for all who serve you. In the midst of many competing loyalties, help us to see your mission constantly before us.

Saturday, February 23, 2013

Week of Lent 1

Polycarp, Bishop of Smyrna, martyr, died 156

Psalm 118:26-29

A pilgrimage song of praise

Blessed is the one who comes in the name of the LORD.
  We bless you from the house of the LORD.
The LORD is God,
  and he has given us light.
Bind the festal procession with branches,
  up to the horns of the altar.

You are my God, and I will give thanks to you;
  you are my God, I will extol you.

O give thanks to the LORD, for he is good,
  for his steadfast love endures forever. (Ps. 118:26-29)

Psalm	Additional Reading
Psalm 27	Matthew 23:37-39
The Lord shall keep me safe	*Jesus laments over Jerusalem*

Hymn: Immortal, Invisible, God Only Wise, ELW 834

Almighty God, blessed are the places where people come together to praise you. Increase our knowledge of your rich blessings so that our worshiping assemblies may ring with sounds of thanksgiving.

Sunday, February 24, 2013

Second Sunday in Lent

Luke 13:31-35

A hen gathering her brood

At that very hour some Pharisees came and said to [Jesus], "Get away from here, for Herod wants to kill you." He said to them, "Go and tell that fox for me, 'Listen, I am casting out demons and performing cures today and tomorrow, and on the third day I finish my work. Yet today, tomorrow, and the next day I must be on my way, because it is impossible for a prophet to be killed outside of Jerusalem.' Jerusalem, Jerusalem, the city that kills the prophets and stones those who are sent to it! How often have I desired to gather your children together as a hen gathers her brood under her wings, and you were not willing! See, your house is left to you. And I tell you, you will not see me until the time comes when you say, 'Blessed is the one who comes in the name of the Lord.' " (Luke 13:31-35)

Psalm	Additional Readings	
Psalm 27	Genesis 15:1-12, 17-18	Philippians 3:17—4:1
The Lord shall keep me safe	*The covenant with Abram*	*Our citizenship is in heaven*

Hymn: When Twilight Comes, ELW 566

God of the covenant, in the mystery of the cross you promise everlasting life to the world. Gather all peoples into your arms, and shelter us with your mercy, that we may rejoice in the life we share in your Son, Jesus Christ, our Savior and Lord, who lives and reigns with you and the Holy Spirit, one God, now and forever.

Monday, February 25, 2013

Week of Lent 2

Elizabeth Fedde, deaconess, died 1921

Psalm 105:1-15 [16-41] 42
God's covenant with Abraham

O give thanks to the Lord, call on his name,
  make known his deeds among the peoples.
Sing to him, sing praises to him;
  tell of all his wonderful works.
Glory in his holy name;
  let the hearts of those who seek the Lord rejoice.
Seek the Lord and his strength;
  seek his presence continually. (Ps. 105:1-4)

Additional Readings
Exodus 33:1-6   Romans 4:1-12
Abraham's descendants lament   *The faith of Abraham*

Hymn: Praise and Thanksgiving, ELW 689

*O God, the beauty of your creation and your power to restore our lives
has inspired poets and musicians to acclaim you. May your great works
continue to prompt the songs of our grateful hearts.*

Tuesday, February 26, 2013

Week of Lent 2

1 Corinthians 10:1-13
God is faithful

I do not want you to be unaware, brothers and sisters, that our ancestors were all under the cloud, and all passed through the sea, and all were baptized into Moses in the cloud and in the sea, and all ate the same spiritual food, and all drank the same spiritual drink. For they drank from the spiritual rock that followed them, and the rock was Christ. Nevertheless, God was not pleased with most of them, and they were struck down in the wilderness. (1 Cor. 10:1-5)

Psalm
Psalm 105:1-15 [16-41] 42
God's covenant with Abraham

Additional Reading
Numbers 14:10b-24
Moses intercedes for the people

Hymn: Jesus, Still Lead On, ELW 624

Most faithful God, you have protected and saved your people in countless ways in the past. Continue to nourish and strengthen us in our time that we may pass along your blessings to those who do not yet know of your power and love.

Wednesday, February 27, 2013

Week of Lent 2

2 Chronicles 20:1-22

The king prays for Jerusalem

Jehoshaphat stood in the assembly of Judah and Jerusalem, in the house of the LORD, before the new court, and said, "O LORD, God of our ancestors, are you not God in heaven? Do you not rule over all the kingdoms of the nations? In your hand are power and might, so that no one is able to withstand you. Did you not, O our God, drive out the inhabitants of this land before your people Israel, and give it forever to the descendants of your friend Abraham? They have lived in it, and in it have built you a sanctuary for your name, saying, 'If disaster comes upon us, the sword, judgment, or pestilence, or famine, we will stand before this house, and before you, for your name is in this house, and cry to you in our distress, and you will hear and save'." (2 Chron. 20:5-9)

Psalm
Psalm 105:1-15 [16-41] 42
God's covenant with Abraham

Additional Reading
Luke 13:22-31
The narrow door

Hymn: Lead On, O King Eternal! ELW 805

O Lord our God, even in the midst of terrifying forces you are near us and able to provide comfort. Help us to believe in your watchful care and continue to hope in your steadfast love that endures forever.

Thursday, February 28, 2013

Week of Lent 2

Psalm 63:1-8
O God, eagerly I seek you

O God, you are my God, I seek you,
   my soul thirsts for you;
my flesh faints for you,
   as in a dry and weary land where there is no water.
So I have looked upon you in the sanctuary,
   beholding your power and glory.
Because your steadfast love is better than life,
   my lips will praise you.
So I will bless you as long as I live;
   I will lift up my hands and call on your name. (Ps. 63:1-4)

Additional Readings

Daniel 3:19-30
Servants of God vindicated

Revelation 2:8-11
Warning to the church in Smyrna

Hymn: All My Hope on God Is Founded, ELW 757

O God, many people in our world hunger and thirst for the very basic necessities of life. Show us ways to enlarge access to the benefits that many of us take for granted, so that all peoples throughout the world may come to know of your blessings.

_____

_____

_____

_____

_____

_____

_____

_____

_____

_____

_____

_____

Friday, March 1, 2013

Week of Lent 2

George Herbert, hymnwriter, died 1633

Revelation 3:1-6

Warning to the church in Sardis

"And to the angel of the church in Sardis write: These are the words of him who has the seven spirits of God and the seven stars:

"I know your works; you have a name of being alive, but you are dead. Wake up, and strengthen what remains and is on the point of death, for I have not found your works perfect in the sight of my God. Remember then what you received and heard; obey it, and repent. If you do not wake up, I will come like a thief, and you will not know at what hour I will come to you. Yet you have still a few persons in Sardis who have not soiled their clothes; they will walk with me, dressed in white, for they are worthy. If you conquer, you will be clothed like them in white robes, and I will not blot your name out of the book of life; I will confess your name before my Father and before his angels." (Rev. 3:1-5)

Psalm
Psalm 63:1-8
O God, eagerly I seek you

Additional Reading
Daniel 12:1-4
God sends Michael

Hymn: Come, My Way, My Truth, My Life, ELW 816

Wake us up, O God. Stir us up in ways we have never imagined, to paths we never dared, and down passageways of faithfulness we could not ever have seen, save for your light and love.

Saturday, March 2, 2013

Week of Lent 2

John Wesley, died 1791; Charles Wesley, died 1788; renewers of the church

Isaiah 5:1-7
The song of the vineyard

Let me sing for my beloved
   my love-song concerning his vineyard:
My beloved had a vineyard
   on a very fertile hill.
He dug it and cleared it of stones,
   and planted it with choice vines;
he built a watchtower in the midst of it,
   and hewed out a wine vat in it;
he expected it to yield grapes,
   but it yielded wild grapes.

And now, inhabitants of Jerusalem
   and people of Judah,
judge between me
   and my vineyard.
What more was there to do for my vineyard
   that I have not done in it?
When I expected it to yield grapes,
   why did it yield wild grapes? (Isa. 5:1-4)

Psalm
Psalm 63:1-8
O God, eagerly I seek you

Additional Reading
Luke 6:43-45
A tree and its fruits

Hymn: Lord of Glory, You Have Bought Us, ELW 707

*Holy One of Israel, in every age your people sing songs of praise to you,
the love songs of heaven and earth. You plant us, and we become your
vineyard. You call us to bear the fruits of faith and love.*

78

Sunday, March 3, 2013

Third Sunday in Lent

Luke 13:1-9

The parable of the fig tree

Then [Jesus] told this parable: "A man had a fig tree planted in his vineyard; and he came looking for fruit on it and found none. So he said to the gardener, 'See here! For three years I have come looking for fruit on this fig tree, and still I find none. Cut it down! Why should it be wasting the soil?' He replied, 'Sir, let it alone for one more year, until I dig around it and put manure on it. If it bears fruit next year, well and good; but if not, you can cut it down'. " (Luke 13:6-9)

Psalm

Psalm 63:1-8
O God, eagerly I seek you

Additional Readings

Isaiah 55:1-9
Come to the water

1 Corinthians 10:1-13
Israel, baptized in cloud and seas

Hymn: I Heard the Voice of Jesus Say, ELW 611

Eternal God, your kingdom has broken into our troubled world through the life, death, and resurrection of your Son. Help us to hear your word and obey it, and bring your saving love to fruition in our lives, through Jesus Christ, our Savior and Lord, who lives and reigns with you and the Holy Spirit, one God, now and forever.

Monday, March 4, 2013

Week of Lent 3

Psalm 39
My hope is in God

"LORD, let me know my end,
  and what is the measure of my days;
  let me know how fleeting my life is.
You have made my days a few handbreadths,
  and my lifetime is as nothing in your sight.
Surely everyone stands as a mere breath.
  Surely everyone goes about like a shadow.
Surely for nothing they are in turmoil;
  they heap up, and do not know who will gather.

"And now, O Lord, what do I wait for?
  My hope is in you." (Ps. 39:4-7)

Additional Readings
Jeremiah 11:1-17   Romans 2:1-11
Judgment against the olive tree   *Divine judgment applies to all*

Hymn: O God, Our Help in Ages Past, ELW 632

*O Lord, in the endless time that is yours, our days are but a glimpse
of all that is eternal. In the endless love that defines you, we breathe
alongside your compassion, and with your help we breathe healing into
this broken world.*

Tuesday, March 5, 2013

Week of Lent 3

Romans 2:12-16

What the law requires is written on the heart

All who have sinned apart from the law will also perish apart from the law, and all who have sinned under the law will be judged by the law. For it is not the hearers of the law who are righteous in God's sight, but the doers of the law who will be justified. When Gentiles, who do not possess the law, do instinctively what the law requires, these, though not having the law, are a law to themselves. They show that what the law requires is written on their hearts, to which their own conscience also bears witness; and their conflicting thoughts will accuse or perhaps excuse them on the day when, according to my gospel, God, through Jesus Christ, will judge the secret thoughts of all. (Rom. 2:12-16)

Psalm

Psalm 39

My hope is in God

Additional Reading

Ezekiel 17:1-10

Allegory of the vine

Hymn: Salvation unto Us Has Come, ELW 590

In our hearts, in our hands, in our work, and in our deeds, O God, there let our love for you be shown.

Wednesday, March 6, 2013

Week of Lent 3

Numbers 13:17-27

The fruit of the promised land

Moses sent them to spy out the land of Canaan, and said to them, "Go up there into the Negeb, and go up into the hill country, and see what the land is like, and whether the people who live in it are strong or weak, whether they are few or many."

At the end of forty days they returned from spying out the land. And they came to Moses and Aaron and to all the congregation of the Israelites in the wilderness of Paran, at Kadesh; they brought back word to them and to all the congregation, and showed them the fruit of the land. And they told him, "We came to the land to which you sent us; it flows with milk and honey, and this is its fruit." (Num. 13:17-18, 25-27)

Psalm	Additional Reading
Psalm 39	Luke 13:18-21
My hope is in God	*Parables of the mustard seed, yeast*

Hymn: O Bread of Life from Heaven, ELW 480

Eternal God, the land is holy, the rivers are holy, the sky is holy, the fields are holy. Each spring when we plow the earth for planting, remind us to turn all of our lives over to you.

Thursday, March 7, 2013

Week of Lent 3

Perpetua and Felicity and companions, martyrs at Carthage, died 202

Psalm 32
Be glad, you righteous

Happy are those whose transgression is forgiven,
  whose sin is covered.
Happy are those to whom the LORD imputes no iniquity,
  and in whose spirit there is no deceit.

Be glad in the LORD and rejoice, O righteous,
  and shout for joy, all you upright in heart. (Ps. 32:1-2, 11)

Additional Readings
Joshua 4:1-13   2 Corinthians 4:16—5:5
Joshua leads the people across the Jordan   *Paul comforts with a promise of glory*

Hymn: In All Our Grief, ELW 615

In the darkness of our souls, O God, and in the secret quietness of our hearts, there we find you and watch while you erase the sin, the guilt, and the shame to make our lives whole again.

Friday, March 8, 2013

Week of Lent 3

2 Corinthians 5:6-15
Walking by faith and not by sight

So we are always confident; even though we know that while we are at home in the body we are away from the Lord—for we walk by faith, not by sight. Yes, we do have confidence, and we would rather be away from the body and at home with the Lord. So whether we are at home or away, we make it our aim to please him. For all of us must appear before the judgment seat of Christ, so that each may receive recompense for what has been done in the body, whether good or evil. (2 Cor. 5:6-10)

Psalm
Psalm 32
Be glad, you righteous

Additional Reading
Joshua 4:14-24
God's people come through the waters dry-shod

Hymn: We Walk by Faith, ELW 635

One foot before the other, dear God, and one heartbeat following the one before, we walk down the paths of life knowing that you are present in the silence.

Saturday, March 9, 2013

Week of Lent 3

Exodus 32:7-14
Moses begs forgiveness

Moses implored the LORD his God, and said, "O LORD, why does your wrath burn hot against your people, whom you brought out of the land of Egypt with great power and with a mighty hand? Why should the Egyptians say, 'It was with evil intent that he brought them out to kill them in the mountains, and to consume them from the face of the earth'? Turn from your fierce wrath; change your mind and do not bring disaster on your people. Remember Abraham, Isaac, and Israel, your servants, how you swore to them by your own self, saying to them, 'I will multiply your descendants like the stars of heaven, and all this land that I have promised I will give to your descendants, and they shall inherit it forever.' " And the LORD changed his mind about the disaster that he planned to bring on his people. (Exod. 32:11-14)

Psalm
Psalm 32
Be glad, you righteous

Additional Reading
Luke 15:1-10
Parables of a lost sheep and a lost coin

Hymn: Come, Thou Fount of Every Blessing, ELW 807

Holy God, let your anger turn away from us. Let us become residents of your holy love, as many and as often as the stars we see above on a moonlit night.

Sunday, March 10, 2013

Fourth Sunday in Lent

Luke 15:1-3, 11b-32

The parable of the forgiving father

"[The elder son] answered his father, 'Listen! For all these years I have been working like a slave for you, and I have never disobeyed your command; yet you have never given me even a young goat so that I might celebrate with my friends. But when this son of yours came back, who has devoured your property with prostitutes, you killed the fatted calf for him!' Then the father said to him, 'Son, you are always with me, and all that is mine is yours. But we had to celebrate and rejoice, because this brother of yours was dead and has come to life; he was lost and has been found'. " (Luke 15:29-32)

Psalm

Psalm 32

Be glad, you righteous

Additional Readings

Joshua 5:9-12

Israel eats bread and grain

2 Corinthians 5:16-21

The mystery and ministry of reconciliation

Hymn: Our Father, We Have Wandered, ELW 606

God of compassion, you welcome the wayward, and you embrace us all with your mercy. By our baptism clothe us with garments of your grace, and feed us at the table of your love, through Jesus Christ, our Savior and Lord, who lives and reigns with you and the Holy Spirit, one God, now and forever.

Monday, March 11, 2013

Week of Lent 4

Psalm 53
Restoring our fortunes

God looks down from heaven on humankind
  to see if there are any who are wise,
  who seek after God.

They have all fallen away, they are all alike perverse;
  there is no one who does good,
  no, not one.

O that deliverance for Israel would come from Zion!
  When God restores the fortunes of his people,
  Jacob will rejoice; Israel will be glad. (Ps. 53:2-3, 6)

Additional Readings
Leviticus 23:26-41   Revelation 19:1-8
Days for confession and celebration   *The marriage supper of the Lamb*

Hymn: Restore in Us, O God, ELW 328

*Eternal God, restore us, reform us, and reshape us into humankind that
is kind indeed. When you forgive you give us life again, so that we will
rejoice and tell your story of love.*

Tuesday, March 12, 2013

Week of Lent 4

Gregory the Great, Bishop of Rome, died 604

Revelation 19:9-10
Blessed are those invited to the marriage supper

And the angel said to me, "Write this: Blessed are those who are invited to the marriage supper of the Lamb." And he said to me, "These are true words of God." Then I fell down at his feet to worship him, but he said to me, "You must not do that! I am a fellow servant with you and your comrades who hold the testimony of Jesus. Worship God! For the testimony of Jesus is the spirit of prophecy." (Rev. 19:9-10)

Psalm
Psalm 53
Restoring our fortunes

Additional Reading
Leviticus 25:1-19
The jubilee celebration

Hymn: I Received the Living God, ELW 477

Holy One, so often we want to worship the angels, the messengers, the prophets, the saints, the teachers, and our mentors in life, but then we remember that it is only your kindness and love that remains always and forever.

Wednesday, March 13, 2013

Week of Lent 4

Luke 9:10-17
Jesus feeds 5000

The day was drawing to a close, and the twelve came to [Jesus] and said, "Send the crowd away, so that they may go into the surrounding villages and countryside, to lodge and get provisions; for we are here in a deserted place." But he said to them, "You give them something to eat." They said, "We have no more than five loaves and two fish—unless we are to go and buy food for all these people." For there were about five thousand men. And he said to his disciples, "Make them sit down in groups of about fifty each." They did so and made them all sit down. And taking the five loaves and the two fish, he looked up to heaven, and blessed and broke them, and gave them to the disciples to set before the crowd. And all ate and were filled. What was left over was gathered up, twelve baskets of broken pieces. (Luke 9:12-17)

Psalm
Psalm 53
Restoring our fortunes

Additional Reading
2 Kings 4:1-7
The widow saved

Hymn: You Satisfy the Hungry Heart, ELW 484

Five loaves of barley, two fish, five thousand, circles of fifty. How your living presence is multiplied. With all the multiplicity of your grace, nourish us and those we love.

Thursday, March 14, 2013

Week of Lent 4

Psalm 126
Sowing with tears, reaping with joy

Restore our fortunes, O Lord,
  like the watercourses in the Negeb.
May those who sow in tears
  reap with shouts of joy.
Those who go out weeping,
  bearing the seed for sowing,
shall come home with shouts of joy,
  carrying their sheaves. (Ps. 126:4-6)

Additional Readings
Isaiah 43:1-7   Philippians 2:19-24
God will gather through fire and water   *Apostolic visits are promised*

Hymn: As the Sun with Longer Journey, ELW 329

Dear God, turn our tears into joy, our grief into laughter, our pain into pleasure, and our aching hearts into a living witness of your grace and everlasting caring.

Friday, March 15, 2013

Week of Lent 4

Isaiah 43:8-15
God is Lord, Holy One, Creator, Ruler

I, I am the LORD,
>and besides me there is no savior.
>I declared and saved and proclaimed,
>>when there was no strange god among you;
>>and you are my witnesses, says the LORD.
>I am God, and also henceforth I am He;
>>there is no one who can deliver from my hand;
>>I work and who can hinder it?
Thus says the LORD,
>your Redeemer, the Holy One of Israel:
>For your sake I will send to Babylon
>>and break down all the bars,
>>and the shouting of the Chaldeans will be turned to lamentation.
I am the LORD, your Holy One,
>the Creator of Israel, your King. (Isa. 43:11-15)

Psalm	Additional Reading
Psalm 126	Philippians 2:25—3:1
Sowing with tears, reaping with joy	*Paul praises a coworker*

Hymn: Praise God, from Whom All Blessings Flow, ELW 884/885

Eternal God, each time we are tempted to wander off in search of other powers, you show up in our prayers, our dreams, and in our days' thoughts and ponderings. To you we shout and sing: you are the one and only!

Saturday, March 16, 2013

Week of Lent 4

Exodus 12:21-27

Passover instituted to celebrate the exodus

Then Moses called all the elders of Israel and said to them, "Go, select lambs for your families, and slaughter the passover lamb. Take a bunch of hyssop, dip it in the blood that is in the basin, and touch the lintel and the two doorposts with the blood in the basin. None of you shall go outside the door of your house until morning. For the Lord will pass through to strike down the Egyptians; when he sees the blood on the lintel and on the two doorposts, the Lord will pass over that door and will not allow the destroyer to enter your houses to strike you down. You shall observe this rite as a perpetual ordinance for you and your children. When you come to the land that the Lord will give you, as he has promised, you shall keep this observance." (Exod. 12:21-25)

Psalm

Psalm 126

Sowing with tears, reaping with joy

Additional Reading

John 11:45-57

Plotting against Jesus during Passover

Hymn: A Lamb Goes Uncomplaining Forth, ELW 340

Faithful God, in the yearly remembrance of Christ's passage from death to life, the ancient Passover ritual is retold, remembered, and relived. As you once brought salvation to your people, so save us now.

Sunday, March 17, 2013

Fifth Sunday in Lent

Patrick, bishop, missionary to Ireland, died 461

John 12:1-8

Mary anoints Jesus for his burial

Mary took a pound of costly perfume made of pure nard, anointed Jesus' feet, and wiped them with her hair. The house was filled with the fragrance of the perfume. But Judas Iscariot, one of his disciples (the one who was about to betray him), said, "Why was this perfume not sold for three hundred denarii and the money given to the poor?" (He said this not because he cared about the poor, but because he was a thief; he kept the common purse and used to steal what was put into it.) Jesus said, "Leave her alone. She bought it so that she might keep it for the day of my burial." (John 12:3-8)

Psalm

Psalm 126

Sowing with tears, reaping with joy

Additional Readings

Isaiah 43:16-21

The Lord gives water in the wilderness

Philippians 3:4b-14

To know Christ and his resurrection

Hymn: Take My Life, That I May Be, ELW 685

Creator God, you prepare a new way in the wilderness, and your grace waters our desert. Open our hearts to be transformed by the new thing you are doing, that our lives may proclaim the extravagance of your love given to all through your Son, Jesus Christ, our Savior and Lord, who lives and reigns with you and the Holy Spirit, one God, now and forever.

Monday, March 18, 2013

Week of Lent 5

Psalm 20
Victory for God's anointed

Now I know that the LORD will help his anointed;
  he will answer him from his holy heaven
  with mighty victories by his right hand.
Some take pride in chariots, and some in horses,
  but our pride is in the name of the LORD our God.
They will collapse and fall,
  but we shall rise and stand upright.

Give victory to the king, O LORD;
  answer us when we call. (Ps. 20:6-9)

Additional Readings
Exodus 40:1-15   Hebrews 10:19-25
Anointing the holy things   *Jesus, priest for the people of God*

Hymn: Jesus Is a Rock in a Weary Land, ELW 333

*O heavenly Lord, you listen, remember, and recall your love for us.
Whenever we speak to you, answer us through starry nights and calm
our troubled hearts.*

Tuesday, March 19, 2013

Joseph, Guardian of Jesus

Matthew 1:16, 18-21, 24a

The Lord appears to Joseph in a dream

Now the birth of Jesus the Messiah took place in this way. When his mother Mary had been engaged to Joseph, but before they lived together, she was found to be with child from the Holy Spirit. Her husband Joseph, being a righteous man and unwilling to expose her to public disgrace, planned to dismiss her quietly. But just when he had resolved to do this, an angel of the Lord appeared to him in a dream and said, "Joseph, son of David, do not be afraid to take Mary as your wife, for the child conceived in her is from the Holy Spirit. She will bear a son, and you are to name him Jesus, for he will save his people from their sins." (Matt. 1:18-21)

Psalm

Psalm 89:1-29

The Lord's steadfast love is established forever

Additional Readings

2 Samuel 7:4, 8-16

God makes a covenant with David

Romans 4:13-18

The promise to those who share Abraham's faith

Hymn: Of the Father's Love Begotten, ELW 295

O God, from the family of your servant David you raised up Joseph to be the guardian of your incarnate Son and the husband of his blessed mother. Give us grace to imitate his uprightness of life and his obedience to your commands, through Jesus Christ, our Savior and Lord, who lives and reigns with you and the Holy Spirit, one God, now and forever.

Wednesday, March 20, 2013

Week of Lent 5

Luke 18:31-34

Jesus foretells his death

Then [Jesus] took the twelve aside and said to them, "See, we are going up to Jerusalem, and everything that is written about the Son of Man by the prophets will be accomplished. For he will be handed over to the Gentiles; and he will be mocked and insulted and spat upon. After they have flogged him, they will kill him, and on the third day he will rise again." But they understood nothing about all these things; in fact, what he said was hidden from them, and they did not grasp what was said. (Luke 18:31-34)

Psalm
Psalm 20
Victory for God's anointed

Additional Reading
Habakkuk 3:2-15
God will save the anointed

Hymn: Jesus, I Will Ponder Now, ELW 345

We do not ever want to give you up, Jesus. We do not want to turn you over to the story of your destruction. Yet within those awful words is our hope and our salvation. Help us grasp the mystery of your saving death.

Thursday, March 21, 2013

Week of Lent 5

Thomas Cranmer, Bishop of Canterbury, martyr, died 1556

Psalm 31:9-16
I commend my spirit

Be gracious to me, O Lord, for I am in distress;
    my eye wastes away from grief,
  my soul and body also.
For my life is spent with sorrow,
    and my years with sighing;
  my strength fails because of my misery,
    and my bones waste away.

But I trust in you, O Lord;
    I say, "You are my God."
My times are in your hand;
    deliver me from the hand of my enemies and persecutors.
Let your face shine upon your servant;
    save me in your steadfast love. (Ps. 31:9-10, 14-16)

Additional Readings
Isaiah 53:10-12
The suffering one bears the sin of many

Hebrews 2:1-9
God's care for humankind

Hymn: Day by Day, ELW 790

Dear God, the losses we have known are more than we can bear or carry. Our eyes are red with tears, and those we thought would love us have run away. Yet we know that you are there, beyond our tears, beyond our fears, leading us from death into life.

Friday, March 22, 2013

Week of Lent 5

Jonathan Edwards, teacher, missionary to American Indians, died 1758

Isaiah 54:9-10
God's love is steadfast

This is like the days of Noah to me:
  Just as I swore that the waters of Noah
  would never again go over the earth,
so I have sworn that I will not be angry with you
  and will not rebuke you.
For the mountains may depart
  and the hills be removed,
but my steadfast love shall not depart from you,
  and my covenant of peace shall not be removed,
  says the LORD, who has compassion on you. (Isa. 54:9-10)

Psalm	Additional Reading
Psalm 31:9-16	Hebrews 2:10-18
I commend my spirit	*Jesus' suffering binds him to humankind*

Hymn: If You But Trust in God to Guide You, ELW 769

When grief like an earthquake commands our souls, when typhoons of tears wash us into despair, be the place of comfort and love for us. Be our home.

Saturday, March 23, 2013

Week of Lent 5

Leviticus 23:1-8
Sabbath and passover

The LORD spoke to Moses, saying: Speak to the people of Israel and say to them: These are the appointed festivals of the LORD that you shall proclaim as holy convocations, my appointed festivals.

Six days shall work be done; but the seventh day is a sabbath of complete rest, a holy convocation; you shall do no work: it is a sabbath to the LORD throughout your settlements. (Lev. 23:1-3)

Psalm
Psalm 31:9-16
I commend my spirit

Additional Reading
Luke 22:1-13
Jesus prepares for Passover with his disciples

Hymn: O Day of Rest and Gladness, ELW 521

We need rest, eternal God. More than mere moments of inactivity, we need true rest for the restoration of our bodies, minds, and souls. If resting is made for humankind, not humankind for resting, let it be so!

Holy Week

On the Sunday of the Passion, Christians enter into Holy Week. This day opens before the Christian community the final period of preparation before the celebration of the Three Days of the Lord's passion, death, and resurrection.

In many churches, palm branches will be given to worshipers for the procession into the worship space. Following an ancient custom, many Christians bring their palms home and place them in the household prayer center, behind a cross or sacred image, or above the indoor lintel of the entryway.

At sunset on Maundy Thursday, Lent comes to an end as the church begins the celebration of the events through which Christ has become the life and the resurrection for all who believe.

Prayer for Placing Palms in the Home

Use this blessing when placing palms in the home after the Palm Sunday liturgy.

Blessed is the One who comes in the name of the Lord!
May we who place these palms receive Christ into our midst
with the joy that marked the entrance to Jerusalem.
May we hold no betrayal in our hearts,
but peacefully welcome Christ,
who lives and reigns with you and the Holy Spirit,
one God, now and forever. Amen.

Sunday, March 24, 2013

Sunday of the Passion
Palm Sunday

Oscar Arnulfo Romero, Bishop of El Salvador, martyr, died 1980

Luke 22:14—23:56
The passion and death of Jesus

Pilate, wanting to release Jesus, addressed [the chief priests, the leaders, and the people] again; but they kept shouting, "Crucify, crucify him!" A third time he said to them, "Why, what evil has he done? I have found in him no ground for the sentence of death; I will therefore have him flogged and then release him." But they kept urgently demanding with loud shouts that he should be crucified; and their voices prevailed. So Pilate gave his verdict that their demand should be granted. He released the man they asked for, the one who had been put in prison for insurrection and murder, and he handed Jesus over as they wished. (Luke 23:20-25)

Psalm
Psalm 31:9-16
I commend my spirit

Additional Readings
Isaiah 50:4-9a
The servant submits to suffering

Philippians 2:5-11
Death on a cross

Hymn: My Song Is Love Unknown, ELW 343

Everlasting God, in your endless love for the human race you sent our Lord Jesus Christ to take on our nature and to suffer death on the cross. In your mercy enable us to share in his obedience to your will and in the glorious victory of his resurrection, who lives and reigns with you and the Holy Spirit, one God, now and forever.

Monday, March 25, 2013

Monday in Holy Week

Annunciation of Our Lord (transferred to April 1)

Psalm 36:5-11
Refuge under the shadow of your wings

Your steadfast love, O LORD, extends to the heavens,
    your faithfulness to the clouds.
Your righteousness is like the mighty mountains,
    your judgments are like the great deep;
    you save humans and animals alike, O LORD.

How precious is your steadfast love, O God!
    All people may take refuge in the shadow of your wings.
They feast on the abundance of your house,
    and you give them drink from the river of your delights.
For with you is the fountain of life;
    in your light we see light. (Ps. 36:5-9)

Additional Readings

Isaiah 42:1-9	Hebrews 9:11-15	John 12:1-11
The servant brings forth justice	*The blood of Christ redeems for eternal life*	*Mary of Bethany anoints Jesus*

Hymn: Lord, Thee I Love with All My Heart, ELW 750

O God, your Son chose the path that led to pain before joy and to the cross before glory. Plant his cross in our hearts, so that in its power and love we may come at last to joy and glory, through Jesus Christ, our Savior and Lord, who lives and reigns with you and the Holy Spirit, one God, now and forever.

Tuesday, March 26, 2013

Tuesday in Holy Week

Isaiah 49:1-7

The servant brings salvation to earth's ends

And now the LORD says,
   who formed me in the womb to be his servant,
to bring Jacob back to him,
   and that Israel might be gathered to him,
for I am honored in the sight of the LORD,
   and my God has become my strength—
he says,
"It is too light a thing that you should be my servant
   to raise up the tribes of Jacob
   and to restore the survivors of Israel;
I will give you as a light to the nations,
   that my salvation may reach to the end of the earth."
(Isa. 49:5-6)

Psalm	Additional Readings	
Psalm 71:1-14	1 Corinthians 1:18-31	John 12:20-36
From my mother's womb you have been my strength	*The cross of Christ reveals God's power and wisdom*	*Jesus speaks of his death*

Hymn: Will You Let Me Be Your Servant, ELW 659

Lord Jesus, you have called us to follow you. Grant that our love may not grow cold in your service, and that we may not fail or deny you in the time of trial, for you live and reign with the Father and the Holy Spirit, one God, now and forever.

Wednesday, March 27, 2013

Wednesday in Holy Week

Hebrews 12:1-3

Look to Jesus, who endured the cross

Therefore, since we are surrounded by so great a cloud of witnesses, let us also lay aside every weight and the sin that clings so closely, and let us run with perseverance the race that is set before us, looking to Jesus the pioneer and perfecter of our faith, who for the sake of the joy that was set before him endured the cross, disregarding its shame, and has taken his seat at the right hand of the throne of God.

Consider him who endured such hostility against himself from sinners, so that you may not grow weary or lose heart. (Heb. 12:1-3)

Psalm

Psalm 70
Be pleased, O God, to deliver me

Additional Readings

Isaiah 50:4-9a
The servant is vindicated by God

John 13:21-32
Jesus foretells his betrayal

Hymn: Beneath the Cross of Jesus, ELW 338

Almighty God, your Son our Savior suffered at human hands and endured the shame of the cross. Grant that we may walk in the way of his cross and find it the way of life and peace, through Jesus Christ, our Savior and Lord, who lives and reigns with you and the Holy Spirit, one God, now and forever.

THE THREE DAYS

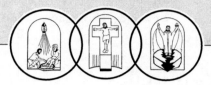

As the sun sets on Maundy Thursday, so Lent ends and the Three Days begin, ending with sunset on Easter Day. During these central days, Christians prepare to celebrate God's gift of new life given in baptism. Indeed, the readings of the Three Days move toward the baptismal font where new brothers and sisters are born of water and the Spirit, and where the baptized renew their baptismal promises.

In the home and in the church community, special attention is given to these days through prayer and the keeping of greater silence until the great Vigil of Easter is celebrated. Many Christians keep a fast from food, work, and entertainment on Good Friday and Holy Saturday. In the home, preparations can be made for the celebration of Easter: cleaning, coloring eggs, baking Easter breads, gathering greens or flowers to adorn crosses and sacred images. In those communities where baptisms will be celebrated, prayers may be offered for those to be received into the church.

Table Prayer for the Three Days

Blessed are you, O Lord our God.
With this food strengthen us on our journey from death to life.
We glory in the cross of Christ.
Raise us, with him, to the joy of the resurrection,
through Jesus Christ our Lord. Amen.

Thursday, March 28, 2013

Maundy Thursday

Exodus 12:1-4 [5-10] 11-14
The passover of the Lord

Tell the whole congregation of Israel that on the tenth of this month they are to take a lamb for each family, a lamb for each household.

This is how you shall eat it: your loins girded, your sandals on your feet, and your staff in your hand; and you shall eat it hurriedly. It is the passover of the LORD. For I will pass through the land of Egypt that night, and I will strike down every firstborn in the land of Egypt, both human beings and animals; on all the gods of Egypt I will execute judgments: I am the LORD. The blood shall be a sign for you on the houses where you live: when I see the blood, I will pass over you, and no plague shall destroy you when I strike the land of Egypt. (Exod. 12:3, 11-13)

Psalm	Additional Readings	
Psalm 116:1-2, 12-19	1 Corinthians	John 13:1-17, 31b-35
The cup of salvation	**11:23-26**	*The service of Christ: footwashing and meal*
	Proclaim the Lord's death	

Hymn: Where Charity and Love Prevail, ELW 359

Holy God, source of all love, on the night of his betrayal, Jesus gave us a new commandment, to love one another as he loves us. Write this commandment in our hearts, and give us the will to serve others as he was the servant of all, your Son, Jesus Christ, our Savior and Lord, who lives and reigns with you and the Holy Spirit, one God, now and forever.

Friday, March 29, 2013

Good Friday

Hans Nielsen Hauge, renewer of the church, died 1824

John 18:1—19:42
The passion and death of Jesus

Joseph of Arimathea, who was a disciple of Jesus, though a secret one because of his fear of the Jews, asked Pilate to let him take away the body of Jesus. Pilate gave him permission; so he came and removed his body. Nicodemus, who had at first come to Jesus by night, also came, bringing a mixture of myrrh and aloes, weighing about a hundred pounds. They took the body of Jesus and wrapped it with the spices in linen cloths, according to the burial custom of the Jews. Now there was a garden in the place where he was crucified, and in the garden there was a new tomb in which no one had ever been laid. And so, because it was the Jewish day of Preparation, and the tomb was nearby, they laid Jesus there. (John 19:38-42)

Psalm
Psalm 22
Why have you forsaken me?

Additional Readings
Isaiah 52:13—53:12
The suffering servant

Hebrews 10:16-25
The way to God is opened

Hymn: There in God's Garden, ELW 342

Almighty God, look with loving mercy on your family, for whom our Lord Jesus Christ was willing to be betrayed, to be given over to the hands of sinners, and to suffer death on the cross; who now lives and reigns with you and the Holy Spirit, one God, forever and ever.

Saturday, March 30, 2013

Resurrection of Our Lord
Vigil of Easter

Romans 6:3-11
Dying and rising with Christ

Do you not know that all of us who have been baptized into Christ
Jesus were baptized into his death? Therefore we have been buried
with him by baptism into death, so that, just as Christ was raised
from the dead by the glory of the Father, so we too might walk in
newness of life.

For if we have been united with him in a death like his, we will
certainly be united with him in a resurrection like his. (Rom. 6:3-5)

Psalm

Psalm 46
The God of Jacob is our stronghold

Additional Readings

**Genesis 7:1-5, 11-18;
8:6-18; 9:8-13**
Flood

John 20:1-18
Seeing the risen Christ

Hymn: Come, You Faithful, Raise the Strain, ELW 363

*Eternal giver of life and light, this holy night shines with the radiance of
the risen Christ. Renew your church with the Spirit given us in baptism,
that we may worship you in sincerity and truth and may shine as a light
in the world, through your Son, Jesus Christ our Lord, who lives and
reigns with you and the Holy Spirit, one God, now and forever.*

Sunday, March 31, 2013

Resurrection of Our Lord
Easter Day

John Donne, poet, died 1631

Luke 24:1-12
Women proclaim the resurrection

But on the first day of the week, at early dawn, the women came to the tomb, taking the spices that they had prepared. They found the stone rolled away from the tomb, but when they went in, they did not find the body. While they were perplexed about this, suddenly two men in dazzling clothes stood beside them. The women were terrified and bowed their faces to the ground, but the men said to them, "Why do you look for the living among the dead? He is not here, but has risen. Remember how he told you, while he was still in Galilee, that the Son of Man must be handed over to sinners, and be crucified, and on the third day rise again." Then they remembered his words, and returning from the tomb, they told all this to the eleven and to all the rest. (Luke 24:1-9)

Psalm
Psalm 118:1-2, 14-24
On this day God has acted

Additional Readings
Acts 10:34-43
God raised Jesus on the third day

1 Corinthians 15:19-26
Christ raised from the dead

Hymn: Now All the Vault of Heaven Resounds, ELW 367

O God, you gave your only Son to suffer death on the cross for our redemption, and by his glorious resurrection you delivered us from the power of death. Make us die every day to sin, that we may live with him forever in the joy of the resurrection, through your Son, Jesus Christ our Lord, who lives and reigns with you and the Holy Spirit, one God, now and forever.

EASTER

The Three Days flow into the rejoicing of the fifty days of Easter. During this "week of weeks," Christians explore the meaning of the central actions of baptism for daily life: renouncing evil and professing faith, washing in water, being marked with the cross, being clothed in the white robe, receiving the light of the paschal/Easter candle, and eating and drinking the bread of life and the cup of salvation.

The fifty days were once called *Pentecost*, Greek for "fifty." On the fiftieth day of Easter, Christians celebrate the pentecostal mystery of the risen Christ breathing on the church the breath, the wind, and the fire of the Holy Spirit.

Table Prayer for the Season of Easter

O God of our risen Lord, we praise you, we bless you,
we worship you for the gifts of life you give us.
Always you offer us life, and for this we bless your holy name.
And we ask you,
give your life also to all who know only hunger and the pangs of death.
So may the whole world be raised to life,
through Jesus Christ, our Savior and Lord. Amen.

PRAYER LIST FOR APRIL

_____

_____

_____

_____

_____

_____

_____

_____

_____

_____

Monday, April 1, 2013

Annunciation of Our Lord (*transferred*)

Luke 1:26-38
The angel greets Mary

In the sixth month the angel Gabriel was sent by God to a town in Galilee called Nazareth, to a virgin engaged to a man whose name was Joseph, of the house of David. The virgin's name was Mary. And he came to her and said, "Greetings, favored one! The Lord is with you." But she was much perplexed by his words and pondered what sort of greeting this might be. The angel said to her, "Do not be afraid, Mary, for you have found favor with God. And now, you will conceive in your womb and bear a son, and you will name him Jesus." (Luke 1:26-31)

Psalm
Psalm 45
*Your name will be
remembered*

Additional Readings
Isaiah 7:10-14
*A young woman will bear
a son*

Hebrews 10:4-10
*The offering of Jesus' body
sanctifies us*

Hymn: The Angel Gabriel from Heaven Came, ELW 265

Pour your grace into our hearts, O God, that we who have known the incarnation of your Son, Jesus Christ, announced by an angel, may by his cross and passion be brought to the glory of his resurrection; for he lives and reigns with you, in the unity of the Holy Spirit, one God, now and forever.

Tuesday, April 2, 2013

Week of Easter 1

Revelation 12:1-12

The woman, the dragon, the child

Then I heard a loud voice in heaven, proclaiming,
"Now have come the salvation and the power
   and the kingdom of our God
   and the authority of his Messiah,
for the accuser of our comrades has been thrown down,
   who accuses them day and night before our God.
But they have conquered him by the blood of the Lamb
   and by the word of their testimony,
for they did not cling to life even in the face of death.
Rejoice then, you heavens
   and those who dwell in them!
But woe to the earth and the sea,
   for the devil has come down to you
with great wrath,
   because he knows that his time is short!" (Rev. 12:10-12)

Psalm
Psalm 118:1-2, 14-24
On this day God has acted

Additional Reading
Judges 4:17-23; 5:24-31a
Jael kills Sisera

Hymn: At the Lamb's High Feast We Sing, ELW 362

*Help us realize, O Lord, that your kingdom is present and that your love
surrounds us now. Guide us to give thanks that this day is ours to use
for proclaiming and sharing your grace with all people.*

Wednesday, April 3, 2013

Week of Easter 1

2 Samuel 6:1-15

David dances before the ark

It was told King David, "The LORD has blessed the household of Obed-edom and all that belongs to him, because of the ark of God." So David went and brought up the ark of God from the house of Obed-edom to the city of David with rejoicing; and when those who bore the ark of the LORD had gone six paces, he sacrificed an ox and a fatling. David danced before the LORD with all his might; David was girded with a linen ephod. So David and all the house of Israel brought up the ark of the LORD with shouting, and with the sound of the trumpet. (2 Sam. 6:12-15)

Psalm

Psalm 118:1-2, 14-24
On this day God has acted

Additional Reading

Luke 24:1-12
Women proclaim the resurrection

Hymn: Oh, Sing to the Lord, ELW 822

Holy Lord, so fill us with your resurrection praise that our shouts of Easter joy will be heard above this world's noise and strife, that people in need will come to the sounds of love and find hope.

Thursday, April 4, 2013

Week of Easter 1

Benedict the African, confessor, died 1589

Psalm 150
Let everything praise the Lord

Praise the LORD!
Praise God in his sanctuary;
　praise him in his mighty firmament!
Praise him for his mighty deeds;
　praise him according to his surpassing greatness!

Praise him with trumpet sound;
　praise him with lute and harp!
Praise him with tambourine and dance;
　praise him with strings and pipe!
Praise him with clanging cymbals;
　praise him with loud clashing cymbals!
Let everything that breathes praise the LORD!
Praise the LORD! (Ps. 150:1-6)

Additional Readings
1 Samuel 17:1-23
The enemy Goliath taunts Israel

Acts 5:12-16
Signs and wonders by the apostles

Hymn: When in Our Music God Is Glorified, ELW 851

Make our every breath a prayer, O God. Make every breath a song in praise of you alone. Make us living witnesses who proclaim your mercy, love, and forgiveness through our daily words and actions.

Friday, April 5, 2013

Week of Easter 1

Acts 5:17-26

The apostles freed from prison

Then the high priest took action; he and all who were with him (that is, the sect of the Sadducees), being filled with jealousy, arrested the apostles and put them in the public prison. But during the night an angel of the Lord opened the prison doors, brought them out, and said, "Go, stand in the temple and tell the people the whole message about this life." When they heard this, they entered the temple at daybreak and went on with their teaching. (Acts 5:17-21)

Psalm

Psalm 150

Let everything praise the Lord

Additional Reading

1 Samuel 17:19-32

David announces he will fight Goliath

Hymn: With High Delight Let Us Unite, ELW 368

No matter what happens to us this day, O Lord, we trust your promise that you are with us. We will share your word of life in our churches, in our workplaces, and in our homes.

Saturday, April 6, 2013

Week of Easter 1

Albrecht Dürer, died 1528; Matthias Grünewald, died 1529; Lucas Cranach, died 1553; artists

1 Samuel 17:32-51
David conquers Goliath

When the Philistine drew nearer to meet David, David ran quickly toward the battle line to meet the Philistine. David put his hand in his bag, took out a stone, slung it, and struck the Philistine on his forehead; the stone sank into his forehead, and he fell face down on the ground.

So David prevailed over the Philistine with a sling and a stone, striking down the Philistine and killing him; there was no sword in David's hand. Then David ran and stood over the Philistine; he grasped his sword, drew it out of its sheath, and killed him; then he cut off his head with it.

When the Philistines saw that their champion was dead, they fled. (1 Sam. 17:48-51)

Psalm
Psalm 150
Let everything praise the Lord

Additional Reading
Luke 24:36-40
Beholding the wounds of the risen Christ

Hymn: Thine Is the Glory, ELW 376

Wounded and broken, we come to you, O God, asking for your mercy. Do not cut us off from the land of the living, but restore us through faith to love and serve you as we serve all people in need.

Sunday, April 7, 2013

Second Sunday of Easter

John 20:19-31

Beholding the wounds of the risen Christ

A week later his disciples were again in the house, and Thomas was with them. Although the doors were shut, Jesus came and stood among them and said, "Peace be with you." Then he said to Thomas, "Put your finger here and see my hands. Reach out your hand and put it in my side. Do not doubt but believe." Thomas answered him, "My Lord and my God!" Jesus said to him, "Have you believed because you have seen me? Blessed are those who have not seen and yet have come to believe." (John 20:26-29)

Psalm
Psalm 118:14-29
Glad songs of victory

Additional Readings
Acts 5:27-32
The God of our ancestors raised up Jesus

Revelation 1:4-8
Jesus Christ, firstborn of the dead

Hymn: The Risen Christ, ELW 390

O God of life, you reach out to us amid our fears with the wounded hands of your risen Son. By your Spirit's breath revive our faith in your mercy, and strengthen us to be the body of your Son, Jesus Christ, our Savior and Lord, who lives and reigns with you and the Holy Spirit, one God, now and forever.

Monday, April 8, 2013

Week of Easter 2

Psalm 122

Peace in Jerusalem

I was glad when they said to me,
   "Let us go to the house of the LORD!"
Our feet are standing
   within your gates, O Jerusalem.

Pray for the peace of Jerusalem:
   "May they prosper who love you.
Peace be within your walls,
   and security within your towers."
For the sake of my relatives and friends
   I will say, "Peace be within you." (Ps. 122:1-2, 6-8)

Additional Readings

Esther 7:1-10   Revelation 1:9-20

Esther prevails over Haman   *A vision of Christ*

Hymn: Grant Peace, We Pray, in Mercy, Lord, ELW 784

*Bless all who strive to bring peace to families, neighborhoods, and cities.
Guide all who work for peace among nations. Keep those safe who do
not yet know peace. Give us a firm vision of your peaceable kingdom.*

Tuesday, April 9, 2013

Week of Easter 2

Dietrich Bonhoeffer, theologian, died 1945

Esther 8:1-17
Destruction of the Jews is averted

Then Mordecai went out from the presence of the king, wearing royal robes of blue and white, with a great golden crown and a mantle of fine linen and purple, while the city of Susa shouted and rejoiced. For the Jews there was light and gladness, joy and honor. In every province and in every city, wherever the king's command and his edict came, there was gladness and joy among the Jews, a festival and a holiday. Furthermore, many of the peoples of the country professed to be Jews, because the fear of the Jews had fallen upon them. (Esther 8:15-17)

Psalm
Psalm 122
Peace in Jerusalem

Additional Reading
Revelation 2:8-11
Words to the church at Smyrna

Hymn: By Gracious Powers, ELW 626

In every generation, Lord, you send messengers who remind us of your love, encourage us to work against evil, and call us to remain faithful as our daily lives witness to the power of mercy, forgiveness, hope, and grace.

Wednesday, April 10, 2013

Week of Easter 2

Mikael Agricola, Bishop of Turku, died 1557

Luke 12:4-12

The courage to confess Christ

[Jesus said,] "And I tell you, everyone who acknowledges me before others, the Son of Man also will acknowledge before the angels of God; but whoever denies me before others will be denied before the angels of God. And everyone who speaks a word against the Son of Man will be forgiven; but whoever blasphemes against the Holy Spirit will not be forgiven. When they bring you before the synagogues, the rulers, and the authorities, do not worry about how you are to defend yourselves or what you are to say; for the Holy Spirit will teach you at that very hour what you ought to say." (Luke 12:8-12)

Psalm
Psalm 122
Peace in Jerusalem

Additional Reading
Esther 9:1-5, 18-23
Purim celebrates victory

Hymn: If God My Lord Be for Me, ELW 788

Strengthen us, O Lord, through your word and sacraments and through our prayer and praise to proclaim your love. Help us each day to speak for those who cannot speak and to bring compassion to those who feel left out.

Thursday, April 11, 2013

Week of Easter 2

Psalm 30

My wailing turns to dancing

I will extol you, O LORD, for you have drawn me up,
  and did not let my foes rejoice over me.
O LORD my God, I cried to you for help,
  and you have healed me.
O LORD, you brought up my soul from Sheol,
  restored me to life from among those gone down to the Pit.
(Ps. 30:1-3)

Additional Readings

Isaiah 5:11-17
Appetites that lead to hunger

Revelation 3:14-22
Words to the church at Laodicea

Hymn: All Glory Be to God on High, ELW 410

In our darkest moments, Lord, you promise to light our steps and help us find the way to your arms. Help us reflect your light so we can guide others into your loving embrace to experience healing.

Friday, April 12, 2013

Week of Easter 2

Isaiah 6:1-4
Heaven's holy, holy, holy

In the year that King Uzziah died, I saw the Lord sitting on a throne, high and lofty; and the hem of his robe filled the temple. Seraphs were in attendance above him; each had six wings: with two they covered their faces, and with two they covered their feet, and with two they flew. And one called to another and said:

"Holy, holy, holy is the LORD of hosts;
the whole earth is full of his glory."

The pivots on the thresholds shook at the voices of those who called, and the house filled with smoke. (Isa. 6:1-4)

Psalm
Psalm 30
My wailing turns to dancing

Additional Reading
Revelation 4:1-11
Heaven's holy, holy, holy

Hymn: You Are Holy, ELW 525

As we continue to celebrate the resurrection's joy, fill us with song and set our hearts to dancing so that we may rejoice in the power of your victory over death now and eternally.

Saturday, April 13, 2013

Week of Easter 2

Genesis 18:1-8

Abraham and Sarah's hospitality to the Lord

The LORD appeared to Abraham by the oaks of Mamre, as he sat at the entrance of his tent in the heat of the day. He looked up and saw three men standing near him. When he saw them, he ran from the tent entrance to meet them, and bowed down to the ground. He said, "My lord, if I find favor with you, do not pass by your servant. Let a little water be brought, and wash your feet, and rest yourselves under the tree. Let me bring a little bread, that you may refresh yourselves, and after that you may pass on—since you have come to your servant." So they said, "Do as you have said." (Gen. 18:1-5)

Psalm
Psalm 30
My wailing turns to dancing

Additional Reading
Luke 14:12-14
Welcome those in need to your table

Hymn: Let Us Talents and Tongues Employ, ELW 674

Lord, your hands are open, providing for our needs. Encourage us always to welcome the stranger, seeking creative ways to provide for widows, orphans, and those who are brokenhearted, hungry, lost, or lonely who desire to be fed at our tables.

Sunday, April 14, 2013

Third Sunday of Easter

John 21:1-19

Jesus appears to the disciples

When [the disciples] had finished breakfast, Jesus said to Simon Peter, "Simon son of John, do you love me more than these?" He said to him, "Yes, Lord; you know that I love you." Jesus said to him, "Feed my lambs." A second time he said to him, "Simon son of John, do you love me?" He said to him, "Yes, Lord; you know that I love you." Jesus said to him, "Tend my sheep." He said to him the third time, "Simon son of John, do you love me?" Peter felt hurt because he said to him the third time, "Do you love me?" And he said to him, "Lord, you know everything; you know that I love you." Jesus said to him, "Feed my sheep. Very truly, I tell you, when you were younger, you used to fasten your own belt and to go wherever you wished. But when you grow old, you will stretch out your hands, and someone else will fasten a belt around you and take you where you do not wish to go." (He said this to indicate the kind of death by which he would glorify God.) After this he said to him, "Follow me." (John 21:15-19)

Psalm	Additional Readings	
Psalm 30	**Acts 9:1-6 [7-20]**	**Revelation 5:11-14**
My wailing turns to dancing	*Paul's conversion, baptism, and preaching*	*The song of the living creatures to the Lamb*

Hymn: God Is Here! ELW 526

Eternal and all-merciful God, with all the angels and all the saints we laud your majesty and might. By the resurrection of your Son, show yourself to us and inspire us to follow Jesus Christ, our Savior and Lord, who lives and reigns with you and the Holy Spirit, one God, now and forever.

Monday, April 15, 2013

Week of Easter 3

Psalm 121
God will preserve your life

The Lord is your keeper;
   the Lord is your shade at your right hand.
The sun shall not strike you by day,
   nor the moon by night.

The Lord will keep you from all evil;
   he will keep your life.
The Lord will keep
   your going out and your coming in
   from this time on and forevermore. (Ps. 121:5-8)

Additional Readings
Ezekiel 1:1-25   **Acts 9:19b-31**
Ezekiel's vision of four living creatures   *Saul joins the apostles in Jerusalem*

Hymn: To You, before the Close of Day, ELW 567

Great God, your blessings fill our lives as we begin each day. Your presence surrounds us as we walk in faith. Watch over our service in your name so at evening's rest we may sing and give thanks for your goodness.

Tuesday, April 16, 2013

Week of Easter 3

Ezekiel 1:26—2:1
Ezekiel's vision of God's glory

And above the dome over their heads there was something like a throne, in appearance like sapphire; and seated above the likeness of a throne was something that seemed like a human form. Upward from what appeared like the loins I saw something like gleaming amber, something that looked like fire enclosed all around; and downward from what looked like the loins I saw something that looked like fire, and there was a splendor all around. Like the bow in a cloud on a rainy day, such was the appearance of the splendor all around. This was the appearance of the likeness of the glory of the Lord.

When I saw it, I fell on my face, and I heard the voice of someone speaking.

He said to me: O mortal, stand up on your feet, and I will speak with you. (Ezek. 1:26—2:1)

Psalm
Psalm 121
God will preserve your life

Additional Reading
Acts 26:1-18
Paul preaches before Agrippa

Hymn: Let All Mortal Flesh Keep Silence, ELW 490

O Lord, in your good creation and in the community of faith, you give us glimpses of your glory. Help us turn our visions into action to bring the goodness and peace that is your kingdom into our neighborhoods and communities.

Wednesday, April 17, 2013

Week of Easter 3

Luke 5:1-11
Simon's catch of fish

Once while Jesus was standing beside the lake of Gennesaret, and the crowd was pressing in on him to hear the word of God, he saw two boats there at the shore of the lake; the fishermen had gone out of them and were washing their nets. He got into one of the boats, the one belonging to Simon, and asked him to put out a little way from the shore. Then he sat down and taught the crowds from the boat. When he had finished speaking, he said to Simon, "Put out into the deep water and let down your nets for a catch." Simon answered, "Master, we have worked all night long but have caught nothing. Yet if you say so, I will let down the nets." When they had done this, they caught so many fish that their nets were beginning to break. (Luke 5:1-6)

Psalm
Psalm 121
God will preserve your life

Additional Reading
Isaiah 6:1-8
Isaiah in the presence of God

Hymn: Praise, Praise! You Are My Rock, ELW 862

Lord God, sometimes we think we cannot do enough for your kingdom. Often we feel we cannot do any more. Send your Spirit to renew us, so that we can go in peace to love and serve all your children.

Thursday, April 18, 2013

Week of Easter 3

Psalm 23
God our shepherd

The LORD is my shepherd, I shall not want.
  He makes me lie down in green pastures;
he leads me beside still waters;
  he restores my soul.
He leads me in right paths
  for his name's sake.

Even though I walk through the darkest valley,
  I fear no evil;
for you are with me;
  your rod and your staff—
  they comfort me. (Ps. 23:1-4)

Additional Readings
Ezekiel 11:1-25
Ezekiel prophesies against the shepherds of Israel

Revelation 5:1-10
The throne and the elders

Hymn: The Lord's My Shepherd, ELW 778

God, when we wander off, you find us. When we need nourishment, you give us your body and blood. When we grow fearful, you comfort us with your word. When we struggle with doubt, you give us yourself. Thank you.

Friday, April 19, 2013

Week of Easter 3

Olavus Petri, priest, died 1552; Laurentius Petri, Bishop of Uppsala, died 1573; renewers of the church

Revelation 6:1—7:4

The servants of God are sealed

After this I saw four angels standing at the four corners of the earth, holding back the four winds of the earth so that no wind could blow on earth or sea or against any tree. I saw another angel ascending from the rising of the sun, having the seal of the living God, and he called with a loud voice to the four angels who had been given power to damage earth and sea, saying, "Do not damage the earth or the sea or the trees, until we have marked the servants of our God with a seal on their foreheads."

And I heard the number of those who were sealed, one hundred forty-four thousand, sealed out of every tribe of the people of Israel. (Rev. 7:1-4)

Psalm	**Additional Reading**
Psalm 23	Ezekiel 20:39-44
God our shepherd	*God will gather the scattered people*

Hymn: Lift High the Cross, ELW 660

Rising from the baptismal water, we are "sealed by the Holy Spirit and marked with the cross of Christ forever." Thank you, Lord, that from generation to generation you set your mark upon those who teach us how to love and serve you.

Saturday, April 20, 2013

Week of Easter 3

Ezekiel 28:25-26

God gathers the people into safety

Thus says the Lord GOD: When I gather the house of Israel from the peoples among whom they are scattered, and manifest my holiness in them in the sight of the nations, then they shall settle on their own soil that I gave to my servant Jacob. They shall live in safety in it, and shall build houses and plant vineyards. They shall live in safety, when I execute judgments upon all their neighbors who have treated them with contempt. And they shall know that I am the LORD their God. (Ezek. 28:25-26)

Psalm

Psalm 23
God our shepherd

Additional Reading

Luke 12:29-32
Do not fear, little flock

Hymn: Have No Fear, Little Flock, ELW 764

Where there is joy, there is no fear. Lord, bring us joy. Where there is hope, there is no despair. Lord, bring us hope. Where there is love, there is no uncertainty. Lord, bring us love. Lord, bring us your very self.

Sunday, April 21, 2013

Fourth Sunday of Easter

Anselm, Bishop of Canterbury, died 1109

John 10:22-30
Jesus promises life to his sheep

[Jesus said,] "My sheep hear my voice. I know them, and they follow me. I give them eternal life, and they will never perish. No one will snatch them out of my hand. What my Father has given me is greater than all else, and no one can snatch it out of the Father's hand. The Father and I are one." (John 10:27-30)

Psalm

Psalm 23
God our shepherd

Additional Readings

Acts 9:36-43
Peter raises Tabitha from the dead

Revelation 7:9-17
A multitude sings before the Lamb

Hymn: The King of Love My Shepherd Is, ELW 502

O God of peace, you brought again from the dead our Lord Jesus Christ, the great shepherd of the sheep. By the blood of your eternal covenant, make us complete in everything good that we may do your will, and work among us all that is well-pleasing in your sight, through Jesus Christ, our Savior and Lord, who lives and reigns with you and the Holy Spirit, one God, now and forever.

Monday, April 22, 2013

Week of Easter 4

Psalm 100
We are God's sheep

Make a joyful noise to the LORD, all the earth.
Worship the LORD with gladness;
come into his presence with singing.

Know that the LORD is God.
It is he that made us, and we are his;
we are his people, and the sheep of his pasture.

Enter his gates with thanksgiving,
and his courts with praise.
Give thanks to him, bless his name.

For the LORD is good;
his steadfast love endures forever,
and his faithfulness to all generations. (Ps. 100:1-5)

Additional Readings

Ezekiel 37:15-28
God will unite the flock

Revelation 15:1-4
The song of the Lamb

Hymn: All People That on Earth Do Dwell, ELW 883

*Holy Lord, you give us the gifts of music and song, prayer and praise.
You gather us into communities of faith where we give thanks for your
mercy. You send us out rejoicing to share your love with all in need.*

Tuesday, April 23, 2013

Week of Easter 4

Toyohiko Kagawa, renewer of society, died 1960

Acts 9:32-35
The healing of paralyzed Aeneas

Now as Peter went here and there among all the believers, he came down also to the saints living in Lydda. There he found a man named Aeneas, who had been bedridden for eight years, for he was paralyzed. Peter said to him, "Aeneas, Jesus Christ heals you; get up and make your bed!" And immediately he got up. And all the residents of Lydda and Sharon saw him and turned to the Lord. (Acts 9:32-35)

Psalm	Additional Reading
Psalm 100	Ezekiel 45:1-9
We are God's sheep	*God promises a sanctuary*

Hymn: Open Now Thy Gates of Beauty, ELW 533

In every generation, O Lord, you send faithful servants to give witness in their words and deeds to your abiding grace and power. As we remember their lives, keep us faithful to that same call to love and serve others.

Wednesday, April 24, 2013

Week of Easter 4

Jeremiah 50:17-20
Israel will be fed

Israel is a hunted sheep driven away by lions. First the king of Assyria
devoured it, and now at the end King Nebuchadrezzar of Babylon
has gnawed its bones. Therefore, thus says the LORD of hosts, the God
of Israel: I am going to punish the king of Babylon and his land, as I
punished the king of Assyria. I will restore Israel to its pasture, and it
shall feed on Carmel and in Bashan, and on the hills of Ephraim and
in Gilead its hunger shall be satisfied. In those days and at that time,
says the LORD, the iniquity of Israel shall be sought, and there shall be
none; and the sins of Judah, and none shall be found; for I will pardon
the remnant that I have spared. (Jer. 50:17-20)

Psalm	Additional Reading
Psalm 100	John 10:31-42
We are God's sheep	*The Son and the Father are one*

Hymn: We Come to the Hungry Feast, ELW 479

*Lord, in Christ's life, death, and resurrection, you give us everything
that is in your heart. You make us one with you and call us your
children. Increase our zeal to proclaim your kingdom's coming for the
sake of the world.*

Thursday, April 25, 2013

Mark, Evangelist

Mark 1:1-15

The beginning of the gospel of Jesus Christ

The beginning of the good news of Jesus Christ, the Son of God.

As it is written in the prophet Isaiah,
"See, I am sending my messenger ahead of you,
   who will prepare your way;
the voice of one crying out in the wilderness:
   'Prepare the way of the Lord,
   make his paths straight,' "
John the baptizer appeared in the wilderness, proclaiming a baptism
of repentance for the forgiveness of sins. And people from the whole
Judean countryside and all the people of Jerusalem were going out to
him, and were baptized by him in the river Jordan, confessing their
sins. (Mark 1:1-5)

Psalm

Psalm 57
Be merciful to me, O God

Additional Readings

Isaiah 52:7-10
The messenger announces salvation

2 Timothy 4:6-11, 18
The good fight of faith

Hymn: When Jesus Came to Jordan, ELW 305

Almighty God, you have enriched your church with Mark's proclamation of the gospel. Give us grace to believe firmly in the good news of salvation and to walk daily in accord with it, through Jesus Christ, our Savior and Lord, who lives and reigns with you and the Holy Spirit, one God, now and forever.

Friday, April 26, 2013

Week of Easter 4

Daniel 7:13-14

An everlasting dominion is given

As I watched in the night visions,
I saw one like a human being
    coming with the clouds of heaven.
And he came to the Ancient One
    and was presented before him.
To him was given dominion
    and glory and kingship,
that all peoples, nations, and languages
    should serve him.
His dominion is an everlasting dominion
    that shall not pass away,
and his kingship is one
    that shall never be destroyed. (Dan. 7:13-14)

Psalm
Psalm 148
God's splendor is over earth and heaven

Additional Reading
Revelation 11:15
God's reign at the end of time

Hymn: Immortal, Invisible, God Only Wise, ELW 834

All things are yours, O Lord. From the beginning of your good creation, you have held our past and our future in your hands and promise to be always with us. We live each day trusting your goodness and love.

Saturday, April 27, 2013

Week of Easter 4

Revelation 11:16-19

God's reign at the end of time

Then the twenty-four elders who sit on their thrones before God fell
on their faces and worshiped God, singing,
  "We give you thanks, Lord God Almighty,
    who are and who were,
  for you have taken your great power
    and begun to reign.
  The nations raged,
    but your wrath has come,
    and the time for judging the dead,
  for rewarding your servants, the prophets
    and saints and all who fear your name,
    both small and great,
  and for destroying those who destroy the earth." (Rev. 11:16-18)

Psalm

Psalm 148

God's splendor is over earth and heaven

Additional Reading

Daniel 7:27

A dominion for the holy ones of the Most High

Hymn: Blessing and Honor, ELW 854

*Lord, we are thankful for the blessings you have given us, for filling us
with the breath of life. From generation to generation we praise your
name and seek to do your will for our neighbors and all in need.*

Sunday, April 28, 2013

Fifth Sunday of Easter

John 13:31-35

Love one another

When he had gone out, Jesus said, "Now the Son of Man has been glorified, and God has been glorified in him. If God has been glorified in him, God will also glorify him in himself and will glorify him at once. Little children, I am with you only a little longer. You will look for me; and as I said to the Jews so now I say to you, 'Where I am going, you cannot come.' I give you a new commandment, that you love one another. Just as I have loved you, you also should love one another. By this everyone will know that you are my disciples, if you have love for one another." (John 13:31-35)

Psalm	Additional Readings	
Psalm 148	**Acts 11:1-18**	**Revelation 21:1-6**
God's splendor is over earth and heaven	*God saves the Gentiles*	*New heaven, new earth*

Hymn: Ubi caritas et amor, ELW 642

O Lord God, you teach us that without love, our actions gain nothing. Pour into our hearts your most excellent gift of love, that, made alive by your Spirit, we may know goodness and peace, through your Son, Jesus Christ, our Savior and Lord, who lives and reigns with you and the Holy Spirit, one God, now and forever.

Monday, April 29, 2013

Week of Easter 5

Catherine of Siena, theologian, died 1380

Psalm 133
How good it is to live in unity

How very good and pleasant it is
    when kindred live together in unity!
It is like the precious oil on the head,
    running down upon the beard,
on the beard of Aaron,
    running down over the collar of his robes.
It is like the dew of Hermon,
    which falls on the mountains of Zion.
For there the LORD ordained his blessing,
    life forevermore. (Ps. 133:1-3)

Additional Readings
1 Samuel 20:1-23, 35-42   Acts 11:19-26
The love of David and Jonathan   *Christians in Antioch*

Hymn: Blest Be the Tie That Binds, ELW 656

Holy Lord, you see your children today, broken, divided, in disarray, and without harmony. Guide us to your presence where we may find blessing and find our unity restored through love in your name.

Tuesday, April 30, 2013

Week of Easter 5

Acts 11:27-30

Love embodied in care for others

At that time prophets came down from Jerusalem to Antioch. One
of them named Agabus stood up and predicted by the Spirit that
there would be a severe famine over all the world; and this took place
during the reign of Claudius. The disciples determined that according
to their ability, each would send relief to the believers living in
Judea; this they did, sending it to the elders by Barnabas and Saul.
(Acts 11:27-30)

Psalm
Psalm 133
How good it is to live in unity

Additional Reading
2 Samuel 1:4-27
David mourns Jonathan's death

Hymn: Lord, Whose Love in Humble Service, ELW 712

*Lord, you call us to be hospitable, to welcome all people, and to love
our neighbors as we love ourselves. Help us to be generous—in every
circumstance and with everyone we encounter—offering nourishment,
encouragement, and healing.*

_____

_____

_____

_____

_____

_____

_____

_____

_____

_____

_____

_____

Wednesday, May 1, 2013

Philip and James, Apostles

John 14:8-14

The Son and the Father are one

Philip said to Jesus, "Lord, show us the Father, and we will be satisfied." Jesus said to him, "Have I been with you all this time, Philip, and you still do not know me? Whoever has seen me has seen the Father. How can you say, 'Show us the Father'? Do you not believe that I am in the Father and the Father is in me? The words that I say to you I do not speak on my own; but the Father who dwells in me does his works." (John 14:8-10)

Psalm

Psalm 44:1-3, 20-26

Save us for the sake of your love

Additional Readings

Isaiah 30:18-21

God's mercy and justice

2 Corinthians 4:1-6

Proclaiming Jesus Christ as Lord

Hymn: God, Whose Almighty Word, ELW 673

Almighty God, you gave to your apostles Philip and James grace and strength to bear witness to your Son. Grant that we, remembering their victory of faith, may glorify in life and death the name of our Lord Jesus Christ, who lives and reigns with you and the Holy Spirit, one God, now and forever.

Thursday, May 2, 2013

Week of Easter 5

Athanasius, Bishop of Alexandria, died 373

Psalm 67

Let the nations be glad

May God be gracious to us and bless us
    and make his face to shine upon us,
that your way may be known upon earth,
    your saving power among all nations.
Let the peoples praise you, O God;
    let all the peoples praise you.

Let the nations be glad and sing for joy,
    for you judge the peoples with equity
    and guide the nations upon earth.
Let the peoples praise you, O God;
    let all the peoples praise you. (Ps. 67:1-5)

Additional Readings

Acts 15:36-41   Proverbs 2:1-5
Paul and Barnabas part company   *Knowledge of God like silver*

Hymn: You Servants of God, ELW 825

Gracious God, you are creator and ruler over all. Empower us to proclaim you among the nations, both with our lips and in our lives, so that the peoples of the earth may turn and praise you.

Friday, May 3, 2013

Week of Easter 5

Proverbs 2:6-8
God gives wisdom

For the LORD gives wisdom;
 from his mouth come knowledge and understanding;
he stores up sound wisdom for the upright;
 he is a shield to those who walk blamelessly,
guarding the paths of justice
 and preserving the way of his faithful ones. (Prov. 2:6-8)

Psalm
Psalm 67
Let the nations be glad

Additional Reading
Acts 16:1-8
Timothy accompanies Paul

Hymn: Earth and All Stars! ELW 731

Heavenly Father, true wisdom comes from you. Let your wisdom light up the paths of our lives so that we may walk with integrity in obedience to your word and reflect your justice and righteousness in our world.

Saturday, May 4, 2013

Week of Easter 5

Monica, mother of Augustine, died 387

Proverbs 2:9-15
Wisdom makes a home in your heart

Then you will understand righteousness and justice
   and equity, every good path;
for wisdom will come into your heart,
   and knowledge will be pleasant to your soul;
prudence will watch over you;
   and understanding will guard you. (Prov. 2:9-11)

Psalm
Psalm 67
Let the nations be glad

Additional Reading
Luke 19:1-10
Salvation makes a home with Zacchaeus

Hymn: Evening and Morning, ELW 761

Father, you sent your Son to bring us salvation; you sent your Holy Spirit to live in our hearts. Grant that we may open our hearts to welcome you, so that you may make your home in us.

Sunday, May 5, 2013

Sixth Sunday of Easter

John 14:23-39
The Father will send the Holy Spirit

[Jesus said,] "I have said these things to you while I am still with you. But the Advocate, the Holy Spirit, whom the Father will send in my name, will teach you everything, and remind you of all that I have said to you. Peace I leave with you; my peace I give to you. I do not give to you as the world gives. Do not let your hearts be troubled, and do not let them be afraid." (John 14:25-27)

Psalm
Psalm 67
Let the nations be glad

Additional Readings
Acts 16:9-15
Lydia and her household are baptized

Revelation 21:10, 22—22:5
The Lamb is the light of God's city

Hymn: Alleluia! Jesus Is Risen! ELW 377

Bountiful God, you gather your people into your realm, and you promise us food from your tree of life. Nourish us with your word, that empowered by your Spirit we may love one another and the world you have made, through Jesus Christ, our Savior and Lord, who lives and reigns with you and the Holy Spirit, one God, now and forever.

Monday, May 6, 2013

Week of Easter 6

Psalm 93

God reigns above the floods

The LORD is king, he is robed in majesty;
   the LORD is robed, he is girded with strength.
He has established the world; it shall never be moved;
   your throne is established from of old;
   you are from everlasting.

The floods have lifted up, O LORD,
   the floods have lifted up their voice;
   the floods lift up their roaring.
More majestic than the thunders of mighty waters,
   more majestic than the waves of the sea,
   majestic on high is the LORD!

Your decrees are very sure;
   holiness befits your house,
   O LORD, forevermore. (Ps. 93:1-5)

Additional Readings

1 Chronicles 12:16-22   Revelation 21:5-14
The spirit of God on Amasai   *Vision of the holy city*

Hymn: Come, Thou Almighty King, ELW 408

Holy, holy, holy Lord, you are mighty and majestic, the Alpha and the Omega, the beginning and the end. We lift our voices, our hands, and our hearts to magnify your holy name.

Tuesday, May 7, 2013

Week of Easter 6

Revelation 21:15-22
Vision of the holy city

The foundations of the wall of the city are adorned with every jewel;
the first was jasper, the second sapphire, the third agate, the fourth
emerald, the fifth onyx, the sixth carnelian, the seventh chrysolite,
the eighth beryl, the ninth topaz, the tenth chrysoprase, the eleventh
jacinth, the twelfth amethyst. And the twelve gates are twelve pearls,
each of the gates is a single pearl, and the street of the city is pure
gold, transparent as glass.

I saw no temple in the city, for its temple is the Lord God the
Almighty and the Lamb. (Rev. 21:19-22)

Psalm
Psalm 93
God reigns above the floods

Additional Reading
2 Chronicles 15:1-15
The spirit of God on Azariah

Hymn: Crown Him with Many Crowns, ELW 855

*Almighty God, in his death Jesus took away the sin of the world.
Cleansed and forgiven, we now enjoy the privilege of standing in your
holy presence. Keep us humble and holy always.*

Wednesday, May 8, 2013

Week of Easter 6

Julian of Norwich, renewer of the church, died around 1416

2 Chronicles 34:20-33
Josiah consults the prophet Huldah

"But as to the king of Judah, who sent you to inquire of the LORD,
thus shall you say to him: Thus says the LORD, the God of Israel:
Regarding the words that you have heard, because your heart was
penitent and you humbled yourself before God when you heard his
words against this place and its inhabitants, and you have humbled
yourself before me, and have torn your clothes and wept before
me, I also have heard you, says the LORD. I will gather you to your
ancestors and you shall be gathered to your grave in peace; your eyes
shall not see all the disaster that I will bring on this place and its
inhabitants." (2 Chron. 34:26-28)

Psalm
Psalm 93
God reigns above the floods

Additional Reading
Luke 2:25-38
The spirit of God on Simeon and Anna

Hymn: Lord Jesus, Think on Me, ELW 599

*Merciful Lord, you are always ready to forgive and restore those who
turn to you in humble repentance. We are sorry that we have grieved
you. We thank you for your patient love and costly grace.*

Thursday, May 9, 2013

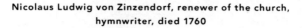

Ascension of Our Lord

**Nicolaus Ludwig von Zinzendorf, renewer of the church,
hymnwriter, died 1760**

Acts 1:1-11

Jesus sends the apostles

So when [the disciples] had come together, they asked [Jesus], "Lord,
is this the time when you will restore the kingdom to Israel?" He
replied, "It is not for you to know the times or periods that the Father
has set by his own authority. But you will receive power when the
Holy Spirit has come upon you; and you will be my witnesses in
Jerusalem, in all Judea and Samaria, and to the ends of the earth."
When he had said this, as they were watching, he was lifted up, and a
cloud took him out of their sight. While he was going and they were
gazing up toward heaven, suddenly two men in white robes stood
by them. They said, "Men of Galilee, why do you stand looking up
toward heaven? This Jesus, who has been taken up from you into
heaven, will come in the same way as you saw him go into heaven."
(Acts 1:6-11)

Psalm

Psalm 47
*God has gone up with a
shout*

Additional Readings

Ephesians 1:15-23
*Seeing the risen and
ascended Christ*

Luke 24:44-53
*Christ present in all times
and places*

Hymn: A Hymn of Glory Let Us Sing! ELW 393

*Almighty God, your only Son was taken into the heavens and in your
presence intercedes for us. Receive us and our prayers for all the world,
and in the end bring everything into your glory, through Jesus Christ,
our Sovereign and Lord, who lives and reigns with you and the Holy
Spirit, one God, now and forever.*

Friday, May 10, 2013

Week of Easter 6

Psalm 97

Light dawns for the righteous

The Lord loves those who hate evil;
    he guards the lives of his faithful;
    he rescues them from the hand of the wicked.
Light dawns for the righteous,
    and joy for the upright in heart.
Rejoice in the Lord, O you righteous,
    and give thanks to his holy name! (Ps. 97:10-12)

Additional Readings

Exodus 33:12-17
Moses prays for the people

Revelation 22:6-9
A trustworthy testimony

Hymn: All Creatures, Worship God Most High! ELW 835

*Holy God, you chose your servant Moses to save and serve your beloved
people. Raise up for your church wise and compassionate leaders who
will shepherd your people with integrity and commitment, in the name
of Jesus, our Good Shepherd.*

Saturday, May 11, 2013

Week of Easter 6

Exodus 33:18-23

Moses asks to see God's glory

Moses said, "Show me your glory, I pray." And he said, "I will make all my goodness pass before you, and will proclaim before you the name, 'The LORD'; and I will be gracious to whom I will be gracious, and will show mercy on whom I will show mercy. But," he said, "you cannot see my face; for no one shall see me and live." And the LORD continued, "See, there is a place by me where you shall stand on the rock; and while my glory passes by I will put you in a cleft of the rock, and I will cover you with my hand until I have passed by; then I will take away my hand, and you shall see my back; but my face shall not be seen." (Exod. 33:18-23)

Psalm
Psalm 97
Light dawns for the righteous

Additional Reading
John 1:14-18
We have seen the glory of God

Hymn: Rock of Ages, Cleft for Me, ELW 623

Gracious Lord, you revealed your glory to your servant Moses. In your Son Jesus, you manifested your glory to the whole world. Let our lives bring glory to you, Father, Son, and Holy Spirit.

Blessing for Mother's Day (May 12)

Under your wings, O Lord, you have held us,
as a mother holds her young.
Look with favor on all those women
who have sheltered children in their loving care.
Guide that they may lead;
strengthen that they may be tender;
grant wisdom that the people may live;
and hold all in your loving gaze
until we see you face-to-face.
Amen.

Sunday, May 12, 2013

Seventh Sunday of Easter

John 17:20-26
Christ's prayer for his disciples

[Jesus prayed,] "I ask not only on behalf of these, but also on behalf of those who will believe in me through their word, that they may all be one. As you, Father, are in me and I am in you, may they also be in us, so that the world may believe that you have sent me. The glory that you have given me I have given them, so that they may be one, as we are one, I in them and you in me, that they may become completely one, so that the world may know that you have sent me and have loved them even as you have loved me. Father, I desire that those also, whom you have given me, may be with me where I am, to see my glory, which you have given me because you loved me before the foundation of the world." (John 17:20-24)

Psalm
Psalm 97
Light dawns for the righteous

Additional Readings
Acts 16:16-34
A jailer is baptized

Revelation 22:12-14, 16-17, 20-21
Blessed are those who wash their robes

Hymn: Thine the Amen, ELW 826

O God, form the minds of your faithful people into your one will. Make us love what you command and desire what you promise, that, amid all the changes of this world, our hearts may be fixed where true joy is found, your Son, Jesus Christ our Lord, who lives and reigns with you and the Holy Spirit, one God, now and forever.

Monday, May 13, 2013

Week of Easter 7

Psalm 29
The glory of God

Ascribe to the LORD, O heavenly beings,
    ascribe to the LORD glory and strength.
Ascribe to the LORD the glory of his name;
    worship the LORD in holy splendor.

The voice of the LORD is over the waters;
    the God of glory thunders,
    the LORD, over mighty waters.
The voice of the LORD is powerful;
    the voice of the LORD is full of majesty. (Ps. 29:1-4)

Additional Readings
Exodus 40:16-38   **Acts 16:35-40**
God's glory on the tabernacle   *The magistrates apologize to Paul and Silas*

Hymn: Praise the Lord! O Heavens, ELW 823

Almighty and all-powerful God, you reign supreme over all creation and over all peoples. In the fullness of your time, may every living being kneel before you and let your glory fill all the earth.

Tuesday, May 14, 2013

Matthias, Apostle

Luke 6:12-16
Jesus calls the Twelve

Now during those days he went out to the mountain to pray; and he spent the night in prayer to God. And when day came, he called his disciples and chose twelve of them, whom he also named apostles: Simon, whom he named Peter, and his brother Andrew, and James, and John, and Philip, and Bartholomew, and Matthew, and Thomas, and James son of Alphaeus, and Simon, who was called the Zealot, and Judas son of James, and Judas Iscariot, who became a traitor. (Luke 6:12-16)

Psalm
Psalm 56
I am bound by the vow I made to you

Additional Readings
Isaiah 66:1-2
Heaven is God's throne, earth is God's footstool

Acts 1:15-26
The apostles cast lots for Matthias

Hymn: The Son of God, Our Christ, ELW 584

Almighty God, you chose your faithful servant Matthias to be numbered among the twelve. Grant that your church may always be taught and guided by faithful and true pastors, through Jesus Christ our shepherd, who lives and reigns with you and the Holy Spirit, one God, now and forever.

Wednesday, May 15, 2013

Week of Easter 7

Ezekiel 3:12-21
God's glory commissions the prophet

At the end of seven days, the word of the LORD came to me: Mortal, I have made you a sentinel for the house of Israel; whenever you hear a word from my mouth, you shall give them warning from me. If I say to the wicked, "You shall surely die," and you give them no warning, or speak to warn the wicked from their wicked way, in order to save their life, those wicked persons shall die for their iniquity; but their blood I will require at your hand. But if you warn the wicked, and they do not turn from their wickedness, or from their wicked way, they shall die for their iniquity; but you will have saved your life. (Ezek. 3:16-19)

Psalm
Psalm 29
The glory of God

Additional Reading
Luke 9:18-27
God's glory and discipleship

Hymn: My Lord, What a Morning, ELW 438

Holy Lord, your warnings come to us not as harsh judgments but as patient offers of grace. Grant that we may respond with repentance and boldly sound your warnings against the evils that rage in our world.

Thursday, May 16, 2013

Week of Easter 7

Psalm 104:24-34, 35b
Renewing the face of the earth

O LORD, how manifold are your works!
  In wisdom you have made them all;
  the earth is full of your creatures.
Yonder is the sea, great and wide,
  creeping things innumerable are there,
  living things both small and great.
There go the ships,
  and Leviathan that you formed to sport in it.

These all look to you
  to give them their food in due season;
when you give to them, they gather it up;
  when you open your hand, they are filled with good things.
(Ps. 104:24-28)

Additional Readings
Isaiah 32:11-17
The spirit poured out to renew the earth

Galatians 5:16-25
The fruit of the Spirit

Hymn: God of the Sparrow, ELW 740

God our provider, you created the earth and everything in it. For giving us all we need to live—and much more—we humbly say thanks.

Friday, May 17, 2013

Week of Easter 7

Galatians 6:7-10

Reaping eternal life from the Spirit

Do not be deceived; God is not mocked, for you reap whatever you sow. If you sow to your own flesh, you will reap corruption from the flesh; but if you sow to the Spirit, you will reap eternal life from the Spirit. So let us not grow weary in doing what is right, for we will reap at harvest time, if we do not give up. So then, whenever we have an opportunity, let us work for the good of all, and especially for those of the family of faith. (Gal. 6:7-10)

Psalm
Psalm 104:24-34, 35b
Renewing the face of the earth

Additional Reading
Isaiah 44:1-4
The spirit poured out to renew the faithful

Hymn: Lord of All Hopefulness, ELW 765

O faithful God, you promise a rich harvest to your faithful ones. In our weakness and weariness, strengthen and encourage us to persevere in faith, trusting in you for your great blessings.

Saturday, May 18, 2013

Vigil of Pentecost

Erik, King of Sweden, martyr, died 1160

John 7:37-39

Jesus, the true living water

On the last day of the festival, the great day, while Jesus was standing there, he cried out, "Let anyone who is thirsty come to me, and let the one who believes in me drink. As the scripture has said, 'Out of the believer's heart shall flow rivers of living water.' " Now he said this about the Spirit, which believers in him were to receive; for as yet there was no Spirit, because Jesus was not yet glorified. (John 7:37-39)

Psalm

Psalm 33:12-22

The Lord is our helper and our shield

Additional Readings

Exodus 19:1-9

The covenant at Sinai

Romans 8:14-17, 22-27

Praying with the Spirit

Hymn: Like the Murmur of the Dove's Song, ELW 403

Almighty and ever-living God, you fulfilled the promise of Easter by sending the gift of your Holy Spirit. Look upon your people gathered in prayer, open to receive the Spirit's flame. May it come to rest in our hearts and heal the divisions of word and tongue, that with one voice and one song we may praise your name in joy and thanksgiving; through Jesus Christ, our Savior and Lord, who lives and reigns with you and the Holy Spirit, one God, now and forever.

Pentecost

Christians pray to God "in the power of the Spirit." The gifts of the Spirit are faith, hope, and love. Whenever two or more gather in Jesus' name, the Spirit is present. At every baptism and communion, we pray for the Spirit's presence to forgive and strengthen, inspire and refresh. In the household, we pray for the Spirit's guidance, for the deepening of faith, hope, and love, for the patience and wisdom to live in peace with each other and our neighbors.

Table Prayer for Pentecost

Blessed are you, O Lord our God,
who gathers the whole world into the Spirit of your Son.
You have given us food for another day:
blessed be God forever!
We beg you to pour out food for the needy,
that all peoples and languages may praise your name,
through Jesus Christ our Lord.
Amen.

Thanksgiving for the Holy Spirit
Use this prayer during the week following Pentecost Sunday.

O Spirit of God, seek us;
Good Spirit, pray with us;
Spirit of counsel, inform us;
Spirit of might, free us;
Spirit of truth, enlighten us;
Spirit of Christ, raise us;
O Holy Spirit, dwell in us. Amen.

Sunday, May 19, 2013

Day of Pentecost

Acts 2:1-21

Filled with the Spirit

When the day of Pentecost had come, they were all together in one place. And suddenly from heaven there came a sound like the rush of a violent wind, and it filled the entire house where they were sitting. Divided tongues, as of fire, appeared among them, and a tongue rested on each of them. All of them were filled with the Holy Spirit and began to speak in other languages, as the Spirit gave them ability. (Acts 2:1-4)

Psalm
Psalm 104:24-34, 35b
Send forth your spirit

Additional Readings
Romans 8:14-17
The Spirit makes us children of God

John 14:8-17 [25-27]
The Spirit of truth

Hymn: Come, Gracious Spirit, Heavenly Dove, ELW 404

God our creator, the resurrection of your Son offers life to all the peoples of earth. By your Holy Spirit, kindle in us the fire of your love, empowering our lives for service and our tongues for praise, through Jesus Christ, our Savior and Lord, who lives and reigns with you and the Holy Spirit, one God, now and forever.

Monday, May 20, 2013

Time after Pentecost

Psalm 48
The God of Zion

Walk about Zion, go all around it,
    count its towers,
consider well its ramparts;
    go through its citadels,
that you may tell the next generation
    that this is God,
our God forever and ever.
    He will be our guide forever. (Ps. 48:12-14)

Additional Readings

Joel 2:18-29
God's spirit poured out

I Corinthians 2:1-11
About the Spirit of God

Hymn: O Day Full of Grace, ELW 627

Eternal God, you are the one true and only God. By the power of your Spirit that has been poured out upon us, may we bear faithful witness to you in our homes, neighborhoods, and workplaces.

Tuesday, May 21, 2013

Time after Pentecost

Helena, mother of Constantine, died around 330

1 Corinthians 2:12-16

About the Spirit of God

Now we have received not the spirit of the world, but the Spirit that is from God, so that we may understand the gifts bestowed on us by God. And we speak of these things in words not taught by human wisdom but taught by the Spirit, interpreting spiritual things to those who are spiritual.

Those who are unspiritual do not receive the gifts of God's Spirit, for they are foolishness to them, and they are unable to understand them because they are spiritually discerned. Those who are spiritual discern all things, and they are themselves subject to no one else's scrutiny.
   "For who has known the mind of the Lord
      so as to instruct him?"
But we have the mind of Christ. (1 Cor. 2:12-16)

Psalm	Additional Reading
Psalm 48	Ezekiel 11:14-25
The God of Zion	*God will gather the people*

Hymn: Come, Holy Ghost, God and Lord, ELW 395

Almighty God, you have given us your Holy Spirit to dwell within us. Keep us ever sensitive and obedient to the promptings of your Spirit, so that our words and actions may be in conformity with your holy will.

Wednesday, May 22, 2013

Time after Pentecost

Luke 1:26-38

God's Spirit comes on Mary

The angel said to [Mary], "Do not be afraid, Mary, for you have found favor with God. And now, you will conceive in your womb and bear a son, and you will name him Jesus. He will be great, and will be called the Son of the Most High, and the Lord God will give to him the throne of his ancestor David. He will reign over the house of Jacob forever, and of his kingdom there will be no end." Mary said to the angel, "How can this be, since I am a virgin?" The angel said to her, "The Holy Spirit will come upon you, and the power of the Most High will overshadow you; therefore the child to be born will be holy; he will be called Son of God." (Luke 1:30-35)

Psalm	Additional Reading
Psalm 48	Numbers 24:1-14
The God of Zion	*Balaam speaks with God's spirit*

Hymn: Spirit of Gentleness, ELW 396

God Most High, you used your servant Mary to bring salvation to the world. Help us, like Mary, to respond wholeheartedly to your call so that your divine purposes may work in and through our lives.

Thursday, May 23, 2013

Time after Pentecost

Psalm 8

Your majesty is praised above the heavens

O Lord, our Sovereign,
   how majestic is your name in all the earth!

You have set your glory above the heavens.
   Out of the mouths of babes and infants
you have founded a bulwark because of your foes,
   to silence the enemy and the avenger.

When I look at your heavens, the work of your fingers,
   the moon and the stars that you have established;
what are human beings that you are mindful of them,
   mortals that you care for them?

Yet you have made them a little lower than God,
   and crowned them with glory and honor. (Ps. 8:1-5)

Additional Readings

Proverbs 3:13-18   Ephesians 1:17-19
Wisdom is a tree of life   *Wisdom in the Trinity*

Hymn: Glorious Things of You Are Spoken, ELW 647

Creator God, you are the author of the myriad wonders of our world!
Open the eyes of our minds and hearts to understand and embrace the
inexpressible treasure of your love and grace, through Jesus Christ our
Lord.

Friday, May 24, 2013

Time after Pentecost

Nicolaus Copernicus, died 1543; Leonhard Euler, died 1783; scientists

Ephesians 4:1-6
Life in the Trinity

I therefore, the prisoner in the Lord, beg you to lead a life worthy of the calling to which you have been called, with all humility and gentleness, with patience, bearing with one another in love, making every effort to maintain the unity of the Spirit in the bond of peace. There is one body and one Spirit, just as you were called to the one hope of your calling, one Lord, one faith, one baptism, one God and Father of all, who is above all and through all and in all. (Eph. 4:1-6)

Psalm
Psalm 8
Your majesty is praised above the heavens

Additional Reading
Proverbs 3:19-26
By wisdom God creates and preserves

Hymn: Many and Great, O God, ELW 837

Eternal God, you are Father, Son, and Holy Spirit, our three-in-one God. Let your church radiate the wonder of your unity, the beauty of your oneness, and so glorify you now and forever.

Saturday, May 25, 2013

Time after Pentecost

Proverbs 4:1-9
Choose God's wisdom

"The beginning of wisdom is this: Get wisdom,
  and whatever else you get, get insight.
Prize her highly, and she will exalt you;
  she will honor you if you embrace her.
She will place on your head a fair garland;
  she will bestow on you a beautiful crown." (Prov. 4:7-9)

Psalm
Psalm 8
Your majesty is praised above the heavens

Additional Reading
Luke 2:41-52
Jesus increases in wisdom

Hymn: O God of Mercy, God of Light, ELW 714

Fount of blessing, you are the source and summit of all wisdom. Let our hearts yearn for your guidance so that we, like Jesus, may always be found devoted to your work.

Time after Pentecost

Summer

The weeks and months following the Day of Pentecost coincide with the natural seasons of summer, autumn, and late autumn/November. Christian communities refer to this time in different ways. Whatever time is used to describe the many weeks between Pentecost and Christ the King (the last Sunday of the year), the seasons and calendars of North America offer some distinctive periods by which we may shape prayer in the household.

The Day of Pentecost is celebrated close to the end of the school year. A connection exists between graduations/new beginnings and our prayer for the Spirit's guidance in new endeavors. For many people, the months of June, July, and August signal a slightly altered schedule attuned to the weather, harvests, and vacations. Summer months offer their unique grace to those who spend time in discerning the many images that link the scriptures and the patient growth of the seed in the soil.

Table Prayer for Summer

O God of wonder,
the whole earth is full of your glory.
We give you thanks for the gifts of summer
and the blessings of this meal.
Teach us to share what we have received,
for you are the giver of all good things.
We ask this through Christ our Lord. Amen.

Sunday, May 26, 2013

The Holy Trinity

John 16:12-15

The Spirit will guide you into the truth

[Jesus said,] "I still have many things to say to you, but you cannot bear them now. When the Spirit of truth comes, he will guide you into all the truth; for he will not speak on his own, but will speak whatever he hears, and he will declare to you the things that are to come. He will glorify me, because he will take what is mine and declare it to you. All that the Father has is mine. For this reason I said that he will take what is mine and declare it to you." (John 16:12-15)

Psalm

Psalm 8

Your majesty is praised above the heavens

Additional Readings

Proverbs 8:1-4, 22-31

Wisdom rejoices in the creation

Romans 5:1-5

God's love poured into our hearts

Hymn: Father Most Holy, ELW 415

Almighty Creator and ever-living God: we worship your glory, eternal Three-in-One, and we praise your power, majestic One-in-Three. Keep us steadfast in this faith, defend us in all adversity, and bring us at last into your presence, where you live in endless joy and love, Father, Son, and Holy Spirit, one God, now and forever.

Monday, May 27, 2013

Time after Pentecost

John Calvin, renewer of the church, died 1564

Psalm 124
We have escaped like a bird

If it had not been the LORD who was on our side
   —let Israel now say—
if it had not been the LORD who was on our side,
    when our enemies attacked us,
then they would have swallowed us up alive,
    when their anger was kindled against us;
then the flood would have swept us away,
    the torrent would have gone over us;
then over us would have gone
    the raging waters. (Psalm 124:1-5)

Additional Readings
Proverbs 7:1-4　　　　　　　　**Ephesians 4:7-16**
Wisdom is your sister　　　　　　*Building up the body of Christ*

Hymn: Eternal Father, Strong to Save, ELW 756

O God, our helper, you are always beside us, before us, behind us, and within us to guard and to guide us. Grant your church the grace to know you more clearly, love you more dearly, and grow daily in holiness.

Tuesday, May 28, 2013

Time after Pentecost

Ephesians 5:15-20
Living as wise ones in the Trinity

Be careful then how you live, not as unwise people but as wise, making the most of the time, because the days are evil. So do not be foolish, but understand what the will of the Lord is. Do not get drunk with wine, for that is debauchery; but be filled with the Spirit, as you sing psalms and hymns and spiritual songs among yourselves, singing and making melody to the Lord in your hearts, giving thanks to God the Father at all times and for everything in the name of our Lord Jesus Christ. (Eph. 5:15-20)

Psalm
Psalm 124
We have escaped like a bird

Additional Reading
Proverbs 8:4-21
Wisdom's riches

Hymn: Let the Whole Creation Cry, ELW 876

Sovereign Lord, you gave us the precious gift of life. By your grace help us live out the brief span of our lives wisely, harnessing all our resources, abilities, and energies for your glory.

Wednesday, May 29, 2013

Time after Pentecost

Jiří Tranovský, hymnwriter, died 1637

Daniel 1:1-21
Daniel's wisdom

At the end of the time that the king had set for them to be brought in, the palace master brought them into the presence of Nebuchadnezzar, and the king spoke with them. And among them all, no one was found to compare with Daniel, Hananiah, Mishael, and Azariah; therefore they were stationed in the king's court. In every matter of wisdom and understanding concerning which the king inquired of them, he found them ten times better than all the magicians and enchanters in his whole kingdom. And Daniel continued there until the first year of King Cyrus. (Dan. 1:18-21)

Psalm
Psalm 124
We have escaped like a bird

Additional Reading
Luke 1:46b-55
Mary sings of God

Hymn: Canticle of the Turning, ELW 723

Lord, you blessed your servant Daniel with wisdom. Let our words and actions be guided by your wisdom, so that our lives may sing sweetly of your greatness in a world that so often fails to acknowledge you.

Thursday, May 30, 2013

Time after Pentecost

Psalm 96:1-9
Praise to God among the nations

O sing to the LORD a new song;
  sing to the LORD, all the earth.
Sing to the LORD, bless his name;
  tell of his salvation from day to day.
Declare his glory among the nations,
  his marvelous works among all the peoples.
For great is the LORD, and greatly to be praised;
  he is to be revered above all gods. (Ps. 96:1-4)

Additional Readings
1 Kings 6:23-38
The splendor of God's temple

2 Corinthians 5:11-17
Beyond a human point of view

Hymn: How Great Thou Art, ELW 856

Lord of the universe, you are great and glorious indeed! Let the witness of your church be a resounding song of praise that captures the minds of the nations and turns the hearts of the peoples toward you in faith.

Friday, May 31, 2013

Visit of Mary to Elizabeth

Luke 1:39-57
Mary greets Elizabeth

In those days Mary set out and went with haste to a Judean town in the hill country, where she entered the house of Zechariah and greeted Elizabeth. When Elizabeth heard Mary's greeting, the child leaped in her womb. And Elizabeth was filled with the Holy Spirit and exclaimed with a loud cry, "Blessed are you among women, and blessed is the fruit of your womb." (Luke 1:39-42)

Psalm
Psalm 113
God, the helper of the needy

Additional Readings
1 Samuel 2:1-10
Hannah's thanksgiving

Romans 12:9-16b
Rejoice with those who rejoice

Hymn: Unexpected and Mysterious, ELW 258

Mighty God, by whose grace Elizabeth rejoiced with Mary and greeted her as the mother of the Lord: look with favor on your lowly servants that, with Mary, we may magnify your holy name and rejoice to acclaim her Son as our Savior, who lives and reigns with you and the Holy Spirit, one God, now and forever.

PRAYER LIST FOR JUNE

_____

_____

_____

_____

_____

_____

_____

_____

_____

_____

_____

Saturday, June 1, 2013

Time after Pentecost

Justin, martyr at Rome, died around 165

Luke 4:31-37
Healing the man with an unclean spirit

Jesus went down to Capernaum, a city in Galilee, and was teaching them on the sabbath. They were astounded at his teaching, because he spoke with authority. In the synagogue there was a man who had the spirit of an unclean demon, and he cried out with a loud voice, "Let us alone! What have you to do with us, Jesus of Nazareth? Have you come to destroy us? I know who you are, the Holy One of God." But Jesus rebuked him, saying, "Be silent, and come out of him!" When the demon had thrown him down before them, he came out of him without having done him any harm. They were all amazed and kept saying to one another, "What kind of utterance is this? For with authority and power he commands the unclean spirits, and out they come!" And a report about him began to reach every place in the region. (Luke 4:31-37)

Psalm
Psalm 96:1-9
Praise to God among the nations

Additional Reading
1 Kings 8:31-40
God knows every human heart

Hymn: O Christ, the Healer, We Have Come, ELW 610

Lord, not only can you see the dark places inside of us, but you can command light to scatter them. Speak a powerful word in the name of Jesus against the world's darkness today.

Sunday, June 2, 2013

Time after Pentecost

Luke 7:1-10

Jesus heals the centurion's slave

When [Jesus] was not far from the house, the centurion sent friends to say to him, "Lord, do not trouble yourself, for I am not worthy to have you come under my roof; therefore I did not presume to come to you. But only speak the word, and let my servant be healed. For I also am a man set under authority, with soldiers under me; and I say to one, 'Go,' and he goes, and to another, 'Come,' and he comes, and to my slave, 'Do this,' and the slave does it." When Jesus heard this he was amazed at him, and turning to the crowd that followed him, he said, "I tell you, not even in Israel have I found such faith." When those who had been sent returned to the house, they found the slave in good health. (Luke 7:6-10)

Psalm

Psalm 96:1-9

Praise to God among the nations

Additional Readings

1 Kings 8:22-23, 41-43

God's everlasting covenant for all

Galatians 1:1-12

Beware of contrary gospels

Hymn: Lord of All Nations, Grant Me Grace, ELW 716

Merciful Lord God, we do not presume to come before you trusting in our own righteousness, but in your great and abundant mercies. Revive our faith, we pray; heal our bodies, and mend our communities, that we may evermore dwell in your Son, Jesus Christ, our Savior and Lord.

Monday, June 3, 2013

Time after Pentecost

The Martyrs of Uganda, died 1886
John XXIII, Bishop of Rome, died 1963

Psalm 5
God's favor like a shield

But let all who take refuge in you rejoice;
  let them ever sing for joy.
Spread your protection over them,
  so that those who love your name may exult in you.
For you bless the righteous, O LORD;
  you cover them with favor as with a shield. (Ps. 5:11-12)

Additional Readings
Jonah 4:1-11
God's mercy on the Ninevites

Acts 8:26-40
The gospel is shared with an Ethiopian

Hymn: Thy Holy Wings, ELW 613

What comfort, what bliss, what peace there is when we abide in your love. May we trust with confidence that your arms are open to all who seek you.

Tuesday, June 4, 2013

Time after Pentecost

Acts 3:1-10
Healing the crippled beggar

One day Peter and John were going up to the temple at the hour of prayer, at three o'clock in the afternoon. And a man lame from birth was being carried in. People would lay him daily at the gate of the temple called the Beautiful Gate so that he could ask for alms from those entering the temple. When he saw Peter and John about to go into the temple, he asked them for alms. Peter looked intently at him, as did John, and said, "Look at us." And he fixed his attention on them, expecting to receive something from them. But Peter said, "I have no silver or gold, but what I have I give you; in the name of Jesus Christ of Nazareth, stand up and walk." (Acts 3:1-6)

Psalm
Psalm 5
God's favor like a shield

Additional Reading
Nehemiah 1:1-11
Asking God to gather the people

Hymn: Healer of Our Every Ill, ELW 612

In the name of Jesus Christ, may we speak the truth in love, bring hope to the hopeless, offer words of healing, and bear your light to a world in need.

Wednesday, June 5, 2013

Time after Pentecost

Boniface, Bishop of Mainz, missionary to Germany, martyr, died 754

Mark 7:24-30
The Syrophoenician woman's faith

From there [Jesus] set out and went away to the region of Tyre. He entered a house and did not want anyone to know he was there. Yet he could not escape notice, but a woman whose little daughter had an unclean spirit immediately heard about him, and she came and bowed down at his feet. Now the woman was a Gentile, of Syrophoenician origin. She begged him to cast the demon out of her daughter. He said to her, "Let the children be fed first, for it is not fair to take the children's food and throw it to the dogs." But she answered him, "Sir, even the dogs under the table eat the children's crumbs." Then he said to her, "For saying that, you may go—the demon has left your daughter." So she went home, found the child lying on the bed, and the demon gone. (Mark 7:24-30)

Psalm
Psalm 5
God's favor like a shield

Additional Reading
Isaiah 56:1-8
God welcomes the outcasts

Hymn: We Come to You for Healing, Lord, ELW 617

Lord, you sometimes surprise us with your mercy. Give us bold hearts to ask you for the bread of life that only you can give.

Thursday, June 6, 2013

Time after Pentecost

Psalm 30
My God, you restored me to health

To you, O Lord, I cried,
    and to the Lord I made supplication:
"What profit is there in my death,
    if I go down to the Pit?
Will the dust praise you?
    Will it tell of your faithfulness?
Hear, O Lord, and be gracious to me!
    O Lord, be my helper!"

You have turned my mourning into dancing;
    you have taken off my sackcloth
    and clothed me with joy,
so that my soul may praise you and not be silent.
    O Lord my God, I will give thanks to you forever. (Ps. 30:8-12)

Additional Readings
2 Samuel 14:1-11
A woman pretends to be a widow

Acts 22:6-21
Paul, the persecutor, is healed

Hymn: We've Come This Far by Faith, ELW 633

We pray for healing rest for those whose bodies and spirits are broken, weary, and hurting. Surround them with your care and love.

Friday, June 7, 2013

Time after Pentecost

Seattle, chief of the Duwamish Confederacy, died 1866

2 Samuel 14:12-24

A plea to restore a lost son

Then the woman said, "Please let your servant speak a word to my lord the king." He said, "Speak." The woman said, "Why then have you planned such a thing against the people of God? For in giving this decision the king convicts himself, inasmuch as the king does not bring his banished one home again. We must all die; we are like water spilled on the ground, which cannot be gathered up. But God will not take away a life; he will devise plans so as not to keep an outcast banished forever from his presence." (2 Sam. 14:12-14)

Psalm

Psalm 30

My God, you restored me to health

Additional Reading

Acts 26:1-11

Paul pursued believers even to foreign cities

Hymn: On Jordan's Stormy Bank I Stand, ELW 437

Lord, we pray for healing time, when we can focus on you and your renewing love. Amid our busy lives, help us to stop, focus, and rest in you. May we see our lives as the precious gifts they are.

Saturday, June 8, 2013

Time after Pentecost

2 Samuel 14:25-33
David welcomes the return of Absalom

So Absalom lived two full years in Jerusalem, without coming into the king's presence. Then Absalom sent for Joab to send him to the king; but Joab would not come to him. He sent a second time, but Joab would not come. Then he said to his servants, "Look, Joab's field is next to mine, and he has barley there; go and set it on fire." So Absalom's servants set the field on fire. Then Joab rose and went to Absalom at his house, and said to him, "Why have your servants set my field on fire?" Absalom answered Joab, "Look, I sent word to you: Come here, that I may send you to the king with the question, 'Why have I come from Geshur? It would be better for me to be there still.' Now let me go into the king's presence; if there is guilt in me, let him kill me!" Then Joab went to the king and told him; and he summoned Absalom. So he came to the king and prostrated himself with his face to the ground before the king; and the king kissed Absalom. (2 Sam. 14:28-33)

Psalm	Additional Reading
Psalm 30	Matthew 9:2-8
My God, you restored me to health	*Forgiveness and healing*

Hymn: Restore in Us, O God, ELW 328

O God, we pray for healing words between peoples and places where violence, mistrust, anger, and division reign. May your Spirit bring much-needed peace to our relationships and our world.

Sunday, June 9, 2013

Time after Pentecost

Columba, died 597; Aidan, died 651; Bede, died 735; renewers of the church

Luke 7:11-17

Jesus revives a widow's son

[Jesus] said, "Young man, I say to you, rise!" The dead man sat up and began to speak, and Jesus gave him to his mother. Fear seized all of them; and they glorified God, saying, "A great prophet has risen among us!" and "God has looked favorably on his people!" This word about him spread throughout Judea and all the surrounding country. (Luke 7:14b-17)

Psalm

Psalm 30

My God, you restored me to health

Additional Readings

1 Kings 17:17-24

Elijah revives a widow's son

Galatians 1:11-24

Jesus Christ is revealed

Hymn: Awake, O Sleeper, Rise from Death, ELW 452

Compassionate God, you have assured the human family of eternal life through Jesus Christ. Deliver us from the death of sin, and raise us to new life in your Son, Jesus Christ, our Savior and Lord.

Monday, June 10, 2013

Time after Pentecost

Psalm 68:1-10, 19-20
God protects the widows

Sing to God, sing praises to his name;
  lift up a song to him who rides upon the clouds—
his name is the LORD—
  be exultant before him.

Father of orphans and protector of widows
  is God in his holy habitation.
God gives the desolate a home to live in;
  he leads out the prisoners to prosperity,
    but the rebellious live in a parched land. (Ps. 68:4-6)

Additional Readings
Genesis 22:1-14
God saves Isaac from death

Galatians 2:1-10
Paul and the pillars of the church

Hymn: Oh, Sing to God Above, ELW 555

*Attentive God, your gaze rests on the powerless and marginalized.
Bestow on them your favor, and use us to offer care and compassion to
the widow, the orphan, the poor, and all those in need.*

Tuesday, June 11, 2013

Barnabas, Apostle

Acts 11:19-30; 13:1-3
Barnabas and Saul are set apart

Now in the church at Antioch there were prophets and teachers: Barnabas, Simeon who was called Niger, Lucius of Cyrene, Manaen a member of the court of Herod the ruler, and Saul. While they were worshiping the Lord and fasting, the Holy Spirit said, "Set apart for me Barnabas and Saul for the work to which I have called them." Then after fasting and praying they laid their hands on them and sent them off. (Acts 13:1-3)

Psalm
Psalm 112
Happy are the God-fearing

Additional Readings
Isaiah 42:5-12
The Lord calls us in righteousness

Matthew 10:7-16
Jesus sends out the Twelve

Hymn: Lord, You Give the Great Commission, ELW 579

We praise you, O God, for the life of your faithful servant Barnabas, who, seeking not his own renown but the well-being of your church, gave generously of his life and possessions for the relief of the poor and the spread of the gospel. Grant that we may follow his example and by our actions give glory to you, Father, Son, and Holy Spirit, now and forever.

Wednesday, June 12, 2013

Time after Pentecost

Jeremiah 8:14-22
A balm in Gilead

My joy is gone, grief is upon me,
   my heart is sick.
Hark, the cry of my poor people
   from far and wide in the land:
"Is the LORD not in Zion?
   Is her King not in her?"
("Why have they provoked me to anger with their images,
   with their foreign idols?")
"The harvest is past, the summer is ended,
   and we are not saved."
For the hurt of my poor people I am hurt,
   I mourn, and dismay has taken hold of me.

Is there no balm in Gilead?
   Is there no physician there?
Why then has the health of my poor people
   not been restored? (Jer. 8:18-22)

Psalm
Psalm 68:1-10, 19-20
God protects the widows

Additional Reading
Luke 8:40-56
A girl raised to life, a woman healed

Hymn: There Is a Balm in Gilead, ELW 614

The cries of the broken rise to you, O Lord, trusting that in your great mercy you will hear and respond. Guide our hearts and hands as we walk with those in pain.

Thursday, June 13, 2013

Time after Pentecost

Psalm 32

You forgive the guilt of my sin

Happy are those whose transgression is forgiven,
    whose sin is covered.
Happy are those to whom the LORD imputes no iniquity,
    and in whose spirit there is no deceit.

While I kept silence, my body wasted away
    through my groaning all day long.
For day and night your hand was heavy upon me;
    my strength was dried up as by the heat of summer.

Then I acknowledged my sin to you,
    and I did not hide my iniquity;
I said, "I will confess my transgressions to the LORD,"
    and you forgave the guilt of my sin. (Ps. 32:1-5)

Additional Readings

2 Samuel 13:23-39
Absalom avenges Tamar's rape

James 4:1-7
God gives grace to the humble

Hymn: Come, Ye Disconsolate, ELW 607

*Great God, at times the weight of sin and guilt can be too great to bear.
We are grateful for your refreshing words of forgiveness. Give us courage
to confess our failings and humble hearts to remind us of our constant
need for your grace.*

Friday, June 14, 2013

Time after Pentecost

**Basil the Great, Bishop of Caesarea, died 379;
Gregory, Bishop of Nyssa, died around 385;
Gregory of Nazianzus, Bishop of Constantinople, died around 389;
Macrina, teacher, died around 379**

Romans 11:1-10
A remnant chosen by grace

I ask, then, has God rejected his people? By no means! I myself am an Israelite, a descendant of Abraham, a member of the tribe of Benjamin. God has not rejected his people whom he foreknew. Do you not know what the scripture says of Elijah, how he pleads with God against Israel? "Lord, they have killed your prophets, they have demolished your altars; I alone am left, and they are seeking my life." But what is the divine reply to him? "I have kept for myself seven thousand who have not bowed the knee to Baal." (Rom. 11:1-4)

Psalm
Psalm 32
You forgive the guilt of my sin

Additional Reading
2 Samuel 15:1-12
Absalom plots against David

Hymn: Goodness Is Stronger than Evil, ELW 721

Could it be, O Lord, that despite our human frailties you have chosen us to be your people? Change our hearts from the inside out so our lives might reflect your gracious favor.

Saturday, June 15, 2013

Time after Pentecost

Luke 5:17-26

Jesus forgives sins and heals

Then the scribes and the Pharisees began to question, "Who is this who is speaking blasphemies? Who can forgive sins but God alone?" When Jesus perceived their questionings, he answered them, "Why do you raise such questions in your hearts? Which is easier, to say, 'Your sins are forgiven you,' or to say, 'Stand up and walk'? But so that you may know that the Son of Man has authority on earth to forgive sins"—he said to the one who was paralyzed—"I say to you, stand up and take your bed and go to your home." Immediately he stood up before them, took what he had been lying on, and went to his home, glorifying God. (Luke 5:21-25)

Psalm
Psalm 32
You forgive the guilt of my sin

Additional Reading
2 Samuel 18:28—19:8
David mourns Absalom

Hymn: There's a Wideness in God's Mercy, ELW 587/588

Lord, the depth of your forgiveness is beyond our comprehension. Help us to name what paralyzes us on our faith journeys and to testify to the ways you give us strength to walk with Jesus.

Blessing for Father's Day (June 16)

As a loving father cares for his children,
so you, O God, have compassion for us.
Look with favor on all those men
who guide and protect their children.
Hold them in your good care
and strengthen them for the holy task
which you have entrusted to them,
that all your children may flourish
in an atmosphere of wise love. Amen.

Sunday, June 16, 2013

Time after Pentecost

Luke 7:36—8:3

The woman anointing Jesus is forgiven

Then turning toward the woman, [Jesus] said to Simon, "Do you see this woman? I entered your house; you gave me no water for my feet, but she has bathed my feet with her tears and dried them with her hair. You gave me no kiss, but from the time I came in she has not stopped kissing my feet. You did not anoint my head with oil, but she has anointed my feet with ointment. Therefore, I tell you, her sins, which were many, have been forgiven; hence she has shown great love. But the one to whom little is forgiven, loves little." Then he said to her, "Your sins are forgiven." (Luke 7:44-48)

Psalm

Psalm 32
You forgive the guilt of my sin

Additional Readings

2 Samuel 11:26—12:10, 13-15
Nathan tells the story of the lamb

Galatians 2:15-21
Justification through grace

Hymn: O Jesus, Joy of Loving Hearts, ELW 658

O God, throughout the ages you judge your people with mercy, and you inspire us to speak your truth. By your Spirit, anoint us for lives of faith and service, and bring all people into your forgiveness, through Jesus Christ, our Savior and Lord.

Monday, June 17, 2013

Time after Pentecost

Psalm 130
Prayer for mercy

Out of the depths I cry to you, O LORD.
    Lord, hear my voice!
Let your ears be attentive
    to the voice of my supplications!

If you, O LORD, should mark iniquities,
    Lord, who could stand?
But there is forgiveness with you,
    so that you may be revered. (Ps. 130:1-4)

Additional Readings
2 Chronicles 29:1-19   **Galatians 3:1-9**
Hezekiah renews worship of God   *Abraham believed God*

Hymn: Out of the Depths I Cry to You, ELW 600

In times of sorrow, pain, and suffering, O Lord, you make your presence known. Turn our hearts to you, and open our hearts to your soothing word.

Tuesday, June 18, 2013

Time after Pentecost

Galatians 3:10-14

Blessing comes to the Gentiles

For all who rely on the works of the law are under a curse; for it is written, "Cursed is everyone who does not observe and obey all the things written in the book of the law." Now it is evident that no one is justified before God by the law; for "The one who is righteous will live by faith." But the law does not rest on faith; on the contrary, "Whoever does the works of the law will live by them." Christ redeemed us from the curse of the law by becoming a curse for us—for it is written, "Cursed is everyone who hangs on a tree"—in order that in Christ Jesus the blessing of Abraham might come to the Gentiles, so that we might receive the promise of the Spirit through faith. (Gal. 3:10-14)

Psalm	Additional Reading
Psalm 130	2 Chronicles 30:1-12
Prayer for mercy	*The people return to the Lord*

Hymn: Salvation unto Us Has Come, ELW 590

God Most High, by taking on the curse of sin and death, your Son has redeemed us from the grave and promised us eternity with you. Fill our mouths with praise and thanksgiving that we might share our gratitude with joyful hearts.

Wednesday, June 19, 2013

Time after Pentecost

2 Chronicles 30:13-27

The people are forgiven and healed

For a multitude of the people, many of them from Ephraim, Manasseh, Issachar, and Zebulun, had not cleansed themselves, yet they ate the passover otherwise than as prescribed. But Hezekiah prayed for them, saying, "The good Lord pardon all who set their hearts to seek God, the Lord the God of their ancestors, even though not in accordance with the sanctuary's rules of cleanness." The Lord heard Hezekiah, and healed the people. The people of Israel who were present at Jerusalem kept the festival of unleavened bread seven days with great gladness; and the Levites and the priests praised the Lord day by day, accompanied by loud instruments for the Lord. (2 Chron. 30:18-21)

Psalm
Psalm 130
Prayer for mercy

Additional Reading
Mark 2:1-12
Jesus forgives and heals

Hymn: The Trumpets Sound, the Angels Sing, ELW 531

Even when we fail to keep your commandments, O Lord, you call us back to you. Accept our penitent prayers when we ask for your forgiveness, and renew our faith in the name of your Son, Jesus Christ.

Thursday, June 20, 2013

Time after Pentecost

Psalm 22:19-28

I will praise you

But you, O LORD, do not be far away!
   O my help, come quickly to my aid!
Deliver my soul from the sword,
   my life from the power of the dog!
   Save me from the mouth of the lion!

From the horns of the wild oxen you have rescued me.
I will tell of your name to my brothers and sisters;
   in the midst of the congregation I will praise you:
You who fear the LORD, praise him!
   All you offspring of Jacob, glorify him;
   stand in awe of him, all you offspring of Israel! (Ps. 22:19-23)

Additional Readings

Isaiah 56:9-12
Israel's leaders are corrupt

Romans 2:17-29
Real circumcision is a matter of the heart

Hymn: Dear Christians, One and All, Rejoice, ELW 594

In times of trouble, Lord, you have the power to save and defend. Come quickly to the aid of the oppressed; those who do not have a safe place to stay, enough to eat, freedom to worship, or hope for the future.

Friday, June 21, 2013

Time after Pentecost

Onesimos Nesib, translator, evangelist, died 1931

Galatians 3:15-22

The purpose of the law

Brothers and sisters, I give an example from daily life: once a person's will has been ratified, no one adds to it or annuls it. Now the promises were made to Abraham and to his offspring; it does not say, "And to offsprings," as of many; but it says, "And to your offspring," that is, to one person, who is Christ. My point is this: the law, which came four hundred thirty years later, does not annul a covenant previously ratified by God, so as to nullify the promise. For if the inheritance comes from the law, it no longer comes from the promise; but God granted it to Abraham through the promise. (Gal. 3:15-18)

Psalm
Psalm 22:19-28
I will praise you

Additional Reading
Isaiah 57:1-13
The righteous perish and no one cares

Hymn: Give to Our God Immortal Praise! ELW 848

Lord, your faithfulness extends from one generation to the next. Unite your people through your Holy Spirit that we might see your mighty hand at work through our world yesterday, today, and tomorrow.

Saturday, June 22, 2013

Time after Pentecost

Isaiah 59:1-8

Sin creates barriers

See, the LORD's hand is not too short to save,
    nor his ear too dull to hear.
Rather, your iniquities have been barriers
    between you and your God,
and your sins have hidden his face from you
    so that he does not hear.
For your hands are defiled with blood,
    and your fingers with iniquity;
your lips have spoken lies,
    your tongue mutters wickedness. (Isa. 59:1-3)

Psalm
Psalm 22:19-28
I will praise you

Additional Reading
Matthew 9:27-34
Healing the blind, casting out a demon

Hymn: Forgive Our Sins As We Forgive, ELW 605

Accept our prayers of repentance, Lord of mercy, for we need your forgiveness. Turn our hearts to you and show us the ways to live and to love. We ask this in the name of the one who gave his life for us, Jesus Christ.

Sunday, June 23, 2013

Time after Pentecost

Luke 8:26-39
Jesus casts out demons

When the swineherds saw what had happened, they ran off and told it in the city and in the country. Then people came out to see what had happened, and when they came to Jesus, they found the man from whom the demons had gone sitting at the feet of Jesus, clothed and in his right mind. And they were afraid. Those who had seen it told them how the one who had been possessed by demons had been healed. (Luke 8:34-36)

Psalm
Psalm 22:19-28
I will praise you

Additional Readings
Isaiah 65:1-9
The prophet sent to a rebellious people

Galatians 3:23-29
Clothed with Christ in baptism

Hymn: Rise, Shine, You People! ELW 665

O Lord God, we bring before you the cries of a sorrowing world. In your mercy set us free from the chains that bind us, and defend us from everything that is evil, through Jesus Christ, our Savior and Lord.

Monday, June 24, 2013

John the Baptist

Luke 1:57-67 [68-80]
The birth and naming of John

On the eighth day Elizabeth and her neighbors and relatives came
to circumcise the child, and they were going to name him Zechariah
after his father. But his mother said, "No; he is to be called John."
They said to her, "None of your relatives has this name." Then they
began motioning to his father to find out what name he wanted
to give him. He asked for a writing tablet and wrote, "His name is
John." And all of them were amazed. Immediately his mouth was
opened and his tongue freed, and he began to speak, praising God.
(Luke 1:59-64)

Psalm
Psalm 141
My eyes are turned to God

Additional Readings
Malachi 3:1-4
*My messenger, a refiner
and purifier*

Acts 13:13-26
*The gospel for the
descendants of Abraham*

Hymn: Christ, Whose Glory Fills the Skies, ELW 553

*Almighty God, by your gracious providence your servant John the
Baptist was born to Elizabeth and Zechariah. Grant to your people the
wisdom to see your purpose and the openness to hear your will, that the
light of Christ may increase in us, through Jesus Christ, our Savior and
Lord, who lives and reigns with you and the Holy Spirit, one God, now
and forever.*

Tuesday, June 25, 2013

Time after Pentecost

Presentation of the Augsburg Confession, 1530
Philipp Melanchthon, renewer of the church, died 1560

Psalm 64
Prayer for protection

Hear my voice, O God, in my complaint;
    preserve my life from the dread enemy.
Hide me from the secret plots of the wicked,
    from the scheming of evildoers,
who whet their tongues like swords,
    who aim bitter words like arrows,
shooting from ambush at the blameless;
    they shoot suddenly and without fear. (Ps. 64:1-4)

Additional Readings
Job 19:1-22   Ephesians 2:11-22
Job questions God's ways   *One new humanity in Christ*

Hymn: Lord, Keep Us Steadfast in Your Word, ELW 517

*When life's struggles seem too great to bear, Holy God, assure us of your
presence and protection. You promise to hear us when we call to you.
May your Spirit be the strength we need to face each day.*

Wednesday, June 26, 2013

Time after Pentecost

Ezekiel 32:1-10

Evil like a dragon will be destroyed

In the twelfth year, in the twelfth month, on the first day of the
month, the word of the LORD came to me: Mortal, raise a lamentation
over Pharaoh king of Egypt,
and say to him:
You consider yourself a lion among the nations,
   but you are like a dragon in the seas;
you thrash about in your streams,
   trouble the water with your feet,
   and foul your streams.
Thus says the LORD God:
   In an assembly of many peoples
   I will throw my net over you;
   and I will haul you up in my dragnet. (Ezek. 32:1-3)

Psalm

Psalm 64

Prayer for protection

Additional Reading

Luke 9:37-43a

Jesus heals a boy with a demon

Hymn: Praise the Almighty! ELW 877

*Cast your wide net across our world, protector God, that your love
might overcome all evil and harm. Give strength to your people, that
they might be instruments of your peace in places too often filled with
chaos.*

204

Thursday, June 27, 2013

Time after Pentecost

Cyril, Bishop of Alexandria, died 444

Psalm 16
Protect me, O God

Protect me, O God, for in you I take refuge.
I say to the LORD, "You are my Lord;
    I have no good apart from you."

As for the holy ones in the land, they are the noble,
    in whom is all my delight.

Those who choose another god multiply their sorrows;
    their drink offerings of blood I will not pour out
    or take their names upon my lips.

The LORD is my chosen portion and my cup;
    you hold my lot. (Ps. 16:1-5)

Additional Readings

Leviticus 9:22—10:11
God's fire consumes Aaron's sons

2 Corinthians 13:5-10
Examine yourselves concerning the faith

Hymn: Just a Closer Walk with Thee, ELW 697

Mighty Lord, our world needs your protection. Work through our hands to care for the planet you have made and for its people whom you so love. May we be good and gracious stewards of your creation, preserving its goodness for future generations.

Friday, June 28, 2013

Time after Pentecost

Irenaeus, Bishop of Lyons, died around 202

Galatians 4:8-20
Paul reproves the hearers

Formerly, when you did not know God, you were enslaved to beings that by nature are not gods. Now, however, that you have come to know God, or rather to be known by God, how can you turn back again to the weak and beggarly elemental spirits? How can you want to be enslaved to them again? You are observing special days, and months, and seasons, and years. I am afraid that my work for you may have been wasted. (Gal. 4:8-11)

Psalm
Psalm 16
Protect me, O God

Additional Reading
2 Kings 1:1-16
God's fire consumes the king's men

Hymn: Sing Praise to God, the Highest Good, ELW 871

O Lord, we know that you choose us and claim us in baptism. Guide us as we strive to live out of those baptismal promises, as people forgiven, blessed, renewed, and set apart for the sake of the world.

Saturday, June 29, 2013

Peter and Paul, Apostles

John 21:15-19
Jesus says to Peter: Tend my sheep

When they had finished breakfast, Jesus said to Simon Peter, "Simon son of John, do you love me more than these?" He said to him, "Yes, Lord; you know that I love you." Jesus said to him, "Feed my lambs." A second time he said to him, "Simon son of John, do you love me?" He said to him, "Yes, Lord; you know that I love you." Jesus said to him, "Tend my sheep." He said to him the third time, "Simon son of John, do you love me?" Peter felt hurt because he said to him the third time, "Do you love me?" And he said to him, "Lord, you know everything; you know that I love you." Jesus said to him, "Feed my sheep. Very truly, I tell you, when you were younger, you used to fasten your own belt and to go wherever you wished. But when you grow old, you will stretch out your hands, and someone else will fasten a belt around you and take you where you do not wish to go." (He said this to indicate the kind of death by which he would glorify God.) After this he said to him, "Follow me." (John 21:15-19)

Psalm
Psalm 87:1-3, 5-7
Glorious things are spoken of you

Additional Readings
Acts 12:1-11
Peter released from prison

2 Timothy 4:6-8, 17-18
The good fight of faith

Hymn: Faith of Our Fathers, ELW 812

Almighty God, we praise you that your blessed apostles Peter and Paul glorified you by their martyrdoms. Grant that your church throughout the world may always be instructed by their teaching and example, be knit together in unity by your Spirit, and ever stand firm upon the one foundation who is Jesus Christ our Lord, for he lives and reigns with you and the Holy Spirit, one God, now and forever.

Sunday, June 30, 2013

Time after Pentecost

Luke 9:51-62

Jesus says, Follow me

As [Jesus and his disciples] were going along the road, someone said to him, "I will follow you wherever you go." And Jesus said to him, "Foxes have holes, and birds of the air have nests; but the Son of Man has nowhere to lay his head." To another he said, "Follow me." But he said, "Lord, first let me go and bury my father." But Jesus said to him, "Let the dead bury their own dead; but as for you, go and proclaim the kingdom of God." (Luke 9:57-60)

Psalm	Additional Readings	
Psalm 16	1 Kings 19:15-16,	Galatians 5:1, 13-25
Protect me, O God	19-21	*Love is the whole of the law*
	Elijah says, Follow me	

Hymn: O Jesus, I Have Promised, ELW 810

Sovereign God, ruler of all hearts, you call us to obey you, and you favor us with true freedom. Keep us faithful to the ways of your Son, that, leaving behind all that hinders us, we may steadfastly follow your paths, through Jesus Christ, our Savior and Lord.

Bob Hughs Son

People and families in Sarasota

Yvonne

Monday, July 1, 2013

Time after Pentecost

Catherine Winkworth, died 1878; John Mason Neale, died 1866; hymn translators

Psalm 140
Prayer for deliverance

I say to the LORD, "You are my God;
  give ear, O LORD, to the voice of my supplications."
O LORD, my Lord, my strong deliverer,
  you have covered my head in the day of battle.
Do not grant, O LORD, the desires of the wicked;
  do not further their evil plot. (Ps. 140:6-8)

Additional Readings
Genesis 24:34-41, 50-67
Rebekah follows Abraham's servant

1 John 2:7-11
Living in the light of love

Hymn: Thee We Adore, O Savior, ELW 476

God of life, every day we encounter challenges and uncertainties of many kinds. Guide and protect our steps, that we may find refuge in your promises, through our Savior Jesus Christ.

Tuesday, July 2, 2013

Time after Pentecost

Jeremiah 3:15-18

Nations cease to follow their own will

I will give you shepherds after my own heart, who will feed you with knowledge and understanding. And when you have multiplied and increased in the land, in those days, says the LORD, they shall no longer say, "The ark of the covenant of the LORD." It shall not come to mind, or be remembered, or missed; nor shall another one be made. At that time Jerusalem shall be called the throne of the LORD, and all nations shall gather to it, to the presence of the LORD in Jerusalem, and they shall no longer stubbornly follow their own evil will. In those days the house of Judah shall join the house of Israel, and together they shall come from the land of the north to the land that I gave your ancestors for a heritage. (Jer. 3:15-18)

Psalm
Psalm 140
Prayer for deliverance

Additional Reading
Ephesians 5:6-20
The fruit of the light

Hymn: O God of Every Nation, ELW 713

God of the nations, in your compassion you desire all peoples to turn to you and live. Turn us from our self-serving ways, that we may live your vision of plenty and peace, through Christ Jesus our Lord.

Wednesday, July 3, 2013

Thomas, Apostle

John 14:1-7

Jesus, the way, the truth, the life

Thomas said to Jesus, "Lord, we do not know where you are going. How can we know the way?" Jesus said to him, "I am the way, and the truth, and the life. No one comes to the Father except through me. If you know me, you will know my Father also. From now on you do know him and have seen him." (John 14:5-7)

Psalm

Psalm 136:1-4, 23-26

God's mercy endures forever

Additional Readings

Judges 6:36-40

God affirms Gideon's calling

Ephesians 4:11-16

The body of Christ has various gifts

Hymn: Come, My Way, My Truth, My Life, ELW 816

Ever-living God, you strengthened your apostle Thomas with firm and certain faith in the resurrection of your Son. Grant that we too may confess our faith in Jesus Christ, our Lord and our God, who lives and reigns with you and the Holy Spirit, one God, now and forever.

Thursday, July 4, 2013

Time after Pentecost

Psalm 66:1-9
God holds our souls in life

Come and see what God has done:
    he is awesome in his deeds among mortals.
He turned the sea into dry land;
    they passed through the river on foot.
There we rejoiced in him,
    who rules by his might forever,
whose eyes keep watch on the nations—
    let the rebellious not exalt themselves.

Bless our God, O peoples,
    let the sound of his praise be heard,
who has kept us among the living,
    and has not let our feet slip. (Ps. 66:5-9)

Additional Readings
2 Kings 21:1-15
God will wipe Jerusalem as a dish

Romans 7:14-25
I do not do the good I want

Hymn: Lead Me, Guide Me, ELW 768

*Lord of life, every day you shower blessings upon us without number.
Open our eyes to see your gracious work among us, that we may rejoice
in your generosity and share your gifts with others in Christ's name.*

Friday, July 5, 2013

Time after Pentecost

Jeremiah 51:47-58
Let Jerusalem come into your mind

Assuredly, the days are coming
   when I will punish the images of Babylon;
her whole land shall be put to shame,
   and all her slain shall fall in her midst.
Then the heavens and the earth,
   and all that is in them,
shall shout for joy over Babylon;
   for the destroyers shall come against them out of the north,
                        says the LORD.
Babylon must fall for the slain of Israel,
   as the slain of all the earth have fallen because of Babylon.

You survivors of the sword,
   go, do not linger!
Remember the LORD in a distant land,
   and let Jerusalem come into your mind:
We are put to shame, for we have heard insults;
   dishonor has covered our face,
for aliens have come
   into the holy places of the LORD's house. (Jer. 51:47-51)

Psalm
Psalm 66:1-9
God holds our souls in life

Additional Reading
2 Corinthians 8:1-7
Poverty overflows in generosity

Hymn: Come, We That Love the Lord, ELW 625

Righteous God, you have made peace with us through the gift of your Son, Jesus Christ. Following his example, help us to be peacemakers in our words and actions, that violence may cease and your peace prevail.

214

Saturday, July 6, 2013

Time after Pentecost

Jan Hus, martyr, died 1415

Zechariah 14:10-21

Jerusalem shall abide in security

The whole land shall be turned into a plain from Geba to Rimmon south of Jerusalem. But Jerusalem shall remain aloft on its site from the Gate of Benjamin to the place of the former gate, to the Corner Gate, and from the Tower of Hananel to the king's wine presses. And it shall be inhabited, for never again shall it be doomed to destruction; Jerusalem shall abide in security. (Zech. 14:10-11)

Psalm

Psalm 66:1-9

God holds our souls in life

Additional Reading

Luke 9:1-6

The mission of the Twelve

Hymn: Jerusalem, My Happy Home, ELW 628

O God, our true home is your city not made by human hands. As we await the fulfillment of your promises, embolden us to work for your kingdom, that all may know your vision for us in Christ Jesus.

Sunday, July 7, 2013

Time after Pentecost

Luke 10:1-11, 16-20

Jesus sends out seventy disciples

After this the Lord appointed seventy others and sent them on ahead of him in pairs to every town and place where he himself intended to go. He said to them, "The harvest is plentiful, but the laborers are few; therefore ask the Lord of the harvest to send out laborers into his harvest. Go on your way. See, I am sending you out like lambs into the midst of wolves. Carry no purse, no bag, no sandals; and greet no one on the road. Whatever house you enter, first say, 'Peace to this house!' " (Luke 10:1-5)

Psalm

Psalm 66:1-9

God holds our souls in life

Additional Readings

Isaiah 66:10-14

Jerusalem, a nursing mother

Galatians 6:[1-6] 7-16

Do what is right now

Hymn: Spread, Oh, Spread, Almighty Word, ELW 663

O God, the Father of our Lord Jesus, you are the city that shelters us, the mother who comforts us. With your Spirit accompany us on our life's journey, that we may spread your peace in all the world, through your Son, Jesus Christ, our Savior and Lord.

Monday, July 8, 2013

Time after Pentecost

Psalm 119:73-80
Living in faithfulness

Your hands have made and fashioned me;
  give me understanding that I may learn your commandments.
Those who fear you shall see me and rejoice,
  because I have hoped in your word.
I know, O LORD, that your judgments are right,
  and that in faithfulness you have humbled me.
Let your steadfast love become my comfort
  according to your promise to your servant.
Let your mercy come to me, that I may live;
  for your law is my delight. (Ps. 119:73-77)

Additional Readings
Jeremiah 6:10-19
Call to faithfulness

Acts 19:21-27
Demetrius opposes Paul

Hymn: O God, My Faithful God, ELW 806

Nurturing God, you are very close to us, closer than the next breath. Stir us from within by your boundless love, that others may see your work in our words and deeds, through Jesus Christ our Lord.

Tuesday, July 9, 2013

Time after Pentecost

Jeremiah 8:4-13
Call to faithfulness

You shall say to them, Thus says the LORD:
When people fall, do they not get up again?
   If they go astray, do they not turn back?
Why then has this people turned away
   in perpetual backsliding?
They have held fast to deceit,
   they have refused to return.
I have given heed and listened,
   but they do not speak honestly;
no one repents of wickedness,
   saying, "What have I done!"
All of them turn to their own course,
   like a horse plunging headlong into battle. (Jer. 8:4-6)

Psalm
Psalm 119:73-80
Living in faithfulness

Additional Reading
Acts 19:28-41
A riot follows Paul's preaching

Hymn: Word of God, Come Down on Earth, ELW 510

Providential God, all your ways are life giving and are intended for our well-being. Teach us to turn from our self-seeking ways and to follow in your path of self-giving love and care for others in Christ Jesus our Lord.

Wednesday, July 10, 2013

Time after Pentecost

Joshua 23:1-16
Joshua urges faithfulness

A long time afterward, when the LORD had given rest to Israel from all their enemies all around, and Joshua was old and well advanced in years, Joshua summoned all Israel, their elders and heads, their judges and officers, and said to them, "I am now old and well advanced in years; and you have seen all that the LORD your God has done to all these nations for your sake, for it is the LORD your God who has fought for you. I have allotted to you as an inheritance for your tribes those nations that remain, along with all the nations that I have already cut off, from the Jordan to the Great Sea in the west. The LORD your God will push them back before you, and drive them out of your sight; and you shall possess their land, as the LORD your God promised you." (Josh. 23:1-5)

Psalm
Psalm 119:73-80
Living in faithfulness

Additional Reading
Luke 10:13-16
Woe to unrepentant cities

Hymn: Amazing Grace, How Sweet the Sound, ELW 779

God of all nations, you desire all peoples to thrive and to practice the ways of peace. Remind us that you have created us to share land and resources, that all may know your justice, in Jesus Christ our Lord.

Thursday, July 11, 2013

Time after Pentecost

Benedict of Nursia, Abbot of Monte Cassino, died around 540

Psalm 25:1-10
Show me your ways

To you, O Lᴏʀᴅ, I lift up my soul.
O my God, in you I trust;
   do not let me be put to shame;
   do not let my enemies exult over me.
Do not let those who wait for you be put to shame;
   let them be ashamed who are wantonly treacherous.

Make me to know your ways, O Lᴏʀᴅ;
   teach me your paths.
Lead me in your truth, and teach me,
   for you are the God of my salvation;
   for you I wait all day long. (Ps. 25:1-5)

Additional Readings
Genesis 41:14-36   **James 2:14-26**
Joseph plans to feed Egypt   *Faith produces good works*

Hymn: Guide Me Ever, Great Redeemer, ELW 618

O God our protector, daily we are surrounded by both trials and blessings. In your compassion, shield us from all harm and create in us the awareness of your never-failing presence, in Christ our Lord.

Friday, July 12, 2013

Time after Pentecost

Nathan Söderblom, Bishop of Uppsala, died 1931

Genesis 41:37-49
God saves Egypt from starvation

Joseph was thirty years old when he entered the service of Pharaoh king of Egypt. And Joseph went out from the presence of Pharaoh, and went through all the land of Egypt. During the seven plenteous years the earth produced abundantly. He gathered up all the food of the seven years when there was plenty in the land of Egypt, and stored up food in the cities; he stored up in every city the food from the fields around it. So Joseph stored up grain in such abundance—like the sand of the sea—that he stopped measuring it; it was beyond measure. (Gen. 41:46-49)

Psalm	**Additional Reading**
Psalm 25:1-10	Acts 7:9-16
Show me your ways	*Egypt's food rescues Israel*

Hymn: Praise and Thanksgiving, ELW 689

Lord God, in you there is wisdom and insight for every occasion or concern. Inspire all leaders and public officials that they may discern what is good and helpful for those under their care.

Saturday, July 13, 2013

Time after Pentecost

Leviticus 19:1-4, 32-37
Mercy to the alien

You shall rise before the aged, and defer to the old; and you shall fear your God: I am the LORD.

When an alien resides with you in your land, you shall not oppress the alien. The alien who resides with you shall be to you as the citizen among you; you shall love the alien as yourself, for you were aliens in the land of Egypt: I am the LORD your God. (Lev. 19:32-34)

Psalm
Psalm 25:1-10
Show me your ways

Additional Reading
John 3:16-21
God's son saves the world

Hymn: In Christ There Is No East or West, ELW 650

O God, in your hospitality you welcome all peoples into your embrace. Enfold us in your grace that we may extend your welcome to those considered outsiders in our cities and communities, through our Lord Jesus Christ.

Sunday, July 14, 2013

Time after Pentecost

Luke 10:25-37

The parable of the merciful Samaritan

[Jesus said,] "But a Samaritan while traveling came near him; and when he saw him, he was moved with pity. He went to him and bandaged his wounds, having poured oil and wine on them. Then he put him on his own animal, brought him to an inn, and took care of him. The next day he took out two denarii, gave them to the innkeeper, and said, 'Take care of him; and when I come back, I will repay you whatever more you spend.' Which of these three, do you think, was a neighbor to the man who fell into the hands of the robbers?" [The lawyer] said, "The one who showed him mercy." Jesus said to him, "Go and do likewise." (Luke 10:33-37)

Psalm
Psalm 25:1-10
Show me your ways

Additional Readings
Deuteronomy 30:9-14
God delights in your fruitfulness

Colossians 1:1-14
The gospel is bearing fruit

Hymn: Lord of All Nations, Grant Me Grace, ELW 716

O Lord God, your mercy delights us, and the world longs for your loving care. Hear the cries of everyone in need, and turn our hearts to love our neighbors with the love of your Son, Jesus Christ, our Savior and Lord.

Monday, July 15, 2013

Time after Pentecost

Psalm 25:11-20
I take refuge in you, O God

Turn to me and be gracious to me,
    for I am lonely and afflicted.
Relieve the troubles of my heart,
    and bring me out of my distress.
Consider my affliction and my trouble,
    and forgive all my sins.

Consider how many are my foes,
    and with what violent hatred they hate me.
O guard my life, and deliver me;
    do not let me be put to shame, for I take refuge in you.
(Ps. 25:16-20)

Additional Readings
Job 24:1-8
The needy are thrust off the road

James 2:1-7
God has chosen the poor

Hymn: My Faith Looks Up to Thee, ELW 759

Merciful God, you have promised to be with us in every affliction we face. Help us to hear your words of solidarity with us, that we may trust in the assurance of your saving love in Christ our Lord.

Tuesday, July 16, 2013

Time after Pentecost

Proverbs 19:1-17

Kindness to the poor

Laziness brings on deep sleep;
    an idle person will suffer hunger.
Those who keep the commandment will live;
    those who are heedless of their ways will die.
Whoever is kind to the poor lends to the LORD,
    and will be repaid in full. (Prov. 19:15-17)

Psalm
Psalm 25:11-20
I take refuge in you, O God

Additional Reading
1 John 3:11-17
Do not refuse one in need

Hymn: Lord of Glory, You Have Bought Us, ELW 707

Lord God, it is your will that everyone has enough and no one go without. Teach us to live simply and mindfully, that we may both enjoy your gifts to us and have plenty to share with those in need.

Wednesday, July 17, 2013

Time after Pentecost

Bartolomé de Las Casas, missionary to the Indies, died 1566

Ecclesiastes 9:13-18

One bungler destroys much good

There was a little city with few people in it. A great king came against it and besieged it, building the great siegeworks against it. Now there was found in it a poor wise man, and he by his wisdom delivered the city. Yet no one remembered that poor man. So I said, "Wisdom is better than might; yet the poor man's wisdom is despised, and his words are not heeded."

The quiet words of the wise are more to be heeded
    than the shouting of a ruler among fools.
Wisdom is better than weapons of war,
    but one bungler destroys much good. (Eccles. 9:14-18)

Psalm
Psalm 25:11-20
I take refuge in you, O God

Additional Reading
Matthew 25:31-46
As you did it to one of the least of these

Hymn: Lord of Light, ELW 688

Generous God, your counsel may come through unexpected or even unwanted means. Help us to listen to your voice where it may be found, that we may receive a word of hope for today, in Christ Jesus our Lord.

Thursday, July 18, 2013

Time after Pentecost

Psalm 15
Leading a blameless life

O Lord, who may abide in your tent?
    Who may dwell on your holy hill?

Those who walk blamelessly, and do what is right,
    and speak the truth from their heart;
who do not slander with their tongue,
    and do no evil to their friends,
    nor take up a reproach against their neighbors;
in whose eyes the wicked are despised,
    but who honor those who fear the Lord;
who stand by their oath even to their hurt;
who do not lend money at interest,
    and do not take a bribe against the innocent. (Ps. 15:1-5)

Additional Readings
Genesis 12:10-20   **Hebrews 5:1-6**
Pharaoh offers hospitality to Sarai   *Christ did not glorify himself*

Hymn: Son of God, Eternal Savior, ELW 655

O God, you are a friend to sinners and to those who humbly confess their failings. Empower us to take on the mantle of your forgiveness, that we may be blameless in your sight, through Christ our Lord.

Friday, July 19, 2013

Time after Pentecost

Ephesians 3:14-21
The love of Christ surpasses knowledge

For this reason I bow my knees before the Father, from whom every family in heaven and on earth takes its name. I pray that, according to the riches of his glory, he may grant that you may be strengthened in your inner being with power through his Spirit, and that Christ may dwell in your hearts through faith, as you are being rooted and grounded in love. I pray that you may have the power to comprehend, with all the saints, what is the breadth and length and height and depth, and to know the love of Christ that surpasses knowledge, so that you may be filled with all the fullness of God. (Eph. 3:14-19)

Psalm
Psalm 15
Leading a blameless life

Additional Reading
Genesis 13:1-18
Abram and Lot separate peacefully

Hymn: Our Father, by Whose Name, ELW 640

Gracious Lord, the depth of your love for us in Christ Jesus knows no boundary or limit. Open our hearts to receive your immeasurable grace, that we may be strengthened by the fullness of your Spirit.

Saturday, July 20, 2013

Time after Pentecost

Genesis 14:1-16
Lot is rescued

When Abram heard that his nephew had been taken captive, he led forth his trained men, born in his house, three hundred eighteen of them, and went in pursuit as far as Dan. He divided his forces against them by night, he and his servants, and routed them and pursued them to Hobah, north of Damascus. Then he brought back all the goods, and also brought back his nephew Lot with his goods, and the women and the people. (Gen. 14:14-16)

Psalm
Psalm 15
Leading a blameless life

Additional Reading
Luke 8:4-10
Jesus speaks in parables

Hymn: On Our Way Rejoicing, ELW 537

O God, the challenges we face are often fraught with uncertainty and make us anxious. Help us to entrust all our undertakings to you, that our motives may match your own, through Christ Jesus our Lord.

Sunday, July 21, 2013

Time after Pentecost

Luke 10:38-42

Choosing the better part

Now as they went on their way, [Jesus] entered a certain village, where a woman named Martha welcomed him into her home. She had a sister named Mary, who sat at the Lord's feet and listened to what he was saying. But Martha was distracted by her many tasks; so she came to him and asked, "Lord, do you not care that my sister has left me to do all the work by myself? Tell her then to help me." But the Lord answered her, "Martha, Martha, you are worried and distracted by many things; there is need of only one thing. Mary has chosen the better part, which will not be taken away from her." (Luke 10:38-42)

Psalm

Psalm 15
Leading a blameless life

Additional Readings

Genesis 18:1-10a
The hospitality of Abraham and Sarah

Colossians 1:15-28
A hymn to Christ

Hymn: Lord, Thee I Love with All My Heart, ELW 750

Eternal God, you draw near to us in Christ, and you make yourself our guest. Amid the cares of our lives, make us attentive to your presence, that we may treasure your word above all else, through Jesus Christ, our Savior and Lord.

Monday, July 22, 2013

Mary Magdalene, Apostle

John 20:1-2, 11-18
Mary Magdalene meets Jesus in the garden

Jesus said to [Mary Magdalene], "Woman, why are you weeping? Whom are you looking for?" Supposing him to be the gardener, she said to him, "Sir, if you have carried him away, tell me where you have laid him, and I will take him away." Jesus said to her, "Mary!" She turned and said to him in Hebrew, "Rabbouni!" (which means Teacher). Jesus said to her, "Do not hold on to me, because I have not yet ascended to the Father. But go to my brothers and say to them, 'I am ascending to my Father and your Father, to my God and your God.'" Mary Magdalene went and announced to the disciples, "I have seen the Lord"; and she told them that he had said these things to her. (John 20:15-18)

Psalm
Psalm 73:23-28
I will speak of all God's works

Additional Readings
Ruth 1:6-18
Ruth stays with Naomi

Acts 13:26-33a
The raising of Jesus fulfills God's promise

Hymn: For All the Faithful Women, stanza 9, ELW 419

Almighty God, your Son first entrusted the apostle Mary Magdalene with the joyful news of his resurrection. Following the example of her witness, may we proclaim Christ as our living Lord and one day see him in glory, for he lives and reigns with you and the Holy Spirit, one God, now and forever.

Tuesday, July 23, 2013

Time after Pentecost

Birgitta of Sweden, renewer of the church, died 1373

Psalm 119:97-104
God's word like honey

Oh, how I love your law!
  It is my meditation all day long.
Your commandment makes me wiser than my enemies,
  for it is always with me.

How sweet are your words to my taste,
  sweeter than honey to my mouth!
Through your precepts I get understanding;
  therefore I hate every false way. (Ps. 119:97-98, 103-104)

Additional Readings
Proverbs 9:1-18   1 John 2:1-6
The wise and foolish women   *Walking as Christ walked*

Hymn: Let Us Ever Walk with Jesus, ELW 802

Life-giving God, you do not hide your wisdom from us, but freely share it with all who listen. Give us ears to hear your word, that we may grow daily into the likeness of Christ Jesus our Lord.

Wednesday, July 24, 2013

Time after Pentecost

John 6:41-51
Whoever eats this bread will live forever

[Jesus answered,] "Very truly, I tell you, whoever believes has eternal life. I am the bread of life. Your ancestors ate the manna in the wilderness, and they died. This is the bread that comes down from heaven, so that one may eat of it and not die. I am the living bread that came down from heaven. Whoever eats of this bread will live forever; and the bread that I will give for the life of the world is my flesh." (John 6:47-51)

Psalm
Psalm 119:97-104
God's word like honey

Additional Reading
Deuteronomy 12:1-12
The promise to eat before God

Hymn: Bread of Life, Our Host and Meal, ELW 464

Living God, you nourish us with the body and blood of Christ Jesus your Son, our Lord. Bring us to his table with ready hearts, that we may be strengthened for our journey by the promise of your forgiveness.

Thursday, July 25, 2013

James, Apostle

Mark 10:35-45

Whoever wishes to be great must serve

James and John, the sons of Zebedee, came forward to [Jesus] and said to him, "Teacher, we want you to do for us whatever we ask of you." And he said to them, "What is it you want me to do for you?" And they said to him, "Grant us to sit, one at your right hand and one at your left, in your glory." But Jesus said to them, "You do not know what you are asking. Are you able to drink the cup that I drink, or be baptized with the baptism that I am baptized with?" They replied, "We are able." Then Jesus said to them, "The cup that I drink you will drink; and with the baptism with which I am baptized, you will be baptized; but to sit at my right hand or at my left is not mine to grant, but it is for those for whom it has been prepared." (Mark 10:35-40)

Psalm

Psalm 7:1-10
God, my shield and defense

Additional Readings

1 Kings 19:9-18
Elijah hears God in the midst of silence

Acts 11:27—12:3a
James is killed by Herod

Hymn: Jesu, Jesu, Fill Us with Your Love, ELW 708

Gracious God, we remember before you today your servant and apostle James, the first among the twelve to be martyred for the name of Jesus Christ. Pour out on the leaders of your church that spirit of self-denying service which is the true mark of authority among your people, through Jesus Christ our servant, who lives and reigns with you and the Holy Spirit, one God, now and forever.

Friday, July 26, 2013

Time after Pentecost

Psalm 138

Your love endures forever

All the kings of the earth shall praise you, O LORD,
    for they have heard the words of your mouth.
They shall sing of the ways of the LORD,
    for great is the glory of the LORD.
For though the LORD is high, he regards the lowly;
    but the haughty he perceives from far away.

Though I walk in the midst of trouble,
    you preserve me against the wrath of my enemies;
you stretch out your hand,
    and your right hand delivers me.
The LORD will fulfill his purpose for me;
    your steadfast love, O LORD, endures forever.
    Do not forsake the work of your hands. (Ps. 138:4-8)

Additional Readings

Esther 3:7-15   **Acts 2:22-36**
Haman's plot to kill the Jews   *The Messiah is handed over to death*

Hymn: O God beyond All Praising, ELW 880

*Almighty God, in Christ Jesus you have traveled with us and shown us
the way of your freedom. Release us from all that binds us and save us
from all forces that seek to enslave us.*

Saturday, July 27, 2013

Time after Pentecost

Esther 4:1-17

Royal dignity for such a time as this

Then Esther said in reply to Mordecai, "Go, gather all the Jews to be found in Susa, and hold a fast on my behalf, and neither eat nor drink for three days, night or day. I and my maids will also fast as you do. After that I will go to the king, though it is against the law; and if I perish, I perish." Mordecai then went away and did everything as Esther had ordered him. (Esther 4:15-17)

Psalm
Psalm 138
Your love endures forever

Additional Reading
Luke 8:22-25
Jesus' disciples cry out for safety

Hymn: Lost in the Night, ELW 243

Lord God, your Son Jesus Christ bids us to take up our cross and follow, trusting in your mercy to safeguard our path. Empower us on the way, so that our faithful actions may lead to abundant life in your name.

Sunday, July 28, 2013

Time after Pentecost

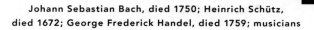

Johann Sebastian Bach, died 1750; Heinrich Schütz, died 1672; George Frederick Handel, died 1759; musicians

Luke 11:1-13
Jesus teaches prayer

[Jesus] was praying in a certain place, and after he had finished, one of his disciples said to him, "Lord, teach us to pray, as John taught his disciples." He said to them, "When you pray, say:
Father, hallowed be your name.

Your kingdom come.

Give us each day our daily bread.

And forgive us our sins,

for we ourselves forgive everyone indebted to us.

And do not bring us to the time of trial." (Luke 11:1-4)

Psalm
Psalm 138
Your love endures forever

Additional Readings
Genesis 18:20-32
Abraham bargains with God

Colossians 2:6-15
[16-19]
Buried with Christ in baptism

Hymn: Our Father, God in Heaven Above, ELW 746

Almighty and ever-living God, you are always more ready to hear than we are to pray, and you gladly give more than we either desire or deserve. Pour upon us your abundant mercy. Forgive us those things that weigh on our conscience, and give us those good things that come only through your Son, Jesus Christ, our Savior and Lord.

Monday, July 29, 2013

Time after Pentecost

Mary, Martha, and Lazarus of Bethany
Olaf, King of Norway, martyr, died 1030

Psalm 55:16-23
Cast your burden on God

My companion laid hands on a friend
   and violated a covenant with me
with speech smoother than butter,
   but with a heart set on war;
with words that were softer than oil,
   but in fact were drawn swords.

Cast your burden on the LORD,
   and he will sustain you;
he will never permit
   the righteous to be moved.

But you, O God, will cast them down
   into the lowest pit;
the bloodthirsty and treacherous
   shall not live out half their days.
But I will trust in you. (Ps. 55:20-23)

Additional Readings

Esther 5:1-14

A banquet guest with a murderous heart

Colossians 2:16—3:1

About false regulations

Hymn: If You But Trust in God to Guide You, ELW 769

Holy God, you are a friend to us when we feel betrayed or ignored. Comfort us with assurance of your presence, that we may find the strength to mend our relationships where they need repair or renewal, in Christ Jesus.

Tuesday, July 30, 2013

Time after Pentecost

Romans 9:30—10:4
Christ is the end of the law

What then are we to say? Gentiles, who did not strive for righteousness, have attained it, that is, righteousness through faith; but Israel, who did strive for the righteousness that is based on the law, did not succeed in fulfilling that law. Why not? Because they did not strive for it on the basis of faith, but as if it were based on works. They have stumbled over the stumbling stone, as it is written,
"See, I am laying in Zion a stone that will make people stumble,
     a rock that will make them fall,
   and whoever believes in him will not be put to shame."
(Rom. 9:30-33)

Psalm
Psalm 55:16-23
Cast your burden on God

Additional Reading
Esther 6:1—7:6
A royal reversal of fortunes

Hymn: All Depends on Our Possessing, ELW 589

Almighty God, in Christ Jesus you revealed your unmerited favor for all people. Give us the faith to trust in your unshakable love, and summon in us the courage to share it with those yet to hear.

Wednesday, July 31, 2013

Time after Pentecost

Matthew 5:43-48

Pray for those who persecute you

[Jesus said,] "You have heard that it was said, 'You shall love your neighbor and hate your enemy.' But I say to you, Love your enemies and pray for those who persecute you, so that you may be children of your Father in heaven; for he makes his sun rise on the evil and on the good, and sends rain on the righteous and on the unrighteous. For if you love those who love you, what reward do you have? Do not even the tax collectors do the same? And if you greet only your brothers and sisters, what more are you doing than others? Do not even the Gentiles do the same? Be perfect, therefore, as your heavenly Father is perfect." (Matt. 5:43-48)

Psalm

Psalm 55:16-23

Cast your burden on God

Additional Reading

Esther 7:7—8:17

Esther saves her people

Hymn: O Spirit of Life, ELW 405

Gracious God, your mercy extends to all people, even to those we would call enemies. Help us to be mindful of your unconditional love, that we may imitate you in your care for all people, in Christ our Lord.

Prayer List for August

_____

_____

_____

_____

_____

_____

_____

_____

_____

_____

_____

Thursday, August 1, 2013

Time after Pentecost

Psalm 49:1-12
The folly of trust in riches

Why should I fear in times of trouble,
    when the iniquity of my persecutors surrounds me,
those who trust in their wealth
    and boast of the abundance of their riches?
Truly, no ransom avails for one's life,
    there is no price one can give to God for it.
For the ransom of life is costly,
    and can never suffice
that one should live on forever
    and never see the grave. (Ps. 49:5-9)

Additional Readings
Proverbs 23:1-11   **Romans 11:33-36**
Resist the allure of becoming rich   *God's riches, wisdom, and knowledge*

Hymn: Jesus Calls Us; o'er the Tumult, ELW 696

Unsearchable Lord, you have shown us that wealth is deceptive and fleeting, and cannot ransom one's life. When we can't buy our way out of life's struggles, remind us to turn back to you, from whom come all things.

Friday, August 2, 2013

Time after Pentecost

Proverbs 24:1-12

By wisdom a house is built

Do not envy the wicked,
   nor desire to be with them;
for their minds devise violence,
   and their lips talk of mischief.

By wisdom a house is built,
   and by understanding it is established;
by knowledge the rooms are filled
   with all precious and pleasant riches. (Prov. 24:1-4)

Psalm

Psalm 49:1-12
The folly of trust in riches

Additional Reading

Ephesians 4:17-24
A new self in the likeness of God

Hymn: Abide, O Dearest Jesus, ELW 539

Our guide, you have given us everything we need to build a house of faith with wisdom and understanding. May we use that knowledge to establish a life built on the foundation of your love and grace.

Saturday, August 3, 2013

Time after Pentecost

Ecclesiastes 1:1-11
Nothing new under the sun

What has been is what will be,
 and what has been done is what will be done;
 there is nothing new under the sun.
Is there a thing of which it is said,
 "See, this is new"?
It has already been,
 in the ages before us.
The people of long ago are not remembered,
 nor will there be any remembrance
of people yet to come
 by those who come after them. (Eccles. 1:9-11)

Psalm
Psalm 49:1-12
The folly of trust in riches

Additional Reading
Mark 10:17-22
Treasure in heaven

Hymn: I Want to Walk as a Child of the Light, ELW 815

Lord, you have seen everything that has been and ever shall be. In our weariness, open the eyes of our hearts to the eternal rhythm of your creation and help us understand that no one is good but you alone.

Sunday, August 4, 2013

Time after Pentecost

Luke 12:13-21

Be rich toward God, your treasure

Then [Jesus] told them a parable: "The land of a rich man produced abundantly. And he thought to himself, 'What should I do, for I have no place to store my crops?' Then he said, 'I will do this: I will pull down my barns and build larger ones, and there I will store all my grain and my goods. And I will say to my soul, 'Soul, you have ample goods laid up for many years; relax, eat, drink, be merry.' But God said to him, 'You fool! This very night your life is being demanded of you. And the things you have prepared, whose will they be?' So it is with those who store up treasures for themselves but are not rich toward God." (Luke 12:16-21)

Psalm

Psalm 49:1-12
The folly of trust in riches

Additional Readings

Ecclesiastes 1:2,
12-14; 2:18-23
Search out wisdom

Colossians 3:1-11
Clothed in Christ

Hymn: God, Whose Giving Knows No Ending, ELW 678

Benevolent God, you are the source, the guide, and the goal of our lives. Teach us to love what is worth loving, to reject what is offensive to you, and to treasure what is precious in your sight, through Jesus Christ, our Savior and Lord.

Monday, August 5, 2013

Time after Pentecost

Psalm 127
Unless the Lord builds the house

Unless the LORD builds the house,
    those who build it labor in vain.
Unless the LORD guards the city,
    the guard keeps watch in vain.
It is in vain that you rise up early
    and go late to rest,
eating the bread of anxious toil;
    for he gives sleep to his beloved.

Sons are indeed a heritage from the LORD,
    the fruit of the womb a reward.
Like arrows in the hand of a warrior
    are the sons of one's youth.
Happy is the man who has
    his quiver full of them.
He shall not be put to shame
    when he speaks with his enemies in the gate. (Ps. 127:1-5)

Additional Readings

Ecclesiastes 2:1-17
The fool accumulates wealth

Colossians 3:18—4:1
A household code

Hymn: In Thee Is Gladness, ELW 867

Great builder, even though you give us every tool we need, we continue to labor in vain, chasing after the wind, eating the bread of anxious toil. May we instead walk from the darkness into your calm and light-giving presence.

Tuesday, August 6, 2013

Time after Pentecost

Colossians 4:2-6

Wise conduct toward outsiders

Devote yourselves to prayer, keeping alert in it with thanksgiving. At the same time pray for us as well that God will open to us a door for the word, that we may declare the mystery of Christ, for which I am in prison, so that I may reveal it clearly, as I should.

Conduct yourselves wisely toward outsiders, making the most of the time. Let your speech always be gracious, seasoned with salt, so that you may know how you ought to answer everyone. (Col. 4:2-6)

Psalm
Psalm 127
Unless the Lord builds the house

Additional Reading
Ecclesiastes 3:16—4:8
Death comes to all

Hymn: What a Friend We Have in Jesus, ELW 742

Determined God, you open doors for your word that it may be clearly revealed. Help us remain alert in it, quietly devoting ourselves to prayer, making the most of our time, and graciously speaking from our hearts.

Wednesday, August 7, 2013

Time after Pentecost

Ecclesiastes 12:1-8, 13-14
Remember God

The end of the matter; all has been heard. Fear God, and keep his commandments; for that is the whole duty of everyone. For God will bring every deed into judgment, including every secret thing, whether good or evil. (Eccles. 12:13-14)

Psalm
Psalm 127
Unless the Lord builds the house

Additional Reading
Luke 12:22-31
Trust in God

Hymn: Be Thou My Vision, ELW 793

Father, the end of the matter is that you will bring every secret deed into judgment, and yet we need not worry about our lives. Help us keep your commandments, trusting that you know what we need before we ask.

Thursday, August 8, 2013

Time after Pentecost

Dominic, founder of the Order of Preachers (Dominicans), died 1221

Psalm 33:12-22
Let your loving kindness be upon us

Our soul waits for the LORD;
　he is our help and shield.
Our heart is glad in him,
　because we trust in his holy name.
Let your steadfast love, O LORD, be upon us,
　even as we hope in you. (Ps. 33:20-22)

Additional Readings

Job 21:1-16
The rich blessed with children despise God

Romans 9:1-9
True descendants of Abraham

Hymn: O God, Our Help in Ages Past, ELW 632

Mighty Lord, you are our help and shield, patiently loving us through the mysteries and injustice of life. May our souls wait for you, trusting and hoping in your steadfast love.

Friday, August 9, 2013

Time after Pentecost

Ecclesiastes 6:1-6

Those who waste life

There is an evil that I have seen under the sun, and it lies heavy upon humankind: those to whom God gives wealth, possessions, and honor, so that they lack nothing of all that they desire, yet God does not enable them to enjoy these things, but a stranger enjoys them. This is vanity; it is a grievous ill. A man may beget a hundred children, and live many years; but however many are the days of his years, if he does not enjoy life's good things, or has no burial, I say that a stillborn child is better off than he. For it comes into vanity and goes into darkness, and in darkness its name is covered; moreover it has not seen the sun or known anything; yet it finds rest rather than he. Even though he should live a thousand years twice over, yet enjoy no good—do not all go to one place? (Eccles. 6:1-6)

Psalm
Psalm 33:12-22
Let your loving kindness be upon us

Additional Reading
Acts 7:1-8
Descendants promised to Abraham

Hymn: O Master, Let Me Walk with You, ELW 818

Great giver of all good gifts, we may lack nothing of all we desire, but if we do not find our rest in you, what good is it? May our hearts be truly thankful for each day under your sun.

Saturday, August 10, 2013

Time after Pentecost

Lawrence, deacon, martyr, died 258

Matthew 6:19-24
Treasures and masters

[Jesus said,] "Do not store up for yourselves treasures on earth, where moth and rust consume and where thieves break in and steal; but store up for yourselves treasures in heaven, where neither moth nor rust consumes and where thieves do not break in and steal. For where your treasure is, there your heart will be also." (Matt. 6:19-21)

Psalm
Psalm 33:12-22
Let your loving kindness be upon us

Additional Reading
Genesis 11:27-32
The ancestors of Abram and Sarai

Hymn: Children of the Heavenly Father, ELW 781

Like Abram and Sarai before us, Father, you lead us through the darkness into your light. Help us resist the temptations on this earth, so that discovering where true treasure lies, our hearts may be there also.

Sunday, August 11, 2013

Time after Pentecost

Clare, Abbess of San Damiano, died 1253

Luke 12:32-40
The treasure of the kingdom

[Jesus said,] "Do not be afraid, little flock, for it is your Father's good pleasure to give you the kingdom. Sell your possessions, and give alms. Make purses for yourselves that do not wear out, an unfailing treasure in heaven, where no thief comes near and no moth destroys. For where your treasure is, there your heart will be also." (Luke 12:32-34)

Psalm

Psalm 33:12-22
Let your loving kindness be upon us

Additional Readings

Genesis 15:1-6
God's promise of a child

Hebrews 11:1-3, 8-16
Abraham's faith

Hymn: Lord Jesus, You Shall Be My Song, ELW 808

Almighty God, you sent your Holy Spirit to be the life and light of your church. Open our hearts to the riches of your grace, that we may be ready to receive you wherever you appear, through Jesus Christ, our Savior and Lord.

Monday, August 12, 2013

Time after Pentecost

Psalm 89:1-18
God's covenant with David

I will sing of your steadfast love, O LORD, forever;
   with my mouth I will proclaim your faithfulness to all generations.
I declare that your steadfast love is established forever;
   your faithfulness is as firm as the heavens.

You said, "I have made a covenant with my chosen one,
   I have sworn to my servant David:
'I will establish your descendants forever,
   and build your throne for all generations'. " (Ps. 89:1-4)

Additional Readings
2 Chronicles 33:1-17
Manasseh returns to God

Hebrews 11:1-7
The ancestors' faith

Hymn: You Servants of God, ELW 825

Steadfast Lord, you have established your descendants forever, with your faithfulness as firm as the heavens. Help us walk in your light and sing of all you have created, declaring to all generations the wonder of your love.

Tuesday, August 13, 2013

Time after Pentecost

**Florence Nightingale, died 1910; Clara Maass, died 1901;
renewers of society**

Hebrews 11:17-28
The faith of Abraham's descendants

By faith Abraham, when put to the test, offered up Isaac. He who
had received the promises was ready to offer up his only son, of
whom he had been told, "It is through Isaac that descendants shall be
named for you." He considered the fact that God is able even to raise
someone from the dead—and figuratively speaking, he did receive
him back. (Heb. 11:17-19)

Psalm
Psalm 89:1-18
God's covenant with David

Additional Reading
2 Chronicles 34:22-33
Huldah preaches the covenant

Hymn: Faith of Our Fathers, ELW 812/813

*God of Abraham, you have poured out sacred promises on your people
since the beginning, providing challenging opportunities for expanding
our faith. When we are put to the test, may we offer you the trust of our
hearts and souls.*

Wednesday, August 14, 2013

Time after Pentecost

Maximilian Kolbe, died 1941; Kaj Munk, died 1944; martyrs

Luke 12:41-48
A parable of the slaves

Peter said, "Lord, are you telling this parable for us or for everyone?" And the Lord said, "Who then is the faithful and prudent manager whom his master will put in charge of his slaves, to give them their allowance of food at the proper time? Blessed is that slave whom his master will find at work when he arrives. Truly I tell you, he will put that one in charge of all his possessions." (Luke 12:41-44)

Psalm
Psalm 89:1-18
God's covenant with David

Additional Reading
Jeremiah 33:14-26
God remembers the covenant

Hymn: We Are an Offering, ELW 692

Righteous Lord, you have entrusted to us your earth and all that is in it until you come again. Motivate us to continue caring for those in our charge, watching faithfully over your flock, and waiting expectantly for your return.

Thursday, August 15, 2013

Mary, Mother of Our Lord

Luke 1:46-55

Mary's thanksgiving

And Mary said,
"My soul magnifies the Lord,
    and my spirit rejoices in God my Savior,
for he has looked with favor on the lowliness of his servant.
    Surely, from now on all generations will call me blessed;
for the Mighty One has done great things for me,
    and holy is his name." (Luke 1:46-49)

Psalm

Psalm 34:1-9
O magnify the Lord with me

Additional Readings

Isaiah 61:7-11
*God will cause
righteousness to spring up*

Galatians 4:4-7
*We are no longer slaves,
but children*

Hymn: Signs and Wonders, ELW 672

*Almighty God, in choosing the virgin Mary to be the mother of your
Son, you made known your gracious regard for the poor, the lowly, and
the despised. Grant us grace to receive your word in humility, and so
to be made one with your Son, Jesus Christ our Savior and Lord, who
lives and reigns with you and the Holy Spirit, one God, now and forever.*

Friday, August 16, 2013

Time after Pentecost

Hebrews 10:32-39
Do not abandon your confidence

But recall those earlier days when, after you had been enlightened, you endured a hard struggle with sufferings, sometimes being publicly exposed to abuse and persecution, and sometimes being partners with those so treated. For you had compassion for those who were in prison, and you cheerfully accepted the plundering of your possessions, knowing that you yourselves possessed something better and more lasting. Do not, therefore, abandon that confidence of yours; it brings a great reward. For you need endurance, so that when you have done the will of God, you may receive what was promised. (Heb. 10:32-36)

Psalm
Psalm 82
O God, rule the earth

Additional Reading
1 Samuel 5:1-12
The Philistines punished

Hymn: Peace, to Soothe Our Bitter Woes, ELW 381

Judge of the earth, you never promised that living faithfully in your will would be easy. Give us the strength, confidence, and endurance to struggle with the suffering of this world, so that we may ultimately receive what you have promised.

Saturday, August 17, 2013

Time after Pentecost

1 Samuel 6:1-16

The Philistines atone for sacrilege

Now the people of Beth-shemesh were reaping their wheat harvest in the valley. When they looked up and saw the ark, they went with rejoicing to meet it. The cart came into the field of Joshua of Beth-shemesh, and stopped there. A large stone was there; so they split up the wood of the cart and offered the cows as a burnt offering to the LORD. The Levites took down the ark of the LORD and the box that was beside it, in which were the gold objects, and set them upon the large stone. Then the people of Beth-shemesh offered burnt offerings and presented sacrifices on that day to the LORD. When the five lords of the Philistines saw it, they returned that day to Ekron. (1 Sam. 6:13-16)

Psalm
Psalm 82
O God, rule the earth

Additional Reading
Matthew 24:15-27
The desolating sacrilege

Hymn: Accept, O Lord, the Gifts We Bring, ELW 691

Surprising God, sometimes in the midst of our daily chores, you send unexpected blessings to us. Open our eyes to recognize your hand in our lives, that we may give you the sacrificial offering of our thankful hearts.

Sunday, August 18, 2013

Time after Pentecost

Luke 12:49-56
Jesus brings fire on earth

[Jesus said,] "I came to bring fire to the earth, and how I wish it were already kindled! I have a baptism with which to be baptized, and what stress I am under until it is completed! Do you think that I have come to bring peace to the earth? No, I tell you, but rather division! From now on five in one household will be divided, three against two and two against three; they will be divided:

father against son
  and son against father,
mother against daughter
  and daughter against mother,
mother-in-law against her daughter-in-law
  and daughter-in-law against mother-in-law." (Luke 12:49-53)

Psalm	Additional Readings	
Psalm 82	Jeremiah 23:23-29	Hebrews 11:29—12:2
O God, rule the earth	*God's word is like fire*	*The faith of the Hebrew people*

Hymn: We've Come This Far by Faith, ELW 633

O God, judge eternal, you love justice and hate oppression, and you call us to share your zeal for truth. Give us courage to take our stand with all victims of bloodshed and greed, and, following your servants and prophets, to look to the pioneer and perfecter of our faith, your Son, Jesus Christ, our Savior and Lord.

Monday, August 19, 2013

Time after Pentecost

Psalm 32
Prayer for forgiveness

Happy are those whose transgression is forgiven,
    whose sin is covered.
Happy are those to whom the LORD imputes no iniquity,
    and in whose spirit there is no deceit.

While I kept silence, my body wasted away
    through my groaning all day long.
For day and night your hand was heavy upon me;
    my strength was dried up as by the heat of summer.

Then I acknowledged my sin to you,
    and I did not hide my iniquity;
I said, "I will confess my transgressions to the LORD,"
    and you forgave the guilt of my sin. (Ps. 32:1-5)

Additional Readings
Jeremiah 23:30-40
False prophets

1 John 4:1-6
False prophets are in the world

Hymn: O Christ, Our Hope, ELW 604

Forgiving Lord, you have covered us with your steadfast, loving grace, but if we keep silent about our sins, guilt cuts us off from you. May we instead offer you our contrite hearts and trust in your faithful counsel.

Tuesday, August 20, 2013

Time after Pentecost

Bernard, Abbot of Clairvaux, died 1153

Acts 7:44-53
Our ancestors persecuted true prophets

[Stephen replied,] "You stiff-necked people, uncircumcised in heart and ears, you are forever opposing the Holy Spirit, just as your ancestors used to do. Which of the prophets did your ancestors not persecute? They killed those who foretold the coming of the Righteous One, and now you have become his betrayers and murderers. You are the ones that received the law as ordained by angels, and yet you have not kept it." (Acts 7:51-53)

Psalm
Psalm 32
Prayer for forgiveness

Additional Reading
Jeremiah 25:15-29
The cup of God's wrath

Hymn: O Jesus, Joy of Loving Hearts, ELW 658

Lord, you have given us your Holy Spirit to guide our lives, but so often we respond with stubborn opposition, just like our ancestors did. As we grow in faith, may we learn to trust your plans for us.

Wednesday, August 21, 2013

Time after Pentecost

Jeremiah 25:30-38
The peaceful flock is devastated

Wail, you shepherds, and cry out;
  roll in ashes, you lords of the flock,
for the days of your slaughter have come—and your dispersions,
  and you shall fall like a choice vessel.
Flight shall fail the shepherds,
  and there shall be no escape for the lords of the flock.
Hark! the cry of the shepherds,
  and the wail of the lords of the flock!
For the LORD is despoiling their pasture,
  and the peaceful folds are devastated,
    because of the fierce anger of the LORD.
Like a lion he has left his covert;
  for their land has become a waste
because of the cruel sword,
  and because of his fierce anger. (Jer. 25:34-38)

Psalm
Psalm 32
Prayer for forgiveness

Additional Reading
Luke 19:45-48
Jesus cleanses the temple

Hymn: O Lord, Hear My Prayer, ELW 751

Mighty Lord, your prophets have warned us of the tempest that will be stirred up by your fierce anger spreading across the earth. May we pay close attention to your words and find our hiding place in you.

Thursday, August 22, 2013

Time after Pentecost

Psalm 103:1-8
Crowned with mercy

Bless the LORD, O my soul,
   and all that is within me,
   bless his holy name.
Bless the LORD, O my soul,
   and do not forget all his benefits—
who forgives all your iniquity,
   who heals all your diseases,
who redeems your life from the Pit,
   who crowns you with steadfast love and mercy,
who satisfies you with good as long as you live
   so that your youth is renewed like the eagle's. (Ps. 103:1-5)

Additional Readings
Numbers 15:32-41
The severity of breaking sabbath law

Hebrews 12:3-17
Call for endurance

Hymn: Praise to the Lord, the Almighty, ELW 858

Merciful and gracious Lord, many are the blessings you have made known to us. We will not forget the benefits of your forgiveness, the vindication of your justice, the discipline that trains us, and your steadfast love.

Friday, August 23, 2013

Time after Pentecost

2 Chronicles 8:12-15

Solomon honors sabbaths

Then Solomon offered up burnt offerings to the Lord on the altar of the Lord that he had built in front of the vestibule, as the duty of each day required, offering according to the commandment of Moses for the sabbaths, the new moons, and the three annual festivals—the festival of unleavened bread, the festival of weeks, and the festival of booths. According to the ordinance of his father David, he appointed the divisions of the priests for their service, and the Levites for their offices of praise and ministry alongside the priests as the duty of each day required, and the gatekeepers in their divisions for the several gates; for so David the man of God had commanded. They did not turn away from what the king had commanded the priests and Levites regarding anything at all, or regarding the treasuries. (2 Chron. 8:12-15)

Psalm
Psalm 103:1-8
Crowned with mercy

Additional Reading
Acts 17:1-9
Paul preaches Christ on the sabbath

Hymn: Let All Things Now Living, ELW 881

Holy Lord, you have commanded your people to leave offerings of thanksgiving at your altar. Fill our hearts with such recognition of your holiness and presence in our lives that we never turn away from what you ask of us.

Saturday, August 24, 2013

Bartholomew, Apostle

John 1:43-51

Jesus says: Follow me

When Jesus saw Nathanael coming toward him, he said of him, "Here is truly an Israelite in whom there is no deceit!" Nathanael asked him, "Where did you get to know me?" Jesus answered, "I saw you under the fig tree before Philip called you." Nathanael replied, "Rabbi, you are the Son of God! You are the King of Israel!" Jesus answered, "Do you believe because I told you that I saw you under the fig tree? You will see greater things than these." And he said to him, "Very truly, I tell you, you will see heaven opened and the angels of God ascending and descending upon the Son of Man." (John 1:47-51)

Psalm

Psalm 12

A plea for help in evil times

Additional Readings

Exodus 19:1-6

Israel is God's priestly kingdom

1 Corinthians 12:27-31a

The body of Christ

Hymn: Listen, God Is Calling, ELW 513

Almighty and everlasting God, you gave to your apostle Bartholomew grace truly to believe and courageously to preach your word. Grant that your church may proclaim the good news to the ends of the earth, through Jesus Christ, our Savior and Lord, who lives and reigns with you and the Holy Spirit, one God, now and forever.

Sunday, August 25, 2013

Time after Pentecost

Luke 13:10-17

Jesus heals on the sabbath

And just then there appeared a woman with a spirit that had crippled her for eighteen years. She was bent over and was quite unable to stand up straight. When Jesus saw her, he called her over and said, "Woman, you are set free from your ailment."

But the leader of the synagogue, indignant because Jesus had cured on the sabbath, kept saying to the crowd, "There are six days on which work ought to be done; come on those days and be cured, and not on the sabbath day." But the LORD answered him and said, "You hypocrites! Does not each of you on the sabbath untie his ox or his donkey from the manger, and lead it away to give it water? And ought not this woman, a daughter of Abraham whom Satan bound for eighteen long years, be set free from this bondage on the sabbath day?" (Luke 13:11-12, 14-16)

Psalm	Additional Readings	
Psalm 103:1-8	Isaiah 58:9b-14	Hebrews 12:18-29
Crowned with mercy	*Do not trample the sabbath*	*Coming to the city of the living God*

Hymn: Praise the One Who Breaks the Darkness, ELW 843

O God, mighty and immortal, you know that as fragile creatures surrounded by great dangers, we cannot by ourselves stand upright. Give us strength of mind and body, so that even when we suffer because of human sin, we may rise victorious through your Son, Jesus Christ, our Savior and Lord.

Monday, August 26, 2013

Time after Pentecost

Psalm 109:21-31
Praise for healing

Help me, O LORD my God!
    Save me according to your steadfast love.

May my accusers be clothed with dishonor;
    may they be wrapped in their own shame as in a mantle.
With my mouth I will give great thanks to the LORD;
    I will praise him in the midst of the throng.
For he stands at the right hand of the needy,
    to save them from those who would condemn them to death.
(Ps. 109:26, 29-31)

Additional Readings
Ezekiel 20:1-17   **Hebrews 3:7—4:11**
The people profaned the sabbath   *Sabbath rest of God's people*

Hymn: O Savior, Precious Savior, ELW 820

*Living God, you have always stood by your people, meeting needs we
don't even realize we have. Though our hearts are pierced within us,
may we recognize your saving help in our lives and give you our thanks
and praise.*

Tuesday, August 27, 2013

Time after Pentecost

Ezekiel 20:18-32
Israel become like the nations

I said to their children in the wilderness, Do not follow the statutes of your parents, nor observe their ordinances, nor defile yourselves with their idols. I the LORD am your God; follow my statutes, and be careful to observe my ordinances, and hallow my sabbaths that they may be a sign between me and you, so that you may know that I the LORD am your God. (Ezek. 20:18-20)

Psalm
Psalm 109:21-31
Praise for healing

Additional Reading
Revelation 3:7-13
The new Jerusalem from heaven

Hymn: We Are Marching in the Light, ELW 866

Lord, our God, you created the structure by which to live our lives, and the rhythm of your sabbath holds us fast to your holiness. Let anyone who has ears to hear listen to your words with patient endurance.

Wednesday, August 28, 2013

Time after Pentecost

Augustine, Bishop of Hippo, died 430
Moses the Black, monk, martyr, died around 400

Luke 6:6-11
Jesus heals on the sabbath

On another sabbath Jesus entered the synagogue and taught, and there was a man there whose right hand was withered. The scribes and the Pharisees watched him to see whether he would cure on the sabbath, so that they might find an accusation against him. Even though he knew what they were thinking, he said to the man who had the withered hand, "Come and stand here." He got up and stood there. Then Jesus said to them, "I ask you, is it lawful to do good or to do harm on the sabbath, to save life or to destroy it?" After looking around at all of them, he said to him, "Stretch out your hand." He did so, and his hand was restored. (Luke 6:6-10)

Psalm
Psalm 109:21-31
Praise for healing

Additional Reading
Ezekiel 20:33-44
God restores rebellious Israel

Hymn: Jesus Lives, My Sure Defense, ELW 621

Lord, you have shown us with your mighty hand and outstretched arm that healing happens in your time, not according to humanly rigid ideas of what is acceptable. Help us remain flexible and open to your presence in our lives.

Thursday, August 29, 2013

Time after Pentecost

Psalm 112
The righteous are merciful

Praise the LORD!
  Happy are those who fear the LORD,
  who greatly delight in his commandments.
Their descendants will be mighty in the land;
  the generation of the upright will be blessed.
Wealth and riches are in their houses,
  and their righteousness endures forever. (Ps. 112:1-3)

Additional Readings
Proverbs 15:13-17
A continual feast for the poor

1 Peter 3:8-12
Repay abuse with a blessing

Hymn: Praise and Thanks and Adoration, ELW 783

Merciful God, you have blessed those who delight in your ways with riches beyond measure and righteousness that endures forever. May we be truly thankful, pursue peace, and live lives filled with unity of spirit, tender hearts, and humble minds.

Friday, August 30, 2013

Time after Pentecost

1 Peter 4:7-11
Be hospitable to one another

The end of all things is near; therefore be serious and discipline yourselves for the sake of your prayers. Above all, maintain constant love for one another, for love covers a multitude of sins. Be hospitable to one another without complaining. Like good stewards of the manifold grace of God, serve one another with whatever gift each of you has received. Whoever speaks must do so as one speaking the very words of God; whoever serves must do so with the strength that God supplies, so that God may be glorified in all things through Jesus Christ. To him belong the glory and the power forever and ever. Amen. (1 Peter 4:7-11)

Psalm
Psalm 112
The righteous are merciful

Additional Reading
Proverbs 18:6-12
Humility precedes honor

Hymn: We Give Thee but Thine Own, ELW 686

Strong tower, you have provided sanctuary and strength to all who ask. May we be good stewards of the gifts you have given us, practicing hospitality and maintaining constant love for one another.

Saturday, August 31, 2013

Time after Pentecost

Proverbs 21:1-4, 24-26
The righteous give and do not hold back

The proud, haughty person, named "Scoffer,"
  acts with arrogant pride.
The craving of the lazy person is fatal,
  for lazy hands refuse to labor.
All day long the wicked covet,
  but the righteous give and do not hold back. (Prov. 21:24-26)

Psalm
Psalm 112
The righteous are merciful

Additional Reading
Matthew 20:20-28
A request for seats of honor

Hymn: Awake, My Soul, and with the Sun, ELW 557

Righteous Father, we know that you weigh our hearts, determining our motives for doing the things we do. Keep us from acting with the arrogant pride of the haughty, and help us give freely of ourselves to those in need.

PRAYER LIST FOR SEPTEMBER

_____

_____

_____

_____

_____

_____

_____

_____

_____

_____

_____

AUTUMN

The days of early autumn (September and October) herald the resumption of a more regular schedule: school begins, church education programs commence, and the steady rhythms of work are accompanied by cooling breezes and the changing colors of the landscape. During these months, various crops are harvested and appear on roadside stands and in grocery stores. In many countries the harvest days of September and October are marked with prayer, feasting, and special care for the poor and hungry.

Table Prayer for Autumn

We praise you and bless you, O God,
for autumn days,
and for the gifts of this table.
Grant us grace to share your goodness,
until all people are fed by the harvest of the earth.
We ask this through Christ our Lord. Amen.

Sunday, September 1, 2013

Time after Pentecost

Luke 14:1, 7-14

Invite the poor to your banquet

[Jesus] said also to the one who had invited him, "When you give a luncheon or a dinner, do not invite your friends or your brothers or your relatives or rich neighbors, in case they may invite you in return, and you would be repaid. But when you give a banquet, invite the poor, the crippled, the lame, and the blind. And you will be blessed, because they cannot repay you, for you will be repaid at the resurrection of the righteous." (Luke 14:12-14)

Psalm

Psalm 112

The righteous are merciful

Additional Readings

Proverbs 25:6-7

Do not put yourself forward

Hebrews 13:1-8, 15-16

God is with us

Hymn: Let Us Go Now to the Banquet, ELW 523

O God, you resist those who are proud and give grace to those who are humble. Give us the humility of your Son, that we may embody the generosity of Jesus Christ, our Savior and Lord.

Monday, September 2, 2013

Time after Pentecost

Nikolai Frederik Severin Grundtvig, bishop, renewer of the church, died 1872

Psalm 119:65-72
God blesses the humble

You have dealt well with your servant,
    O Lord, according to your word.
Teach me good judgment and knowledge,
    for I believe in your commandments.
Before I was humbled I went astray,
    but now I keep your word.
You are good and do good;
    teach me your statutes. (Ps. 119:65-68)

Additional Readings
2 Chronicles 12:1-12   **Hebrews 13:7-21**
King Rehoboam humbles himself   *Call for faithfulness*

Hymn: God's Word Is Our Great Heritage, ELW 509

Gracious God, inspire us through your wisdom, teaching us good judgment and knowledge through your commandments and your word. Deal well with us as we strive to do good and serve Jesus Christ our Lord.

Tuesday, September 3, 2013

Time after Pentecost

Titus 1:1-9
Humble and hospitable leaders

I left you behind in Crete for this reason, so that you should put in order what remained to be done, and should appoint elders in every town, as I directed you: someone who is blameless, married only once, whose children are believers, not accused of debauchery and not rebellious. For a bishop, as God's steward, must be blameless; he must not be arrogant or quick-tempered or addicted to wine or violent or greedy for gain; but he must be hospitable, a lover of goodness, prudent, upright, devout, and self-controlled. He must have a firm grasp of the word that is trustworthy in accordance with the teaching, so that he may be able both to preach with sound doctrine and to refute those who contradict it. (Titus 1:5-9)

Psalm
Psalm 119:65-72
God blesses the humble

Additional Reading
Isaiah 2:12-17
Pride shall be brought low

Hymn: Lord, Whose Love in Humble Service, ELW 712

O God, we remember leaders of the church who have answered your call to serve. Grant them wisdom, grace, and passion to embrace their calling to serve Jesus Christ with a sure confidence in the Holy Spirit to guide their journey.

Wednesday, September 4, 2013

Time after Pentecost

Isaiah 57:14-21
God blesses the humble

It shall be said,
"Build up, build up, prepare the way,
   remove every obstruction from my people's way."
For thus says the high and lofty one
   who inhabits eternity, whose name is Holy:
I dwell in the high and holy place,
   and also with those who are contrite and humble in spirit,
to revive the spirit of the humble,
   and to revive the heart of the contrite.
For I will not continually accuse,
   nor will I always be angry;
for then the spirits would grow faint before me,
   even the souls that I have made. (Isa. 57:14-16)

Psalm
Psalm 119:65-72
God blesses the humble

Additional Reading
Luke 14:15-24
God's hospitality to the humble

Hymn: Built on a Rock, ELW 652

Holy One, as you have prepared the path of many who have come before, so now ready our way to you, removing those obstacles along our paths. May we be ready to receive your gracious hospitality extended though Jesus Christ.

Thursday, September 5, 2013

Time after Pentecost

Psalm 1
Delight in the law

Happy are those
   who do not follow the advice of the wicked,
or take the path that sinners tread,
   or sit in the seat of scoffers;
but their delight is in the law of the LORD,
   and on his law they meditate day and night.
They are like trees
   planted by streams of water,
which yield their fruit in its season,
   and their leaves do not wither.
In all that they do, they prosper. (Ps. 1:1-3)

Additional Readings
Genesis 39:1-23
Joseph does not sin against God

Philippians 2:25-30
Welcome a faithful servant home

Hymn: Great Is Thy Faithfulness, ELW 733

Almighty God, root us in your word, nurture us through the gift of Christian community, and guide our lives so we might bear fruit in its season. May we always delight in the Word made flesh in Jesus Christ.

Friday, September 6, 2013

Time after Pentecost

Colossians 4:7-17

A faithful and beloved brother

Tychicus will tell you all the news about me; he is a beloved brother, a faithful minister, and a fellow servant in the Lord. I have sent him to you for this very purpose, so that you may know how we are and that he may encourage your hearts; he is coming with Onesimus, the faithful and beloved brother, who is one of you. They will tell you about everything here. (Col. 4:7-9)

Psalm

Psalm 1

Delight in the law

Additional Reading

Deuteronomy 7:12-26

The way of obedience

Hymn: We All Are One in Mission, ELW 576

Blessed God, thank you for sending faithful servants of Christ into our lives to encourage our hearts and keep us steadfast in faith. Use our lives and voices to encourage others to be faithful to Jesus Christ, our Savior.

Saturday, September 7, 2013

Time after Pentecost

Deuteronomy 29:2-20
A renewed covenant

You stand assembled today, all of you, before the LORD your God—
the leaders of your tribes, your elders, and your officials, all the men
of Israel, your children, your women, and the aliens who are in your
camp, both those who cut your wood and those who draw your
water—to enter into the covenant of the LORD your God, sworn by an
oath, which the LORD your God is making with you today; in order
that he may establish you today as his people, and that he may be
your God, as he promised you and as he swore to your ancestors, to
Abraham, to Isaac, and to Jacob. (Deut. 29:10-13)

Psalm
Psalm 1
Delight in the law

Additional Reading
Matthew 10:34-42
The cost of discipleship

Hymn: On My Heart Imprint Your Image, ELW 811

*Lord God, in your infinite wisdom you have chosen to be in relationship
with us, despite our limited capacity to love you in return. Inspire us to
live as your people called, gathered, and sanctified by the Holy Spirit to
follow Christ.*

Sunday, September 8, 2013

Time after Pentecost

Luke 14:25-33

Give up your possessions

[Jesus said,] "What king, going out to wage war against another king, will not sit down first and consider whether he is able with ten thousand to oppose the one who comes against him with twenty thousand? If he cannot, then, while the other is still far away, he sends a delegation and asks for the terms of peace. So therefore, none of you can become my disciple if you do not give up all your possessions." (Luke 14:31-33)

Psalm

Psalm 1

Delight in the law

Additional Readings

Deuteronomy
30:15-20
Walk in the way of life

Philemon 1-21
Paul says, Receive Onesimus

Hymn: Jesus, Keep Me Near the Cross, ELW 335

Direct us, O Lord God, in all our doings with your continual help, that in all our works, begun, continued, and ended in you, we may glorify your holy name; and finally, by your mercy, bring us to everlasting life, through Jesus Christ, our Savior and Lord.

Monday, September 9, 2013

Time after Pentecost

Peter Claver, priest, missionary to Colombia, died 1654

Psalm 101
Choosing God's law

I will sing of loyalty and of justice;
    to you, O LORD, I will sing.
I will study the way that is blameless.
    When shall I attain it?

I will walk with integrity of heart
    within my house;
I will not set before my eyes
    anything that is base.

I hate the work of those who fall away;
    it shall not cling to me. (Ps. 101:1-3)

Additional Readings
2 Kings 17:24-41   I Timothy 3:14—4:5
The Assyrians worship other gods   *Behavior in the church*

Hymn: Sing Praise to God, the Highest Good, ELW 871

O God, we sing your praises but also see our neighbors in pain and need. We weep at the injustices of our world. Use our songs and tears to be healing instruments, reflecting the love of Jesus Christ.

Tuesday, September 10, 2013

Time after Pentecost

1 Timothy 4:6-16
Being a servant of Christ

If you put these instructions before the brothers and sisters, you will be a good servant of Christ Jesus, nourished on the words of the faith and of the sound teaching that you have followed. Have nothing to do with profane myths and old wives' tales. Train yourself in godliness, for, while physical training is of some value, godliness is valuable in every way, holding promise for both the present life and the life to come. (1 Tim. 4:6-8)

Psalm
Psalm 101
Choosing God's law

Additional Reading
2 Kings 18:9-18
Transgressing the covenant

Hymn: O Christ, Your Heart, Compassionate, ELW 722

Almighty God, nourish us in your word, creating us to be servants of Christ Jesus. Train us in godly living, even if it means vigorous training, for we aim to reflect the fullness of your reign.

Wednesday, September 11, 2013

Time after Pentecost

Luke 18:18-30
The rich ruler

A certain ruler asked [Jesus], "Good Teacher, what must I do to inherit eternal life?" Jesus said to him, "Why do you call me good? No one is good but God alone. You know the commandments: 'You shall not commit adultery; You shall not murder; You shall not steal; You shall not bear false witness; Honor your father and mother.' " He replied, "I have kept all these since my youth." When Jesus heard this, he said to him, "There is still one thing lacking. Sell all that you own and distribute the money to the poor, and you will have treasure in heaven; then come, follow me." (Luke 18:18-22)

Psalm
Psalm 101
Choosing God's law

Additional Reading
2 Kings 18:19-25; 19:1-7
A king repents, the nation is saved

Hymn: Will You Come and Follow Me, ELW 798

Source of all wisdom, you hear our questions and know we seek answers. Free us from our possessions so we might follow you with open hearts, hands, spirits, and minds; through Jesus Christ our Lord.

Thursday, September 12, 2013

Time after Pentecost

Psalm 51:1-10
Have mercy upon me, O God

Have mercy on me, O God,
  according to your steadfast love;
according to your abundant mercy
  blot out my transgressions.
Wash me thoroughly from my iniquity,
  and cleanse me from my sin.

For I know my transgressions,
  and my sin is ever before me.
Against you, you alone, have I sinned,
  and done what is evil in your sight,
so that you are justified in your sentence
  and blameless when you pass judgment. (Ps. 51:1-4)

Additional Readings

Genesis 6:1-6
Sinful humanity forgets God

I Timothy 1:1-11
About false teachers

Hymn: Chief of Sinners Though I Be, ELW 609

O God, have mercy on us, your servants. Allow our words to be more than idle chatter, but instead may your mercy penetrate to the depths of our being. Embrace us with your tender, steadfast love through Jesus Christ.

Friday, September 13, 2013

Time after Pentecost

John Chrysostom, Bishop of Constantinople, died 407

Genesis 7:6-10; 8:1-5

God remembers faithful Noah

Noah was six hundred years old when the flood of waters came on the earth. And Noah with his sons and his wife and his sons' wives went into the ark to escape the waters of the flood. Of clean animals, and of animals that are not clean, and of birds, and of everything that creeps on the ground, two and two, male and female, went into the ark with Noah, as God had commanded Noah. And after seven days the waters of the flood came on the earth. (Gen. 7:6-10)

Psalm

Psalm 51:1-10

Have mercy upon me, O God

Additional Reading

2 Peter 2:1-10a

God judges and rescues

Hymn: God of the Sparrow, ELW 740

God of all creation, you remembered the faithfulness of Noah and protected his family from the waters of the flood. By the Holy Spirit, inspire us to follow Christ boldly during the storms and calms of this life.

Saturday, September 14, 2013

Holy Cross Day

John 3:13-17
The Son of Man will be lifted up

[Jesus said,] "No one has ascended into heaven except the one who descended from heaven, the Son of Man. And just as Moses lifted up the serpent in the wilderness, so must the Son of Man be lifted up, that whoever believes in him may have eternal life.

"For God so loved the world that he gave his only Son, so that everyone who believes in him may not perish but may have eternal life.

"Indeed, God did not send the Son into the world to condemn the world, but in order that the world might be saved through him." (John 3:13-17)

Psalm	Additional Readings	
Psalm 98:1-4	Numbers 21:4b-9	1 Corinthians 1:18-24
God has done marvelous things	*A bronze serpent in the wilderness*	*The cross is the power of God*

Hymn: When I Survey the Wondrous Cross, ELW 803

Almighty God, your Son Jesus Christ was lifted high upon the cross so that he might draw the whole world to himself. To those who look upon the cross, grant your wisdom, healing, and eternal life, through Jesus Christ, our Savior and Lord, who lives and reigns with you and the Holy Spirit, one God, now and forever.

Sunday, September 15, 2013

Time after Pentecost

Luke 15:1-10

Lost sheep and lost coin

So [Jesus] told them this parable: "Which one of you, having a hundred sheep and losing one of them, does not leave the ninety-nine in the wilderness and go after the one that is lost until he finds it? When he has found it, he lays it on his shoulders and rejoices. And when he comes home, he calls together his friends and neighbors, saying to them, 'Rejoice with me, for I have found my sheep that was lost.' Just so, I tell you, there will be more joy in heaven over one sinner who repents than over ninety-nine righteous persons who need no repentance." (Luke 15:3-7)

Psalm
Psalm 51:1-10
Have mercy upon me, O God

Additional Readings
Exodus 32:7-14
Moses begs forgiveness

1 Timothy 1:12-17
Christ Jesus came for sinners

Hymn: Beloved, God's Chosen, ELW 648

O God, overflowing with mercy and compassion, you lead back to yourself all those who go astray. Preserve your people in your loving care, that we may reject whatever is contrary to you and may follow all things that sustain our life in your Son, Jesus Christ, our Savior and Lord.

Monday, September 16, 2013

Time after Pentecost

Cyprian, Bishop of Carthage, martyr, died around 258

Psalm 73
God is my portion

My flesh and my heart may fail,
   but God is the strength of my heart and my portion forever.

Indeed, those who are far from you will perish;
   you put an end to those who are false to you.
But for me it is good to be near God;
   I have made the Lord GOD my refuge,
   to tell of all your works. (Ps. 73:26-28)

Additional Readings
Amos 7:1-6   I Timothy 1:18-20
God relents from punishing Israel   *The danger of rejecting conscience*

Hymn: A Mighty Fortress Is Our God, ELW 503/504

God of strength, we come to you wearily carrying our burdens and concerns, seeking refuge from the trials and challenges of life. Strengthen our hearts and give us courage to stay near your side, through Jesus Christ.

Tuesday, September 17, 2013

Time after Pentecost

Hildegard, Abbess of Bingen, died 1179

Jonah 3:1-10
God relents from punishing Nineveh

When the news reached the king of Nineveh, he rose from his throne, removed his robe, covered himself with sackcloth, and sat in ashes. Then he had a proclamation made in Nineveh: "By the decree of the king and his nobles: No human being or animal, no herd or flock, shall taste anything. They shall not feed, nor shall they drink water. Human beings and animals shall be covered with sackcloth, and they shall cry mightily to God. All shall turn from their evil ways and from the violence that is in their hands. Who knows? God may relent and change his mind; he may turn from his fierce anger, so that we do not perish."

When God saw what they did, how they turned from their evil ways, God changed his mind about the calamity that he had said he would bring upon them; and he did not do it. (Jonah 3:6-10)

Psalm
Psalm 73
God is my portion

Additional Reading
2 Peter 3:8-13
That all may come to repentance

Hymn: There's a Wideness in God's Mercy, ELW 587/588

Gracious God, you relented from punishing Nineveh and gave that city a second chance. Have mercy on us, your imperfect servants. Remember not our shortcomings, but fortify our faith in Christ Jesus through the Holy Spirit.

Wednesday, September 18, 2013

Time after Pentecost

Dag Hammarskjöld, renewer of society, died 1961

Job 40:6-14; 42:1-6
Job repents

Then the LORD answered Job out of the whirlwind:

"Deck yourself with majesty and dignity;
  clothe yourself with glory and splendor.
Pour out the overflowings of your anger,
  and look on all who are proud, and abase them.
Look on all who are proud, and bring them low;
  tread down the wicked where they stand.
Hide them all in the dust together;
  bind their faces in the world below.
Then I will also acknowledge to you
  that your own right hand can give you victory."
(Job 40:6, 10-14)

Psalm	Additional Reading
Psalm 73	Luke 22:31-33, 54-62
God is my portion	*Peter denies Jesus*

Hymn: Soul, Adorn Yourself with Gladness, ELW 488

Lord, out of the whirlwind you spoke to Job, and in doing so you challenge us to beware of our pride, arrogance, and misplaced trust. We stand in humbled awe of your splendor, majesty, and glory made known in Jesus Christ.

Thursday, September 19, 2013

Time after Pentecost

Psalm 113
Our God lifts up the poor

Who is like the LORD our God,
  who is seated on high,
who looks far down
  on the heavens and the earth?
He raises the poor from the dust,
  and lifts the needy from the ash heap,
to make them sit with princes,
  with the princes of his people. (Ps. 113:5-8)

Additional Readings
Exodus 23:1-9
Justice for all

Romans 3:1-8
The justice of God

Hymn: Hear I Am, Lord, ELW 574

Creator of all, stir our hearts with compassion for the poor, inspire us to share our bounty with those in need, and fill us with joy and thanksgiving as we celebrate your gift of Jesus Christ.

Friday, September 20, 2013

Time after Pentecost

Romans 8:31-39

It is God who justifies

What then are we to say about these things? If God is for us, who is against us? He who did not withhold his own Son, but gave him up for all of us, will he not with him also give us everything else? Who will bring any charge against God's elect? It is God who justifies. Who is to condemn? It is Christ Jesus, who died, yes, who was raised, who is at the right hand of God, who indeed intercedes for us. (Rom. 8:31-34)

Psalm

Psalm 113

Our God lifts up the poor

Additional Reading

Ezekiel 22:17-31

Israel becomes dross to God

Hymn: Neither Death nor Life, ELW 622

Almighty God, there is much we might say, but we cannot deny our connection with Christ Jesus, who died and was raised, who intercedes for us, and who sits on your right hand. Thanks for this glorious gift!

Saturday, September 21, 2013

Matthew, Apostle and Evangelist

Matthew 9:9-13
Jesus calls to Matthew: Follow me

As Jesus was walking along, he saw a man called Matthew sitting at the tax booth; and he said to him, "Follow me." And he got up and followed him.

And as he sat at dinner in the house, many tax collectors and sinners came and were sitting with him and his disciples. When the Pharisees saw this, they said to his disciples, "Why does your teacher eat with tax collectors and sinners?" But when he heard this, he said, "Those who are well have no need of a physician, but those who are sick. Go and learn what this means, 'I desire mercy, not sacrifice.' For I have come to call not the righteous but sinners." (Matt. 9:9-13)

Psalm
Psalm 119:33-40
Give me understanding

Additional Readings
Ezekiel 2:8—3:11
A prophet to the house of Israel

Ephesians 2:4-10
By grace you have been saved

Hymn: Come, Follow Me, the Savior Spake, ELW 799

Almighty God, your Son our Savior called a despised tax collector to become one of his apostles. Help us, like Matthew, to respond to the transforming call of Jesus Christ, who lives and reigns with you and the Holy Spirit, one God, now and forever.

Sunday, September 22, 2013

Time after Pentecost

Luke 16:1-13
Serving God or wealth

[Jesus said,] "Whoever is faithful in a very little is faithful also in
much; and whoever is dishonest in a very little is dishonest also in
much. If then you have not been faithful with the dishonest wealth,
who will entrust to you the true riches? And if you have not been
faithful with what belongs to another, who will give you what is your
own? No slave can serve two masters; for a slave will either hate the
one and love the other, or be devoted to the one and despise the other.
You cannot serve God and wealth." (Luke 16:10-13)

Psalm
Psalm 113
Our God lifts up the poor

Additional Readings
Amos 8:4-7
*Those who trample the
needy*

1 Timothy 2:1-7
One God, one mediator

Hymn: When the Poor Ones, ELW 725

*God among us, we gather in the name of your Son to learn love for
one another. Keep our feet from evil paths. Turn our minds to your
wisdom and our hearts to the grace revealed in your Son, Jesus Christ,
our Savior and Lord.*

Monday, September 23, 2013

Time after Pentecost

Psalm 12
Help for the poor

"Because the poor are despoiled, because the needy groan,
   I will now rise up," says the LORD;
   "I will place them in the safety for which they long."
The promises of the LORD are promises that are pure,
   silver refined in a furnace on the ground,
   purified seven times.

You, O LORD, will protect us;
   you will guard us from this generation forever. (Ps. 12:5-7)

Additional Readings
Proverbs 14:12-31   **Acts 4:1-12**
Oppressing the poor   *Salvation through Jesus Christ*

Hymn: Goodness Is Stronger than Evil, ELW 721

*O Lord, you hear the cries of the outcast and give hope to the poor.
Strengthen our faith and trust in your promises so we might reflect the
beauty of your pure love as shown in Jesus Christ.*

Tuesday, September 24, 2013

Time after Pentecost

1 Corinthians 9:19-23
A servant of the gospel

For though I am free with respect to all, I have made myself a slave to all, so that I might win more of them. To the Jews I became as a Jew, in order to win Jews. To those under the law I became as one under the law (though I myself am not under the law) so that I might win those under the law. To those outside the law I became as one outside the law (though I am not free from God's law but am under Christ's law) so that I might win those outside the law. To the weak I became weak, so that I might win the weak. I have become all things to all people, that I might by all means save some. I do it all for the sake of the gospel, so that I may share in its blessings. (1 Cor. 9:19-23)

Psalm
Psalm 12
Help for the poor

Additional Reading
Proverbs 17:1-5
Oppressing the poor

Hymn: Send Me, Jesus, ELW 549

Almighty God, free us to live for the sake of the gospel so that we are willing to be flexible in those things that do not matter, trusting in the eternal blessing of Jesus Christ through the Holy Spirit.

Wednesday, September 25, 2013

Time after Pentecost

Proverbs 21:10-16

Ears closed to the cry of the poor

The souls of the wicked desire evil;
   their neighbors find no mercy in their eyes.
When a scoffer is punished, the simple become wiser;
   when the wise are instructed, they increase in knowledge.
The Righteous One observes the house of the wicked;
   he casts the wicked down to ruin.
If you close your ear to the cry of the poor,
   you will cry out and not be heard. (Prov. 21:10-13)

Psalm
Psalm 12
Help for the poor

Additional Reading
Luke 20:45—21:4
The rich versus the poor

Hymn: Where Cross the Crowded Ways of Life, ELW 719

O God, you hear the softest of voices crying to you. We ask you to open our ears to the cries of the poor and to open our eyes to our neighbors in need. Do not allow our hearts to become callous, but teach us to share the love of Christ.

Thursday, September 26, 2013

Time after Pentecost

Psalm 146
Justice to the oppressed

Happy are those whose help is the God of Jacob,
    whose hope is in the Lord their God,
who made heaven and earth,
    the sea, and all that is in them;
who keeps faith forever;
    who executes justice for the oppressed;
    who gives food to the hungry. (Ps. 146:5-7a)

Additional Readings
Proverbs 22:2-16   **2 Corinthians 8:8-15**
The rich versus the poor   *Christ became poor*

Hymn: We Come to the Hungry Feast, ELW 479

Creator of the universe, you have created heaven and earth, the sea and everything in it. Happy are those of us who turn to you in times of need and know of your never-failing love in Christ.

Friday, September 27, 2013

Time after Pentecost

Proverbs 28:3-10

The rich versus the poor

Better to be poor and walk in integrity
   than to be crooked in one's ways even though rich.
Those who keep the law are wise children,
   but companions of gluttons shame their parents.
One who augments wealth by exorbitant interest
   gathers it for another who is kind to the poor. (Prov. 28:6-8)

Psalm

Psalm 146

Justice to the oppressed

Additional Reading

Ephesians 2:1-10

God is rich in mercy

Hymn: We Are Called, ELW 720

Guide us, O Lord, to walk on paths of truth and integrity so that we do not go astray. Help us not be consumed by our possessions but see the true treasure of Jesus Christ, our Savior.

Saturday, September 28, 2013

Time after Pentecost

Proverbs 28:11-28

Helpers of the poor lack nothing

The greedy person stirs up strife,
>   but whoever trusts in the LORD will be enriched.
Those who trust in their own wits are fools;
>   but those who walk in wisdom come through safely.
Whoever gives to the poor will lack nothing,
>   but one who turns a blind eye will get many a curse.
When the wicked prevail, people go into hiding;
>   but when they perish, the righteous increase. (Prov. 28:25-28)

Psalm

Psalm 146
Justice to the oppressed

Additional Reading

Luke 9:43b-48
Welcoming little ones

Hymn: O God of Every Nation, ELW 713

God of wisdom, deepen our trust in you, allowing generosity toward the poor to overflow from our lives and generating a life of loving service in the name of Jesus Christ.

Sunday, September 29, 2013

Time after Pentecost

Michael and All Angels (transferred to September 30)

Luke 16:19-31
Poor Lazarus and the rich man

[Jesus said,] "There was a rich man who was dressed in purple and fine linen and who feasted sumptuously every day. And at his gate lay a poor man named Lazarus, covered with sores, who longed to satisfy his hunger with what fell from the rich man's table; even the dogs would come and lick his sores. The poor man died and was carried away by the angels to be with Abraham. The rich man also died and was buried. In Hades, where he was being tormented, he looked up and saw Abraham far away with Lazarus by his side." (Luke 16:19-23)

Psalm	Additional Readings	
Psalm 146	Amos 6:1a, 4-7	1 Timothy 6:6-19
Justice to the oppressed	*Warnings to the wealthy*	*Pursuing God's justice*

Hymn: Will You Let Me Be Your Servant, ELW 659

O God, rich in mercy, you look with compassion on this troubled world. Feed us with your grace, and grant us the treasure that comes only from you, through Jesus Christ, our Savior and Lord.

Monday, September 30, 2013

Michael and All Angels (*transferred*)

Jerome, translator, teacher, died 420

Revelation 12:7-12
Michael defeats Satan in a cosmic battle

And war broke out in heaven; Michael and his angels fought against the dragon. The dragon and his angels fought back, but they were defeated, and there was no longer any place for them in heaven. The great dragon was thrown down, that ancient serpent, who is called the Devil and Satan, the deceiver of the whole world—he was thrown down to the earth, and his angels were thrown down with him. (Rev. 12:7-9)

Psalm
Psalm 103:1-5, 20-22
Bless the Lord, you angels

Additional Readings
Daniel 10:10-14;
12:1-3
Michael shall arise

Luke 10:17-20
Jesus gives his followers authority

Hymn: Ye Watchers and Ye Holy Ones, ELW 424

Everlasting God, you have wonderfully established the ministries of angels and mortals. Mercifully grant that as Michael and the angels contend against the cosmic forces of evil, so by your direction they may help and defend us here on earth, through your Son, Jesus Christ our Lord, who lives and reigns with you and the Holy Spirit, one God whom we worship and praise with angels and archangels and all the company of heaven, now and forever.

_____

_____

_____

_____

_____

_____

_____

_____

_____

_____

_____

Tuesday, October 1, 2013

Time after Pentecost

James 5:1-6
Riches that rot

Come now, you rich people, weep and wail for the miseries that are coming to you. Your riches have rotted, and your clothes are moth-eaten. Your gold and silver have rusted, and their rust will be evidence against you, and it will eat your flesh like fire. You have laid up treasure for the last days. Listen! The wages of the laborers who mowed your fields, which you kept back by fraud, cry out, and the cries of the harvesters have reached the ears of the Lord of hosts. You have lived on the earth in luxury and in pleasure; you have fattened your hearts in a day of slaughter. You have condemned and murdered the righteous one, who does not resist you. (James 5:1-6)

Psalm
Psalm 62
I wait on God

Additional Reading
Hosea 10:9-15
Reaping injustice

Hymn: Christ, Be Our Light, ELW 715

Lord of hosts, you have shown us the error of our selfish ways. Help us to live out your vision of a world where all joyously share in the abundance you have provided.

Wednesday, October 2, 2013

Time after Pentecost

Hosea 12:2-14

I have gained wealth for myself

The LORD has an indictment against Judah,
and will punish Jacob according to his ways,
and repay him according to his deeds.
In the womb he tried to supplant his brother,
and in his manhood he strove with God.
He strove with the angel and prevailed,
he wept and sought his favor;
he met him at Bethel,
and there he spoke with him.
The LORD the God of hosts,
the LORD is his name!
But as for you, return to your God,
hold fast to love and justice,
and wait continually for your God. (Hosea 12:2-6)

Psalm
Psalm 62
I wait on God

Additional Reading
Matthew 19:16-22
Treasure in heaven

Hymn: Come Now, O Prince of Peace, ELW 247

Lord of love, you have met us in the midst of our sin, and you have spoken to us through your word and through your Son, Jesus. Guide us as we again turn our hearts and minds to you.

Thursday, October 3, 2013

Time after Pentecost

Psalm 37:1-9
Commit your way to the Lord

Do not fret because of the wicked;
   do not be envious of wrongdoers,
for they will soon fade like the grass,
   and wither like the green herb.

Trust in the LORD, and do good;
   so you will live in the land, and enjoy security.
Take delight in the LORD,
   and he will give you the desires of your heart.

Commit your way to the LORD;
   trust in him, and he will act. (Ps. 37:1-5)

Additional Readings
2 Kings 18:1-8, 28-36
King Hezekiah trusts in God

Revelation 2:8-11
Be faithful until death

Hymn: Have No Fear, Little Flock, ELW 764

*We place our trust in you, unchanging God. All around us we see
injustice, bigotry, hatred, and pain. Give us hope, faith, and perseverance
so that we may do good for our neighbors, for our community, and for
the world.*

Friday, October 4, 2013

Time after Pentecost

Francis of Assisi, renewer of the church, died 1226
Theodor Fliedner, renewer of society, died 1864

Revelation 2:12-29
Call to faithfulness

[Jesus said,] "To everyone who conquers and continues to do my
works to the end,
    I will give authority over the nations;
  to rule them with an iron rod,
        as when clay pots are shattered—
even as I also received authority from my Father. To the one who
conquers I will also give the morning star." (Rev. 2:26-28)

Psalm
Psalm 37:1-9
Commit your way to the Lord

Additional Reading
2 Kings 19:8-20, 35-37
God saves the people

Hymn: I Want to Walk as a Child of the Light, ELW 815

*God of all nations, all peoples, all languages, we cry to you for peace.
As you have strengthened those who have come before us, empower us
to follow your commandments, heed your call, and serve your glorious
name.*

Saturday, October 5, 2013

Time after Pentecost

Matthew 20:29-34

Mercy on persistent blind men

As they were leaving Jericho, a large crowd followed [Jesus]. There were two blind men sitting by the roadside. When they heard that Jesus was passing by, they shouted, "Lord, have mercy on us, Son of David!" The crowd sternly ordered them to be quiet; but they shouted even more loudly, "Have mercy on us, Lord, Son of David!" Jesus stood still and called them, saying, "What do you want me to do for you?" They said to him, "Lord, let our eyes be opened." Moved with compassion, Jesus touched their eyes. Immediately they regained their sight and followed him. (Matt. 20:29-34)

Psalm
Psalm 37:1-9
Commit your way to the Lord

Additional Reading
Isaiah 7:1-9
Standing firm in faith

Hymn: Amazing Grace, How Sweet the Sound, ELW 779

God of all that is seen and unseen, open our eyes so we may share in your vision for a compassionate world. Open our hearts that we may live as Jesus lived. Open our ears so we may hear your voice this day.

Sunday, October 6, 2013

Time after Pentecost

William Tyndale, translator, martyr, died 1536

Luke 17:5-10
Faith the size of a mustard seed

The apostles said to the Lord, "Increase our faith!" The Lord replied, "If you had faith the size of a mustard seed, you could say to this mulberry tree, 'Be uprooted and planted in the sea,' and it would obey you." (Luke 17:5-6)

Psalm
Psalm 37:1-9
Commit your way to the Lord

Additional Readings
Habakkuk 1:1-4; 2:1-4
The wicked surround the righteous

2 Timothy 1:1-14
Guard the treasure entrusted to you

Hymn: O Spirit of Life, ELW 405

Benevolent, merciful God: When we are empty, fill us. When we are weak in faith, strengthen us. When we are cold in love, warm us, that with fervor we may love our neighbors and serve them for the sake of your Son, Jesus Christ, our Savior and Lord.

Monday, October 7, 2013

Time after Pentecost

Henry Melchior Muhlenberg, pastor in North America, died 1787

Psalm 3
Deliverance comes from God

I lie down and sleep;
  I wake again, for the Lord sustains me.
I am not afraid of ten thousands of people
  who have set themselves against me all around.

Rise up, O Lord!
  Deliver me, O my God!
For you strike all my enemies on the cheek;
  you break the teeth of the wicked.

Deliverance belongs to the Lord;
  may your blessing be on your people! (Ps. 3:5-8)

Additional Readings
Habakkuk 1:5-17   **James 1:2-11**
The wicked swallow the righteous   *Faith produces endurance*

Hymn: God, Who Made the Earth and Heaven, ELW 564

O God, deliver us from all the chaos and darkness that seem to close in from every side. Sustain us as we struggle to find light in the midst of grief, despair, depression, or addiction. May we awaken in the light of your love.

Tuesday, October 8, 2013

Time after Pentecost

1 John 5:1-5, 13-21
Faith overcomes the world

Everyone who believes that Jesus is the Christ has been born of
God, and everyone who loves the parent loves the child. By this we
know that we love the children of God, when we love God and obey
his commandments. For the love of God is this, that we obey his
commandments. And his commandments are not burdensome, for
whatever is born of God conquers the world. And this is the victory
that conquers the world, our faith. Who is it that conquers the world
but the one who believes that Jesus is the Son of God? (1 John 5:1-5)

Psalm
Psalm 3
Deliverance comes from God

Additional Reading
Habakkuk 2:5-11
Those who heap up what is not theirs

Hymn: You Are the Way, ELW 758

*Loving God, in the life of your Son, Jesus Christ, your love for this world
was made known. Help us to see your commandments as fruits of this
love that allow our lives to blossom in joyous service to you and to our
world.*

Wednesday, October 9, 2013

Time after Pentecost

Habakkuk 2:12-20
Knowledge of the glory of God

"Alas for you who build a town by bloodshed,
   and found a city on iniquity!"
Is it not from the LORD of hosts
   that peoples labor only to feed the flames,
   and nations weary themselves for nothing?
But the earth will be filled
   with the knowledge of the glory of the LORD,
   as the waters cover the sea. (Hab. 2:12-14)

Psalm
Psalm 3
Deliverance comes from God

Additional Reading
Mark 11:12-14, 20-24
Faith that moves mountains

Hymn: God, Who Stretched the Spangled Heavens, ELW 771

Fill us, O Lord, with your presence. Cover us, O God of hosts, with your waters of mercy and cleanse us with your compassionate love. Direct the work of our hands, the words of our lips, and the meditations of our hearts to you and your glory.

Thursday, October 10, 2013

Time after Pentecost

Psalm 111

I give thanks with my whole heart

Praise the LORD!
I will give thanks to the LORD with my whole heart,
   in the company of the upright, in the congregation.
Great are the works of the LORD,
   studied by all who delight in them.
Full of honor and majesty is his work,
   and his righteousness endures forever. (Ps. 111:1-3)

Additional Readings

Leviticus 14:33-53   2 Timothy 1:13-18
Cleansing a leprous house   *Paul in prison*

Hymn: Voices Raised to You, ELW 845

We give thanks for the prism of colors that surround us, the symphony of sounds that accompanies our lives, the breathtaking fragility of a butterfly, and the glorious expanse of sky we look to this day as we sing praise, Creator God.

Friday, October 11, 2013

Time after Pentecost

Numbers 4:34—5:4
A census and the exclusion of lepers

The LORD spoke to Moses, saying: Command the Israelites to put out of the camp everyone who is leprous, or has a discharge, and everyone who is unclean through contact with a corpse; you shall put out both male and female, putting them outside the camp; they must not defile their camp, where I dwell among them. The Israelites did so, putting them outside the camp; as the LORD had spoken to Moses, so the Israelites did. (Num. 5:1-4)

Psalm
Psalm 111
I give thanks with my whole heart

Additional Reading
2 Timothy 2:1-7
Share in suffering

Hymn: All Are Welcome, ELW 641

God of mercy, we know you will never exclude us nor refuse to dwell with us, no matter how far we have fallen short of your glory. Praise to you and to Jesus Christ our Lord, through whom your extravagant compassion was revealed.

Saturday, October 12, 2013

Time after Pentecost

Luke 5:12-16
A leper healed

Once, when [Jesus] was in one of the cities, there was a man covered with leprosy. When he saw Jesus, he bowed with his face to the ground and begged him, "Lord, if you choose, you can make me clean." Then Jesus stretched out his hand, touched him, and said, "I do choose. Be made clean." Immediately the leprosy left him. And he ordered him to tell no one. "Go," he said, "and show yourself to the priest, and, as Moses commanded, make an offering for your cleansing, for a testimony to them." But now more than ever the word about Jesus spread abroad; many crowds would gather to hear him and to be cured of their diseases. But he would withdraw to deserted places and pray. (Luke 5:12-16)

Psalm
Psalm 111
I give thanks with my whole heart

Additional Reading
Numbers 12:1-15
Miriam contracts leprosy

Hymn: There Is a Balm in Gilead, ELW 614

Lord of all, you reach out your hand to us this day and cleanse us from all our disease, despair, and dysfunction. Help us realize the healing power of your love and to offer our very lives in response to this merciful gift.

Sunday, October 13, 2013

Time after Pentecost

Luke 17:11-19
One leper gives thanks to God

As [Jesus] entered a village, ten lepers approached him. Keeping their distance, they called out, saying, "Jesus, Master, have mercy on us!" When he saw them, he said to them, "Go and show yourselves to the priests." And as they went, they were made clean. Then one of them, when he saw that he was healed, turned back, praising God with a loud voice. He prostrated himself at Jesus' feet and thanked him. And he was a Samaritan. (Luke 17:12-16)

Psalm	Additional Readings	
Psalm 111	2 Kings 5:1-3, 7-15c	2 Timothy 2:8-15
I give thanks with my whole heart	*Naaman is cleansed*	*We will live with Christ*

Hymn: Baptized in Water, ELW 456

Almighty and most merciful God, your bountiful goodness fills all creation. Keep us safe from all that may hurt us, that, whole and well in body and spirit, we may with grateful hearts accomplish all that you would have us do, through Jesus Christ, our Savior and Lord.

Monday, October 14, 2013

Day of Thanksgiving (Canada)

A Blessing of the Household for Thanksgiving Day is provided on page 367.

Psalm 61
Prayer for a long life

Hear my cry, O God;
   listen to my prayer.
From the end of the earth I call to you,
   when my heart is faint.

Lead me to the rock
   that is higher than I;
for you are my refuge,
   a strong tower against the enemy.

Let me abide in your tent forever,
   find refuge under the shelter of your wings. (Ps. 61:1-4)

Additional Readings
2 Kings 5:15-19a
Naaman seeks to repay Elisha

Acts 26:24-29
Except for these chains

Hymn: O Lord, Hear My Prayer, ELW 751

We pray, O God, that you hear our cries of fear and pain. As you have led you people through the wilderness, lead us now to you. Give us courage. Give us hope. Give us refuge in your promise of unending love.

Tuesday, October 15, 2013

Time after Pentecost

Teresa of Avila, teacher, renewer of the church, died 1582

Ephesians 6:10-20
An ambassador in chains

Finally, be strong in the Lord and in the strength of his power. Put
on the whole armor of God, so that you may be able to stand against
the wiles of the devil. For our struggle is not against enemies of blood
and flesh, but against the rulers, against the authorities, against the
cosmic powers of this present darkness, against the spiritual forces of
evil in the heavenly places. (Eph. 6:10-12)

Psalm
Psalm 61
Prayer for a long life

Additional Reading
2 Kings 5:19b-27
Greed brings leprosy to Gehazi

Hymn: I Bind unto Myself Today, ELW 450

*Clothe us in your love, O Lord, and strengthen us with your presence
as we meet a new day full of both promise and peril. Equip us, we pray,
with your Spirit to go forth and share the light of your Son, Jesus Christ
our Lord.*

Wednesday, October 16, 2013

Time after Pentecost

Matthew 10:5-15
Cure without payment

These twelve Jesus sent out with the following instructions: "Go nowhere among the Gentiles, and enter no town of the Samaritans, but go rather to the lost sheep of the house of Israel. As you go, proclaim the good news, 'The kingdom of heaven has come near.' Cure the sick, raise the dead, cleanse the lepers, cast out demons. You received without payment; give without payment." (Matt. 10:5-8)

Psalm
Psalm 61
Prayer for a long life

Additional Reading
2 Kings 15:1-7
A leprous king lives in isolation

Hymn: The Son of God, Our Christ, ELW 584

Equip us, O God, to share the good news to all as you equipped those first followers of Jesus. Lead us where you would have us take your word of love, inspire us with your word, and encourage us with your unending love.

Thursday, October 17, 2013

Time after Pentecost

Ignatius, Bishop of Antioch, martyr, died around 115

Psalm 121
My help is from the Lord

I lift up my eyes to the hills—
   from where will my help come?
My help comes from the LORD,
   who made heaven and earth.

He will not let your foot be moved;
   he who keeps you will not slumber.
He who keeps Israel
   will neither slumber nor sleep. (Ps. 121:1-4)

Additional Readings
Isaiah 54:11-17
God will vindicate the faithful

Acts 17:22-34
God has fixed a day of judgment

Hymn: All Praise to Thee, My God, This Night, ELW 565

God of Israel, watch over us this day. Watch over all those who must work through the night with the sick, elderly, laboring mothers, and travelers. Watch over those who protect us from harm and those who care for our facilities for work and education.

Friday, October 18, 2013

Luke, Evangelist

Luke 1:1-4; 24:44-53
Luke witnesses to the ministry of Jesus

Since many have undertaken to set down an orderly account of the events that have been fulfilled among us, just as they were handed on to us by those who from the beginning were eyewitnesses and servants of the word, I too decided, after investigating everything carefully from the very first, to write an orderly account for you, most excellent Theophilus, so that you may know the truth concerning the things about which you have been instructed. (Luke 1:1-4)

Psalm	**Additional Readings**	
Psalm 124	Isaiah 43:8-13	2 Timothy 4:5-11
Our help is in God	*You are my witness*	*The good fight of faith*

Hymn: Oh, for a Thousand Tongues to Sing, ELW 886

Almighty God, you inspired your servant Luke to reveal in his gospel the love and healing power of your Son. Give your church the same love and power to heal, and to proclaim your salvation to the nations, to the glory of your name, through Jesus Christ, your Son, our healer, who lives and reigns with you and the Holy Spirit, one God, now and forever.

Saturday, October 19, 2013

Time after Pentecost

Mark 10:46-52

A man who would not be silenced

They came to Jericho. As [Jesus] and his disciples and a large crowd were leaving Jericho, Bartimaeus son of Timaeus, a blind beggar, was sitting by the roadside. When he heard that it was Jesus of Nazareth, he began to shout out and say, "Jesus, Son of David, have mercy on me!" Then Jesus said to him, "What do you want me to do for you?" The blind man said to him, "My teacher, let me see again." Jesus said to him, "Go; your faith has made you well." Immediately he regained his sight and followed him on the way. (Mark 10:46-52)

Psalm

Psalm 121

My help is from the Lord

Additional Reading

Genesis 32:3-21

Jacob sends gifts to Esau

Hymn: Be Thou My Vision, ELW 793

Healing God, empower us to name our afflictions. Grant us the humility to identify our needs and to ask for your miraculous power in our lives so we may follow Jesus free from burden and filled with the light of Christ.

Sunday, October 20, 2013

Time after Pentecost

Luke 18:1-8

A widow begs for justice

Then Jesus told them a parable about their need to pray always and not to lose heart. He said, "In a certain city there was a judge who neither feared God nor had respect for people. In that city there was a widow who kept coming to him and saying, 'Grant me justice against my opponent.' For a while he refused; but later he said to himself, 'Though I have no fear of God and no respect for anyone, yet because this widow keeps bothering me, I will grant her justice, so that she may not wear me out by continually coming.' " (Luke 18:1-5)

Psalm
Psalm 121
My help is from the Lord

Additional Readings
Genesis 32:22-31
Jacob's struggle with the angel

2 Timothy 3:14—4:5
Christ the judge

Hymn: Lord, Listen to Your Children Praying, ELW 752

O Lord God, tireless guardian of your people, you are always ready to hear our cries. Teach us to rely day and night on your care. Inspire us to seek your enduring justice for all this suffering world, through Jesus Christ, our Savior and Lord.

Monday, October 21, 2013

Time after Pentecost

Psalm 57
Vindication from God

Be merciful to me, O God, be merciful to me,
   for in you my soul takes refuge;
in the shadow of your wings I will take refuge,
   until the destroying storms pass by.
I cry to God Most High,
   to God who fulfills his purpose for me.
He will send from heaven and save me,
   he will put to shame those who trample on me.
God will send forth his steadfast love and his faithfulness. (Ps. 57:1-3)

Additional Readings
I Samuel 25:2-22   I Corinthians 6:1-11
David judges against Nabal   *You are washed and sanctified*

Hymn: Thy Holy Wings, ELW 613

Our souls long to feel at rest in you, O God. Our spirits are weary with wondering and wandering and cry to you: fulfill your purpose for us! Be merciful to us and reveal your steadfast love.

Tuesday, October 22, 2013

Time after Pentecost

James 5:7-12

The Judge standing at the doors

Be patient, therefore, beloved, until the coming of the Lord. The farmer waits for the precious crop from the earth, being patient with it until it receives the early and the late rains. You also must be patient. Strengthen your hearts, for the coming of the Lord is near. Beloved, do not grumble against one another, so that you may not be judged. See, the Judge is standing at the doors! As an example of suffering and patience, beloved, take the prophets who spoke in the name of the Lord. Indeed we call blessed those who showed endurance. You have heard of the endurance of Job, and you have seen the purpose of the Lord, how the Lord is compassionate and merciful. (James 5:7-11)

Psalm

Psalm 57

Vindication from God

Additional Reading

1 Samuel 25:23-35

Abigail pleads for life

Hymn: Oh, Worship the King, ELW 842

God of refuge, protect us from the destructive storms that swirl around us. As you have saved your people from injustice, disease, and war, save us now from all the forces of evil that threaten our communities and relationships.

Wednesday, October 23, 2013

Time after Pentecost

James of Jerusalem, martyr, died around 62

Luke 22:39-46

Jesus prays for life

[Jesus] came out and went, as was his custom, to the Mount of Olives; and the disciples followed him. When he reached the place, he said to them, "Pray that you may not come into the time of trial." Then he withdrew from them about a stone's throw, knelt down, and prayed, "Father, if you are willing, remove this cup from me; yet, not my will but yours be done." (Luke 22:39-42)

Psalm

Psalm 57

Vindication from God

Additional Reading

I Samuel 25:36-42

David welcomes Abigail as wife

Hymn: Go to Dark Gethsemane, ELW 347

We pray to you this day as Jesus himself prayed: "not my will but yours be done." May we hear your voice in this moment of quiet contemplation and trust in your vision for our lives.

Thursday, October 24, 2013

Time after Pentecost

Psalm 84:1-7

Happy are they whose strength is in you

How lovely is your dwelling place,
    O Lᴏʀᴅ of hosts!
My soul longs, indeed it faints
    for the courts of the Lᴏʀᴅ;
my heart and my flesh sing for joy
    to the living God.

Even the sparrow finds a home,
    and the swallow a nest for herself,
    where she may lay her young,
at your altars, O Lᴏʀᴅ of hosts,
    my King and my God.
Happy are those who live in your house,
    ever singing your praise.

Happy are those whose strength is in you,
    in whose heart are the highways to Zion. (Ps. 84:1-5)

Additional Readings

Jeremiah 9:1-16

Israel refuses to know God

2 Timothy 3:1-9

Godlessness

Hymn: Beautiful Savior, ELW 838

Lord of hosts, we long for the day when we may live in your house and sing for joy with all of creation. Give us strength to finish our journey while our hearts ache for those who have already come to dwell with you.

Friday, October 25, 2013

Time after Pentecost

Jeremiah 9:17-26

Israel uncircumcised in heart

Thus says the LORD: Do not let the wise boast in their wisdom, do not let the mighty boast in their might, do not let the wealthy boast in their wealth; but let those who boast boast in this, that they understand and know me, that I am the LORD; I act with steadfast love, justice, and righteousness in the earth, for in these things I delight, says the LORD.

The days are surely coming, says the LORD, when I will attend to all those who are circumcised only in the foreskin: Egypt, Judah, Edom, the Ammonites, Moab, and all those with shaven temples who live in the desert. For all these nations are uncircumcised, and all the house of Israel is uncircumcised in heart. (Jer. 9:23-26)

Psalm
Psalm 84:1-7
Happy are they whose strength is in you

Additional Reading
2 Timothy 3:10-15
The persecution of the godly

Hymn: Joyful, Joyful We Adore Thee, ELW 836

O God of Israel, foolishly we strut among our neighbors as if our blessings were given to us of our own merits. Reveal the genuine natures beneath our façades and restore our humility so we may again delight in your name.

Saturday, October 26, 2013

Time after Pentecost

Philipp Nicolai, died 1608; Johann Heermann, died 1647;
Paul Gerhardt, died 1676; hymnwriters

Jeremiah 14:1-6
A drought portends destruction

The word of the LORD that came to Jeremiah concerning the drought:
Judah mourns
    and her gates languish;
they lie in gloom on the ground,
    and the cry of Jerusalem goes up.
Her nobles send their servants for water;
    they come to the cisterns,
they find no water,
    they return with their vessels empty.
They are ashamed and dismayed
    and cover their heads,
because the ground is cracked.
    Because there has been no rain on the land
the farmers are dismayed;
    they cover their heads. (Jer. 14:1-4)

Psalm	Additional Reading
Psalm 84:1-7	Luke 1:46-55
Happy are they whose strength is in you	*Mary's song*

Hymn: O Christ, Our Light, O Radiance True, ELW 675

Lord of famine and feast, hear our plea: do not abandon us! God of grain and grape, listen to our call: provide for us! Nourish our bodies with your abundant creation and nourish our souls with your abundant love.

Sunday, October 27, 2013

Time after Pentecost

Luke 18:9-14

A Pharisee and tax collector pray

[Jesus said,] "Two men went up to the temple to pray, one a Pharisee and the other a tax collector. The Pharisee, standing by himself, was praying thus, 'God, I thank you that I am not like other people: thieves, rogues, adulterers, or even like this tax collector. I fast twice a week; I give a tenth of all my income.' But the tax collector, standing far off, would not even look up to heaven, but was beating his breast and saying, 'God, be merciful to me, a sinner!' I tell you, this man went down to his home justified rather than the other; for all who exalt themselves will be humbled, but all who humble themselves will be exalted." (Luke 18:10-14)

Psalm

Psalm 84:1-7

Happy are they whose strength is in you

Additional Readings

Jeremiah 14:7-10, 19-22

Jerusalem will be defeated

2 Timothy 4:6-8, 16-18

The good fight of faith

Hymn: Just As I Am, without One Plea, ELW 592

Holy God, our righteous judge, daily your mercy surprises us with everlasting forgiveness. Strengthen our hope in you, and grant that all the peoples of the earth may find their glory in you, through Jesus Christ, our Savior and Lord.

Monday, October 28, 2013

Simon and Jude, Apostles

John 14:21-27

Those who love Jesus will keep his word

[Jesus said,] "They who have my commandments and keep them are those who love me; and those who love me will be loved by my Father, and I will love them and reveal myself to them." Judas (not Iscariot) said to him, "Lord, how is it that you will reveal yourself to us, and not to the world?" Jesus answered him, "Those who love me will keep my word, and my Father will love them, and we will come to them and make our home with them. Whoever does not love me does not keep my words; and the word that you hear is not mine, but is from the Father who sent me." (John 14:21-24)

Psalm

Psalm 11

Take refuge in God

Additional Readings

Jeremiah 26:[1-6] 7-16

Jeremiah promises the judgment of God

1 John 4:1-6

Do not believe every spirit of this world

Hymn: Rejoice in God's Saints, ELW 418

O God, we thank you for the glorious company of the apostles, and especially on this day for Simon and Jude. We pray that, as they were faithful and zealous in your mission, so we may with ardent devotion make known the love and mercy of our Savior Jesus Christ, who lives and reigns with you and the Holy Spirit, one God, now and forever.

Tuesday, October 29, 2013

Time after Pentecost

1 Peter 5:1-11
The unfading crown of glory

Now as an elder myself and a witness of the sufferings of Christ, as well as one who shares in the glory to be revealed, I exhort the elders among you to tend the flock of God that is in your charge, exercising the oversight, not under compulsion but willingly, as God would have you do it—not for sordid gain but eagerly. Do not lord it over those in your charge, but be examples to the flock. And when the chief shepherd appears, you will win the crown of glory that never fades away. (1 Peter 5:1-4)

Psalm
Psalm 84:8-12
A doorkeeper in God's house

Additional Reading
Daniel 5:1-12
A hand writing on the wall

Hymn: Savior, like a Shepherd Lead Us, ELW 789

Gracious God, you gave your Son, Jesus, so that we might see your light. Guide us with your word, lead us in your love, and teach us to help others see your glory that never fades away.

Wednesday, October 30, 2013

Time after Pentecost

Matthew 21:28-32

Faith of tax collectors and prostitutes

[Jesus said,] "What do you think? A man had two sons; he went to the first and said, 'Son, go and work in the vineyard today.' He answered, 'I will not'; but later he changed his mind and went. The father went to the second and said the same; and he answered, 'I go, sir'; but he did not go. Which of the two did the will of his father?" They said, "The first." Jesus said to them, "Truly I tell you, the tax collectors and the prostitutes are going into the kingdom of God ahead of you. For John came to you in the way of righteousness and you did not believe him, but the tax collectors and the prostitutes believed him; and even after you saw it, you did not change your minds and believe him." (Matt. 21:28-32)

Psalm
Psalm 84:8-12
A doorkeeper in God's house

Additional Reading
Daniel 5:13-31
Daniel urges humility

Hymn: Lord, Dismiss Us with Your Blessing, ELW 545

God of all people, help us to live out your vision of justice and dismiss the voices that berate, judge, demean, and degrade whole segments of our society. Embolden us to love, respect, and have compassion on each person we encounter this day.

Thursday, October 31, 2013

Reformation Day

Romans 3:19-28

Justified by God's grace as a gift

But now, apart from law, the righteousness of God has been disclosed, and is attested by the law and the prophets, the righteousness of God through faith in Jesus Christ for all who believe. For there is no distinction, since all have sinned and fall short of the glory of God; they are now justified by his grace as a gift, through the redemption that is in Christ Jesus, whom God put forward as a sacrifice of atonement by his blood, effective through faith. He did this to show his righteousness, because in his divine forbearance he had passed over the sins previously committed; it was to prove at the present time that he himself is righteous and that he justifies the one who has faith in Jesus. (Rom. 3:21-26)

Psalm

Psalm 46
The God of Jacob is our stronghold

Additional Readings

Jeremiah 31:31-34
I will write my law in their hearts

John 8:31-36
The truth will set you free

Hymn: The Church of Christ, in Every Age, ELW 729

Almighty God, gracious Lord, we thank you that your Holy Spirit renews the church in every age. Pour out your Holy Spirit on your faithful people. Keep them steadfast in your word, protect and comfort them in times of trial, defend them against all enemies of the gospel, and bestow on the church your saving peace, through Jesus Christ, our Savior and Lord, who lives and reigns with you and the Holy Spirit, one God, now and forever.

PRAYER LIST FOR NOVEMBER

_____

_____

_____

_____

_____

_____

_____

_____

_____

_____

_____

_____

TIME AFTER PENTECOST

NOVEMBER

The month of November is unique in that it begins with All Saints Day (November 1) and ends with the feast of Christ the King (often the last Sunday of November). The Sunday and daily readings seem to extend the harvest, but in a new way: they speak of God's harvest of *human beings* into their heavenly home.

Perhaps it is no coincidence that November's scriptural emphasis on the consummation of all things in Christ is reflected in the landscape and the chilling temperatures. Yet in the midst of this turning of the seasons and the reminders of death's presence, Christians hold forth the central feast of the year: the death and resurrection of Christ present in baptism and the holy supper. In these last days of the church's year, Christians are invited to celebrate the reign of Christ, whose death on the cross has transformed our deaths into the gate of everlasting life.

Table Prayer for November

Stay with us, God of life,
as we share the bounty of this food and drink.
We give you thanks for those who have gone before us in faith.
Bring us, with them, to the harvest of everlasting life,
where all people will feast forever at your abundant table.
We ask this through Christ our Lord. Amen.

Remembering Those Who Have Died

Use this prayer in the home or at the grave.

O God, our help in ages past and our hope for years to come:
We give you thanks for all your faithful people
who have followed the light of your word throughout the centuries
into our time and place.

Here individual names may be spoken.

As we remember these people,
strengthen us to follow Christ through this world
until we are carried into the harvest of eternal life,
where suffering and death will be no more.
Hear our prayer in the name of the good and gracious shepherd,
Jesus Christ, our Savior and Lord. Amen.

or

With reverence and affection we remember before you,
O everlasting God,
all our departed friends and relatives.
Keep us in union with them here
through faith and love toward you,
that hereafter we may enter into your presence
and be numbered with those who serve you
and look upon your face in glory everlasting,
through your Son, Jesus Christ our Lord. Amen.

Friday, November 1, 2013

All Saints Day

Luke 6:20-31

Jesus speaks blessings and woes

Then Jesus looked up at his disciples and said:
"Blessed are you who are poor,
   for yours is the kingdom of God.
"Blessed are you who are hungry now,
   for you will be filled.
"Blessed are you who weep now,
   for you will laugh.

"Blessed are you when people hate you, and when they exclude you, revile you, and defame you on account of the Son of Man. Rejoice in that day and leap for joy, for surely your reward is great in heaven; for that is what their ancestors did to the prophets." (Luke 6:20-23)

Psalm	Additional Readings	
Psalm 149	**Daniel 7:1-3, 15-18**	**Ephesians 1:11-23**
Sing praise for God's goodness	*The holy ones of the Most High*	*God made Christ head over all*

Hymn: Blest Are They, ELW 728

Almighty God, you have knit your people together in one communion in the mystical body of your Son, Jesus Christ our Lord. Grant us grace to follow your blessed saints in lives of faith and commitment, and to know the inexpressible joys you have prepared for those who love you, through Jesus Christ, our Savior and Lord, who lives and reigns with you and the Holy Spirit, one God, now and forever.

Saturday, November 2, 2013

Time after Pentecost

Isaiah 1:1-9
Sinful Judah

Hear, O heavens, and listen, O earth;
    for the LORD has spoken:
I reared children and brought them up,
    but they have rebelled against me.
The ox knows its owner,
    and the donkey its master's crib;
but Israel does not know,
    my people do not understand.

Ah, sinful nation,
    people laden with iniquity,
offspring who do evil,
    children who deal corruptly,
who have forsaken the LORD,
    who have despised the Holy One of Israel,
    who are utterly estranged! (Isa. 1:2-4)

Psalm	Additional Reading
Psalm 32:1-7	John 8:39-47
Praying in time of trouble	*True children of Abraham*

Hymn: All Who Love and Serve Your City, ELW 724

Merciful God, through the waters of baptism you claimed us as your daughters and sons. Help us to listen more carefully when you speak. Teach us to look with kindness on all your children and everything that you have created.

Sunday, November 3, 2013

Time after Pentecost

Martín de Porres, renewer of society, died 1639

Luke 19:1-10
Zacchaeus climbs high to see Jesus

When Jesus came to [Jericho], he looked up and said to [Zacchaeus], "Zacchaeus, hurry and come down; for I must stay at your house today." So he hurried down and was happy to welcome him. All who saw it began to grumble and said, "He has gone to be the guest of one who is a sinner." Zacchaeus stood there and said to the Lord, "Look, half of my possessions, Lord, I will give to the poor; and if I have defrauded anyone of anything, I will pay back four times as much." Then Jesus said to him, "Today salvation has come to this house, because he too is a son of Abraham. For the Son of Man came to seek out and to save the lost." (Luke 19:5-10)

Psalm
Psalm 32:1-7
Praying in time of trouble

Additional Readings
Isaiah 1:10-18
Learn to do good

2 Thessalonians
1:1-4, 11-12
Faith and love amid adversity

Hymn: Blessed Assurance, ELW 638

Merciful God, gracious and benevolent, through your Son you invite all the world to a meal of mercy. Grant that we may eagerly follow his call, and bring us with all your saints into your life of justice and joy, through Jesus Christ, our Savior and Lord.

Monday, November 4, 2013

Time after Pentecost

Psalm 50
A sacrifice of thanksgiving

[God says,] "Mark this, then, you who forget God,
  or I will tear you apart, and there will be no one to deliver.
Those who bring thanksgiving as their sacrifice honor me;
  to those who go the right way
  I will show the salvation of God." (Ps. 50:22-23)

Additional Readings
Nehemiah 13:1-3, 23-31
Israel separates from foreigners

1 Corinthians 5:9-13
Drive out the wicked

Hymn: Lord, I Lift Your Name on High, ELW 857

*Eternal God, you have led your people throughout time in countless
ways. Strengthen our minds to recognize your presence daily. Deliver us
from the things that distract us from you. Inspire us to be ever thankful
for the things you have done.*

Tuesday, November 5, 2013

Time after Pentecost

Jude 5-21
Warning against sinners

But you, beloved, must remember the predictions of the apostles of
our Lord Jesus Christ; for they said to you, "In the last time there will
be scoffers, indulging their own ungodly lusts." It is these worldly
people, devoid of the Spirit, who are causing divisions. But you,
beloved, build yourselves up on your most holy faith; pray in the Holy
Spirit; keep yourselves in the love of God; look forward to the mercy
of our Lord Jesus Christ that leads to eternal life. (Jude 17-21)

Psalm
Psalm 50
A sacrifice of thanksgiving

Additional Reading
Zechariah 7:1-14
Fasting versus justice and mercy

Hymn: Thy Strong Word, ELW 511

*Holy God, you draw all people unto yourself. Make us holy as we strive
toward unity amid adversity and diversity. As you love us, enable us to
love one another and to ground our lives on faith in you.*

Wednesday, November 6, 2013

Time after Pentecost

Amos 5:12-24
God desires justice, not offerings

I hate, I despise your festivals,
  and I take no delight in your solemn assemblies.
Even though you offer me your burnt offerings and grain offerings,
  I will not accept them;
and the offerings of well-being of your fatted animals
  I will not look upon.
Take away from me the noise of your songs;
  I will not listen to the melody of your harps.
But let justice roll down like waters,
  and righteousness like an everflowing stream. (Amos 5:21-24)

Psalm
Psalm 50
A sacrifice of thanksgiving

Additional Reading
Luke 19:11-27
The parable of the pounds

Hymn: Let Justice Flow like Streams, ELW 717

Almighty God, you created us and you know our innermost secrets and thoughts. Keep us genuine in our worship and praise toward you. Give us courage to live boldly, demanding justice for all who are marginalized or oppressed.

Thursday, November 7, 2013

Time after Pentecost

John Christian Frederick Heyer, died 1873; Bartholomaeus Ziegenbalg, died 1719; Ludwig Nommensen, died 1918; missionaries

Psalm 17:1-9

Keep me as the apple of your eye

I call upon you, for you will answer me, O God;
    incline your ear to me, hear my words.
Wondrously show your steadfast love,
    O savior of those who seek refuge
    from their adversaries at your right hand.

Guard me as the apple of the eye;
    hide me in the shadow of your wings,
from the wicked who despoil me,
    my deadly enemies who surround me. (Ps. 17:6-9)

Additional Readings

Deuteronomy 25:5-10
Instructions for levirate marriage

Acts 22:22—23:11
Paul confronts religious leaders

Hymn: What Wondrous Love Is This, ELW 666

Loving God, in your wondrous love you listen to the cries of your people. Guard and protect us each day from the evils that surround us. Keep us safe in your care that we might serve you all the days of our lives.

Friday, November 8, 2013

Time after Pentecost

Acts 24:10-23
Paul testifies to the resurrection

When the governor motioned to him to speak, Paul replied:
"I cheerfully make my defense, knowing that for many years you have
been a judge over this nation. As you can find out, it is not more than
twelve days since I went up to worship in Jerusalem. They did not find
me disputing with anyone in the temple or stirring up a crowd either
in the synagogues or throughout the city. Neither can they prove to
you the charge that they now bring against me. But this I admit to
you, that according to the Way, which they call a sect, I worship the
God of our ancestors, believing everything laid down according to
the law or written in the prophets. I have a hope in God—a hope that
they themselves also accept—that there will be a resurrection of both
the righteous and the unrighteous." (Acts 24:10-15)

Psalm
Psalm 17:1-9
Keep me as the apple of your eye

Additional Reading
Genesis 38:1-26
Tamar and levirate marriage

Hymn: Holy God, Holy and Glorious, ELW 637

*God of new life, you gave your only Son as a sacrifice for our sin. As
we are grateful for the witness of our ancestors, encourage us to be
witnesses to Christ's resurrection, announcing to the world your endless
gifts of grace.*

Saturday, November 9, 2013

Time after Pentecost

Exodus 3:13-20
God appears to Moses

But Moses said to God, "If I come to the Israelites and say to them, 'The God of your ancestors has sent me to you,' and they ask me, 'What is his name?' what shall I say to them?" God said to Moses, "I AM WHO I AM." He said further, "Thus you shall say to the Israelites, 'I AM has sent me to you.' " God also said to Moses, "Thus you shall say to the Israelites, 'The LORD, the God of your ancestors, the God of Abraham, the God of Isaac, and the God of Jacob, has sent me to you':
  This is my name forever,
  and this my title for all generations." (Exod. 3:13-15)

Psalm
Psalm 17:1-9
Keep me as the apple of your eye

Additional Reading
Luke 20:1-8
Jesus' teaching authority

Hymn: The God of Abraham Praise, ELW 831

God of Abraham, Isaac, and Jacob, your love is everlasting from age to age. As our world is full of constant change, continually remain in our lives bringing us hope and peace forevermore.

Sunday, November 10, 2013

Time after Pentecost

Luke 20:27-38

Jesus speaks of the resurrection

Jesus said to [the Sadducees], "Those who belong to this age marry and are given in marriage; but those who are considered worthy of a place in that age and in the resurrection from the dead neither marry nor are given in marriage. Indeed they cannot die anymore, because they are like angels and are children of God, being children of the resurrection. And the fact that the dead are raised Moses himself showed, in the story about the bush, where he speaks of the Lord as the God of Abraham, the God of Isaac, and the God of Jacob. Now he is God not of the dead, but of the living; for to him all of them are alive." (Luke 20:34-38)

Psalm

Psalm 17:1-9

Keep me as the apple of your eye

Additional Readings

Job 19:23-27a

I know that my Redeemer lives

2 Thessalonians 2:1-5, 13-17

The coming of Christ Jesus

Hymn: Sing with All the Saints in Glory, ELW 426

O God, our eternal redeemer, by the presence of your Spirit you renew and direct our hearts. Keep always in our mind the end of all things and the day of judgment. Inspire us for a holy life here, and bring us to the joy of the resurrection, through Jesus Christ, our Savior and Lord.

Monday, November 11, 2013

Time after Pentecost

Martin, Bishop of Tours, died 397
Søren Aabye Kierkegaard, teacher, died 1855

Psalm 123
Our eyes look to God

To you I lift up my eyes,
  O you who are enthroned in the heavens!
As the eyes of servants
  look to the hand of their master,
as the eyes of a maid
  to the hand of her mistress,
so our eyes look to the Lord our God,
  until he has mercy upon us.

Have mercy upon us, O Lord, have mercy upon us,
  for we have had more than enough of contempt.
Our soul has had more than its fill
  of the scorn of those who are at ease,
  of the contempt of the proud. (Ps. 123:1-4)

Additional Readings
Job 20:1-11   2 Peter 1:16-21
Mortals fly away like a dream   *Prophecy comes not by human will*

Hymn: Kyrie! God, Father, ELW 409

*God of the heavens, you have shown mercy to our forbearers. When we
are confronted by death and destruction, pain and sadness, grant to us
the mercy and the peace that only you can give. Bring us healing and
new life.*

Tuesday, November 12, 2013

Time after Pentecost

2 John 1-13
Be on your guard

Many deceivers have gone out into the world, those who do not confess that Jesus Christ has come in the flesh; any such person is the deceiver and the antichrist! Be on your guard, so that you do not lose what we have worked for, but may receive a full reward. Everyone who does not abide in the teaching of Christ, but goes beyond it, does not have God; whoever abides in the teaching has both the Father and the Son. Do not receive into the house or welcome anyone who comes to you and does not bring this teaching; for to welcome is to participate in the evil deeds of such a person. (2 John 7-11)

Psalm
Psalm 123
Our eyes look to God

Additional Reading
Job 21:1, 17-34
Poor and rich lie down in the dust

Hymn: Jesus, Still Lead On, ELW 624

God of knowledge and wisdom, you sent Christ to teach us a new way. Help us live more faithfully in all that we say and do. Lead us to welcome the strangers among us with Christian hospitality.

Wednesday, November 13, 2013

Time after Pentecost

John 5:19-29

The authority of the Son

[Jesus said,] "Very truly, I tell you, the hour is coming, and is now here, when the dead will hear the voice of the Son of God, and those who hear will live. For just as the Father has life in himself, so he has granted the Son also to have life in himself; and he has given him authority to execute judgment, because he is the Son of Man. Do not be astonished at this; for the hour is coming when all who are in their graves will hear his voice and will come out—those who have done good, to the resurrection of life, and those who have done evil, to the resurrection of condemnation." (John 5:25-29)

Psalm
Psalm 123
Our eyes look to God

Additional Reading
Job 25:1—26:14
Even Sheol is naked before God

Hymn: I Am the Bread of Life, ELW 485

God of life, through Christ you have conquered death and the grave. Raise us up to life eternal. Bring us all to your heavenly home where we will join the saints who have gone before us, in your glory.

Thursday, November 14, 2013

Time after Pentecost

Psalm 98
God judges the world

Let the sea roar, and all that fills it;
  the world and those who live in it.
Let the floods clap their hands;
  let the hills sing together for joy
at the presence of the LORD, for he is coming
  to judge the earth.
He will judge the world with righteousness,
  and the peoples with equity. (Ps. 98:7-9)

Additional Readings
1 Samuel 28:3-19   Romans 1:18-25
Saul warned of God's judgment   *The revealing of God's wrath*

Hymn: Light Dawns on a Weary World, ELW 726

God of peace, all of creation sings your praise. Make us holy as you are holy; make us righteous as you are righteous. In your gracious compassion, judge us with kindness and let your face shine upon us.

Friday, November 15, 2013

Time after Pentecost

2 Thessalonians 1:3-12
God's judgment

This is evidence of the righteous judgment of God, and is intended to make you worthy of the kingdom of God, for which you are also suffering. For it is indeed just of God to repay with affliction those who afflict you, and to give relief to the afflicted as well as to us, when the Lord Jesus is revealed from heaven with his mighty angels in flaming fire, inflicting vengeance on those who do not know God and on those who do not obey the gospel of our Lord Jesus. (2 Thess. 1:5-8)

Psalm
Psalm 98
God judges the world

Additional Reading
2 Samuel 21:1-14
Violence comes on Saul's household

Hymn: O Day of Peace, ELW 711

Lord of righteousness, you alone are worthy of praise. Forgive us our sins. Free us from all suffering. By your mercy make us worthy to inherit the kingdom of God.

Saturday, November 16, 2013

Time after Pentecost

Luke 17:20-37
The judgment coming

Then [Jesus] said to the disciples, "The days are coming when you will long to see one of the days of the Son of Man, and you will not see it. They will say to you, 'Look there!' or 'Look here!' Do not go, do not set off in pursuit. For as the lightning flashes and lights up the sky from one side to the other, so will the Son of Man be in his day." (Luke 17:22-24)

Psalm
Psalm 98
God judges the world

Additional Reading
Ezekiel 10:1-19
God's glory leaves Jerusalem

Hymn: Soon and Very Soon, ELW 439

Lord God, you sent Christ to dwell among us. Focus our hearts and minds on the things of Christ. Bring clarity where there is uncertainty, guidance where we lack direction, and renewed hope for Christ's coming again.

Sunday, November 17, 2013

Time after Pentecost

Elizabeth of Hungary, renewer of society, died 1231

Luke 21:5-19

Suffering for Jesus' sake

[Jesus said,] "You will be betrayed even by parents and brothers, by relatives and friends; and they will put some of you to death. You will be hated by all because of my name. But not a hair of your head will perish. By your endurance you will gain your souls." (Luke 21:16-19)

Psalm	Additional Readings	
Psalm 98	**Malachi 4:1-2a**	**2 Thessalonians**
God judges the world	*A day of healing for the righteous*	**3:6-13**
		Do what is right

Hymn: Through the Night of Doubt and Sorrow, ELW 327

O God, the protector of all who trust in you, without you nothing is strong, nothing is holy. Embrace us with your mercy, that with you as our ruler and guide, we may live through what is temporary without losing what is eternal, through Jesus Christ, our Savior and Lord.

Monday, November 18, 2013

Time after Pentecost

Psalm 141
God is my refuge

But my eyes are turned toward you, O GOD, my Lord;
  in you I seek refuge; do not leave me defenseless.
Keep me from the trap that they have laid for me,
  and from the snares of evildoers.
Let the wicked fall into their own nets,
  while I alone escape. (Ps. 141:8-10)

Additional Readings
Ezekiel 11:14-25
Judgment and promised restoration

Ephesians 4:25—5:2
Be imitators of God

Hymn: My Hope Is Built on Nothing Less, ELW 596/597

*Lord of hope, you abide with us even when we feel lonely or afraid.
Defend us from all evil and grant us a safe refuge. Be our sure defense
against all the mental and physical things that seek to harm us.*

Tuesday, November 19, 2013

Time after Pentecost

I Corinthians 10:23—11:1

Do all to the glory of God

So, whether you eat or drink, or whatever you do, do everything
for the glory of God. Give no offense to Jews or to Greeks or to the
church of God, just as I try to please everyone in everything I do, not
seeking my own advantage, but that of many, so that they may be
saved. Be imitators of me, as I am of Christ. (1 Cor. 10:31—11:1)

Psalm

Psalm 141

God is my refuge

Additional Reading

Ezekiel 39:21—40:4

Mercy on the house of Israel

Hymn: Awake, My Soul, and with the Sun, ELW 557

*Lord of all, you know our every need. Inspire us in everything we do,
that our work may glorify you. Remove us from our selfishness and
make us attentive to the needs and cares of others.*

Wednesday, November 20, 2013

Time after Pentecost

Ezekiel 43:1-12

Divine glory returns to the temple

As for you, mortal, describe the temple to the house of Israel, and let them measure the pattern; and let them be ashamed of their iniquities. When they are ashamed of all that they have done, make known to them the plan of the temple, its arrangement, its exits and its entrances, and its whole form—all its ordinances and its entire plan and all its laws; and write it down in their sight, so that they may observe and follow the entire plan and all its ordinances. This is the law of the temple: the whole territory on the top of the mountain all around shall be most holy. This is the law of the temple. (Ezek. 43:10-12)

Psalm

Psalm 141

God is my refuge

Additional Reading

Matthew 23:37—24:14

The last things

Hymn: In His Temple Now Behold Him, ELW 417

Lord of wisdom, the depths of your beauty are beyond human comprehension. Guide the discernment of government and national leaders, writing your word on their hearts as they act on behalf of others.

Thursday, November 21, 2013

Time after Pentecost

Psalm 46
The God of Jacob is our stronghold

There is a river whose streams make glad the city of God,
    the holy habitation of the Most High.
God is in the midst of the city; it shall not be moved;
    God will help it when the morning dawns.
The nations are in an uproar, the kingdoms totter;
    he utters his voice, the earth melts.
The LORD of hosts is with us;
    the God of Jacob is our refuge. (Ps. 46:4-7)

Additional Readings
2 Chronicles 18:12-22   Hebrews 9:23-28
Sheep without a shepherd   *Christ has appeared once for all*

Hymn: O God beyond All Praising, ELW 880

*Lord of the universe, without you we are like sheep without a shepherd.
Make your presence known in our cities and suburban communities;
shine your hope and glory on rural lands. Come, inhabit our homes
and dwell among us.*

Friday, November 22, 2013

Time after Pentecost

1 Peter 1:3-9
An imperishable inheritance

Blessed be the God and Father of our Lord Jesus Christ! By his great mercy he has given us a new birth into a living hope through the resurrection of Jesus Christ from the dead, and into an inheritance that is imperishable, undefiled, and unfading, kept in heaven for you, who are being protected by the power of God through faith for a salvation ready to be revealed in the last time. In this you rejoice, even if now for a little while you have had to suffer various trials, so that the genuineness of your faith—being more precious than gold that, though perishable, is tested by fire—may be found to result in praise and glory and honor when Jesus Christ is revealed. (1 Peter 1:3-7)

Psalm
Psalm 46
The God of Jacob is our stronghold

Additional Reading
Zechariah 11:1-17
Shepherds who desert the flock

Hymn: O Savior, Precious Savior, ELW 820

Blessed God, you have given us an inheritance that knows no ending. In your great mercy put an end to our selfish wants. Turn us from being mindless consumers into faithful believers of the resurrected life.

Saturday, November 23, 2013

Time after Pentecost

Clement, Bishop of Rome, died around 100
Miguel Agustín Pro, martyr, died 1927

Luke 18:15-17
Receiving the kingdom of God

People were bringing even infants to him that he might touch them; and when the disciples saw it, they sternly ordered them not to do it. But Jesus called for them and said, "Let the little children come to me, and do not stop them; for it is to such as these that the kingdom of God belongs. Truly I tell you, whoever does not receive the kingdom of God as a little child will never enter it." (Luke 18:15-17)

Psalm
Psalm 46
The God of Jacob is our stronghold

Additional Reading
Jeremiah 22:18-30
The wind shepherds the shepherds

Hymn: Cradling Children in His Arm, ELW 444

Compassionate God, you care for the smallest of creatures. Watch over the orphans, children of domestic violence, and victims of school bullying. Surround them with your healing love. Hold them in your arms and keep them from being lost and afraid.

Sunday, November 24, 2013

Christ the King

Justus Falckner, died 1723; Jehu Jones, died 1852; William Passavant, died 1894; pastors in North America

Luke 23:33-43

Jesus crucified with two thieves

When they came to the place that is called The Skull, they crucified Jesus there with the criminals, one on his right and one on his left. [Then Jesus said, "Father, forgive them; for they do not know what they are doing."] And they cast lots to divide his clothing. And the people stood by, watching; but the leaders scoffed at him, saying, "He saved others; let him save himself if he is the Messiah of God, his chosen one!" The soldiers also mocked him, coming up and offering him sour wine, and saying, "If you are the King of the Jews, save yourself!" (Luke 23:33-37)

Psalm

Psalm 46
The God of Jacob is our stronghold

Additional Readings

Jeremiah 23:1-6
Coming of the shepherd

Colossians 1:11-20
A hymn to Christ, firstborn of all creation

Hymn: Lord, Enthroned in Heavenly Splendor, ELW 475

O God, our true life, to serve you is freedom, and to know you is unending joy. We worship you, we glorify you, we give thanks to you for your great glory. Abide with us, reign in us, and make this world into a fit habitation for your divine majesty, through Jesus Christ, our Savior and Lord, who lives and reigns with you and the Holy Spirit, one God, now and forever.

Monday, November 25, 2013

Time after Pentecost

Isaac Watts, hymnwriter, died 1748

Psalm 24
The King of glory comes

Lift up your heads, O gates!
  and be lifted up, O ancient doors!
  that the King of glory may come in.
Who is the King of glory?
  The LORD, strong and mighty,
  the LORD, mighty in battle.
Lift up your heads, O gates!
  and be lifted up, O ancient doors!
  that the King of glory may come in.
Who is this King of glory?
  The LORD of hosts,
  he is the King of glory. (Ps. 24:7-10)

Additional Readings
Jeremiah 46:18-28
God will save Israel

Revelation 21:5-27
God reigns in the holy city

Hymn: Praise, My Soul, the King of Heaven, ELW 865

Mighty God, your Son was lifted up on a cross for the salvation of the whole world. By your strength help us to rebuild homes and communities that have been ravaged by war and natural disasters.

Tuesday, November 26, 2013

Time after Pentecost

Revelation 22:8-21
Surely, I am coming soon

"See, I am coming soon; my reward is with me, to repay according to everyone's work. I am the Alpha and the Omega, the first and the last, the beginning and the end."

Blessed are those who wash their robes, so that they will have the right to the tree of life and may enter the city by the gates. (Rev. 22:12-14)

Psalm
Psalm 24
The King of glory comes

Additional Reading
Isaiah 33:17-22
Our God rules

Hymn: Love Divine, All Loves Excelling, ELW 631

Living God, you have promised restoration and renewal for your people. Come quickly as we strive to wait patiently for your coming again. Reshape our world with your grace and bring us new life.

Wednesday, November 27, 2013

Time after Pentecost

Isaiah 60:8-16
The forsaken become majestic

The descendants of those who oppressed you
  shall come bending low to you,
and all who despised you
  shall bow down at your feet;
they shall call you the City of the LORD,
  the Zion of the Holy One of Israel.
Whereas you have been forsaken and hated,
  with no one passing through,
I will make you majestic forever,
  a joy from age to age.
You shall suck the milk of nations,
  you shall suck the breasts of kings;
and you shall know that I, the LORD, am your Savior
  and your Redeemer, the Mighty One of Jacob. (Isa. 60:14-16)

Psalm
Psalm 24
The King of glory comes

Additional Reading
Luke 1:1-4
That you may know the truth

Hymn: Glorious Things of You Are Spoken, ELW 647

Holy God, you are everlasting from age to age. In our sinfulness we demand power and control over one another. Humble us. Remind us that you alone are God and ruler over all.

Blessing of the Household for Thanksgiving Day

We gather this day to give thanks to God for the gifts of this land and its people, for God has been generous to us. As we ask God's blessing upon this food we share, may we be mindful of the lonely and the hungry.

As we prepare to offer thanks to God,
let us listen to the words of scripture:

I give thanks to my God always for you because of the grace of God that has been given you in Christ Jesus, for in every way you have been enriched in him, in speech and knowledge of every kind—just as the testimony of Christ has been strengthened among you—so that you are not lacking in any spiritual gift as you wait for the revealing of our Lord Jesus Christ. He will also strengthen you to the end, so that you may be blameless on the day of our Lord Jesus Christ. (1 Cor. 1:4-8)

Let us pray.
God most provident,
we join all creation in offering you praise through Jesus Christ.
For generations the people of this land have sung of your bounty.
With them, we offer you thanksgiving
for the rich harvest we have received at your hands.
Bless us and this food that we share with grateful hearts.
Continue to make our land fruitful
and let our love for you be seen in our pursuit of justice and peace
and in our generous response to those in need.
We ask this through Christ our Lord. Amen.

May Christ, the living bread, bring us to the feast of eternal life.
Amen.

Thursday, November 28, 2013

Day of Thanksgiving (U.S.A.)

Psalm 122
Gladness in God's house

I was glad when they said to me,
  "Let us go to the house of the LORD!"
Our feet are standing
  within your gates, O Jerusalem.

Jerusalem—built as a city
  that is bound firmly together.
To it the tribes go up,
  the tribes of the LORD,
as was decreed for Israel,
  to give thanks to the name of the LORD.
For there the thrones for judgment were set up,
  the thrones of the house of David. (Ps. 122:1-5)

Additional Readings

Daniel 9:15-19
A plea for forgiveness

James 4:1-10
A plea for God's grace and human humility

Hymn: Open Now Thy Gates of Beauty, ELW 533

Majestic God, you shower us with an abundance of gifts. Keep us thankful each and every day of our lives. Give us glad and generous hearts as we bountifully share with others the gifts you have given us.

Friday, November 29, 2013

Time after Pentecost

Hebrews 11:1-7
Noah acts in faith

By faith Abel offered to God a more acceptable sacrifice than Cain's. Through this he received approval as righteous, God himself giving approval to his gifts; he died, but through his faith he still speaks. By faith Enoch was taken so that he did not experience death; and "he was not found, because God had taken him." For it was attested before he was taken away that "he had pleased God." And without faith it is impossible to please God, for whoever would approach him must believe that he exists and that he rewards those who seek him. By faith Noah, warned by God about events as yet unseen, respected the warning and built an ark to save his household; by this he condemned the world and became an heir to the righteousness that is in accordance with faith. (Heb. 11:4-7)

Psalm
Psalm 122
Gladness in God's house

Additional Reading
Genesis 6:1-10
Humankind's wickedness, Noah's righteousness

Hymn: We Walk by Faith, ELW 635

Gracious God, you saved Noah from the waters of a flood. Strengthen our faith in you. Help us trust in your mercy through trials known and unknown. Direct our lives that they may be holy and pleasing in your sight.

Saturday, November 30, 2013

Andrew, Apostle

John 1:35-42

Jesus calls Andrew

One of the two who heard John speak and followed him was Andrew, Simon Peter's brother. He first found his brother Simon and said to him, "We have found the Messiah" (which is translated Anointed). He brought Simon to Jesus, who looked at him and said, "You are Simon son of John. You are to be called Cephas" (which is translated Peter). (John 1:40-42)

Psalm

Psalm 19:1-6

The heavens declare God's glory

Additional Readings

Ezekiel 3:16-21

A sentinel for the house of Israel

Romans 10:10-18

Faith comes from the word of Christ

Hymn: Jesus Calls Us; o'er the Tumult, ELW 696

Almighty God, you gave your apostle Andrew the grace to obey the call of your Son and to bring his brother to Jesus. Give us also, who are called by your holy word, grace to follow Jesus without delay and to bring into his presence those who are near to us, for he lives and reigns with you and the Holy Spirit, one God, now and forever.

PRAYER LIST FOR DECEMBER

_____

_____

_____

_____

_____

_____

_____

_____

_____

_____

_____

_____

ADVENT

In the days of Advent, Christians prepare to celebrate the presence of God's Word among us in our own day. During these four weeks, we pray that the reign of God, which Jesus preached and lived, would come among us. We pray that God's justice would flourish in our land, that the people of the earth would live in peace, that the weak and the sick and the hungry would be strengthened, healed, and fed with God's merciful presence.

During the last days of Advent, Christians welcome Christ with names inspired by the prophets: wisdom, liberator of slaves, mighty power, radiant dawn and sun of justice, the keystone of the arch of humanity, and Emmanuel—God with us.

Table Prayer for Advent

Blessed are you, O Lord our God,
the one who is, who was, and who is to come.
At this table you fill us with good things.
May these gifts strengthen us
to share with the hungry and all those in need,
as we wait and watch for your coming among us
in Jesus Christ our Lord. Amen.

The Advent Wreath

One of the best-known customs for the season is the Advent wreath. The wreath and winter candle-lighting in the midst of growing darkness strengthen some of the Advent images found in the Bible. The unbroken circle of greens is clearly an image of everlasting life, a victory wreath, the crown of Christ, or the wheel of time itself. Christians use the wreath as a sign that Christ reaches into our time to lead us to the light of everlasting life. The four candles mark the progress of the four weeks of Advent and the growth of light. Sometimes the wreath is embellished with natural dried flowers or fruit. Its evergreen branches lead the household and the congregation to the evergreen Christmas tree. In many homes, the family gathers for prayer around the wreath.

Lighting the Advent Wreath
Use this blessing when lighting the first candle.

Blessed are you, O Lord our God, ruler of the universe.
You call all nations to walk in your light
and to seek your ways of justice and peace,
for the night is past, and the dawn of your coming is near.
Bless us as we light the first candle of this wreath.
Rouse us from sleep,
that we may be ready to greet our Lord when he comes
and welcome him into our hearts and homes,
for he is our light and our salvation.
Blessed be God forever.

Sunday, December 1, 2013

First Sunday of Advent

Matthew 24:36-44

The sudden coming of salvation

[Jesus said,] "But about that day and hour no one knows, neither the angels of heaven, nor the Son, but only the Father. For as the days of Noah were, so will be the coming of the Son of Man. For as in those days before the flood they were eating and drinking, marrying and giving in marriage, until the day Noah entered the ark, and they knew nothing until the flood came and swept them all away, so too will be the coming of the Son of Man." (Matt. 24:36-39)

Psalm

Psalm 122

Gladness in God's house

Additional Readings

Isaiah 2:1-5

War transformed into peace

Romans 13:11-14

Salvation is near; wake from sleep

Hymn: Wake, Awake, for Night Is Flying, ELW 436

Stir up your power, Lord Christ, and come. By your merciful protection save us from the threatening dangers of our sins, and enlighten our walk in the way of your salvation, for you live and reign with the Father and the Holy Spirit, one God, now and forever.

Monday, December 2, 2013

Week of Advent 1

Psalm 124

We have escaped like a bird

Blessed be the LORD,
   who has not given us
   as prey to their teeth.
We have escaped like a bird
   from the snare of the fowlers;
the snare is broken,
   and we have escaped.

Our help is in the name of the LORD,
   who made heaven and earth. (Ps. 124:6-8)

Additional Readings

Romans 6:1-11
Dying and rising with Christ through baptism

Genesis 8:1-19
The flood waters subside

Hymn: Come, Thou Long-Expected Jesus, ELW 254

O God, we know that you will not let us be prey forever. Break the snares that bind us. Help us to escape from all that would hold us captive. Guide us back to you.

Tuesday, December 3, 2013

Week of Advent I

Francis Xavier, missionary to Asia, died 1552

Genesis 9:1-17

Command to be fruitful; sign of the rainbow

God blessed Noah and his sons, and said to them, "Be fruitful and multiply, and fill the earth. The fear and dread of you shall rest on every animal of the earth, and on every bird of the air, on everything that creeps on the ground, and on all the fish of the sea; into your hand they are delivered. Every moving thing that lives shall be food for you; and just as I gave you the green plants, I give you everything." (Gen. 9:1-3)

Psalm

Psalm 124
We have escaped like a bird

Additional Reading

Hebrews 11:32-40
The heroes of faith

Hymn: For the Fruit of All Creation, ELW 679

Creator God, you give us everything we need. Help us to remember all your promises. Make us fruitful and green. Multiply the blessings of your creation and help us to be faithful stewards of all the good gifts you bestow.

Wednesday, December 4, 2013

Week of Advent 1

John of Damascus, theologian and hymnwriter, died around 749

Isaiah 54:1-10
God will save the people

This is like the days of Noah to me:
 Just as I swore that the waters of Noah
 would never again go over the earth,
so I have sworn that I will not be angry with you
 and will not rebuke you.
For the mountains may depart
 and the hills be removed,
but my steadfast love shall not depart from you,
 and my covenant of peace shall not be removed,
 says the LORD, who has compassion on you. (Isa. 54:9-10)

Psalm
Psalm 124
We have escaped like a bird

Additional Reading
Matthew 24:23-35
The end is coming

Hymn: Praise the Lord! O Heavens, ELW 823

Merciful God, help us to remember your covenant and all your promises of peace. Do not rebuke us when we come to you. Hold us steady in your love. Let the floodwaters of anger and anxiety recede.

Thursday, December 5, 2013

Week of Advent 1

Psalm 72:1-7, 18-19
The righteous shall flourish

Give the king your justice, O God,
    and your righteousness to a king's son.
May he judge your people with righteousness,
    and your poor with justice.
May the mountains yield prosperity for the people,
    and the hills, in righteousness.
May he defend the cause of the poor of the people,
    give deliverance to the needy,
        and crush the oppressor. (Ps. 72:1-4)

Additional Readings

Isaiah 4:2-6
God's promised glory for the survivors in Zion

Acts 1:12-17, 21-26
Beginnings of the apostolic ministry

Hymn: Jesus Shall Reign, ELW 434

O God, you know the things that oppress us. Grant us deliverance. In our prosperity, help us remember the poor. In our poverty, remind us of your bountiful blessings. Help us to be righteous in all our circumstances.

Friday, December 6, 2013

Week of Advent I

Nicholas, Bishop of Myra, died around 342

Isaiah 30:19-26

God's promise to be gracious to Zion

Truly, O people in Zion, inhabitants of Jerusalem, you shall weep no more. He will surely be gracious to you at the sound of your cry; when he hears it, he will answer you. Though the Lord may give you the bread of adversity and the water of affliction, yet your Teacher will not hide himself any more, but your eyes shall see your Teacher. And when you turn to the right or when you turn to the left, your ears shall hear a word behind you, saying, "This is the way; walk in it." (Isa. 30:19-21)

Psalm
Psalm 72:1-7, 18-19
The righteous shall flourish

Additional Reading
Acts 13:16-25
Paul's testimony concerning John the Baptist

Hymn: O Zion, Haste, ELW 668

Comforter God, hear us when we weep. Let us feed on the bread that can sustain us. Show us the path that leads away from the water of affliction and toward the purifying water of your love.

Saturday, December 7, 2013

Week of Advent I

Ambrose, Bishop of Milan, died 397

Isaiah 40:1-11

A voice crying in the wilderness

A voice cries out:
"In the wilderness prepare the way of the LORD,
  make straight in the desert a highway for our God.
Every valley shall be lifted up,
  and every mountain and hill be made low;
the uneven ground shall become level,
  and the rough places a plain.
Then the glory of the LORD shall be revealed,
  and all people shall see it together,
  for the mouth of the LORD has spoken." (Isa. 40:3-5)

Psalm	Additional Reading
Psalm 72:1-7, 18-19	John 1:19-28
The righteous shall flourish	*John the Baptist concerning his own ministry*

Hymn: Savior of the Nations, Come, ELW 263

O God, help us to prepare the highway for you, as we make the uneven ground of our lives level. Lead us from the wild areas and smooth out our rough places so that we may glorify you.

Lighting the Advent Wreath
Use this blessing when lighting the first two candles.

Blessed are you, O Lord our God, ruler of the universe.
John the Baptist calls all people to prepare the Lord's way
for the kingdom of heaven is near.
Bless us as we light the candles on this wreath.
Baptize us with the fire of your Spirit,
that we may be a light shining in the darkness
welcoming others as Christ has welcomed us,
for he is our light and our salvation.
Blessed be God forever.

Sunday, December 8, 2013

Second Sunday of Advent

Matthew 3:1-12

Prepare the way of the Lord

In those days John the Baptist appeared in the wilderness of Judea, proclaiming, "Repent, for the kingdom of heaven has come near." This is the one of whom the prophet Isaiah spoke when he said, "The voice of one crying out in the wilderness:
'Prepare the way of the Lord,
   make his paths straight'. " (Matt. 3:1-3)

Psalm

Psalm 72:1-7, 18-19

The righteous shall flourish

Additional Readings

Isaiah 11:1-10

A ruler brings justice and peace

Romans 15:4-13

Living in harmony

Hymn: On Jordan's Bank the Baptist's Cry, ELW 249

Stir up our hearts, Lord God, to prepare the way of your only Son. By his coming nurture our growth as people of repentance and peace; through Jesus Christ, our Savior and Lord, who lives and reigns with you and the Holy Spirit, one God, now and forever.

Monday, December 9, 2013

Week of Advent 2

Psalm 21
God comes with judgment and strength

In your strength the king rejoices, O LORD,
  and in your help how greatly he exults!

For the king trusts in the LORD,
  and through the steadfast love of the Most High he shall not be
    moved.

Your hand will find out all your enemies;
  your right hand will find out those who hate you. (Ps. 21:1, 7-8)

Additional Readings
Isaiah 24:1-16a   I Thessalonians 4:1-12
Judgment is coming, but glorify God   *Live in holiness and love one another*

Hymn: Come Now, O Prince of Peace, ELW 247

*How hard it is to trust you, Lord God. How much we want to rely on our
own power. Help us to know your steadfast love. Convince us to exult in
the true strength that can sustain us.*

Tuesday, December 10, 2013

Week of Advent 2

Romans 15:14-21

Gentiles are also called to the obedience of faith

I myself feel confident about you, my brothers and sisters, that you yourselves are full of goodness, filled with all knowledge, and able to instruct one another. Nevertheless on some points I have written to you rather boldly by way of reminder, because of the grace given me by God to be a minister of Christ Jesus to the Gentiles in the priestly service of the gospel of God, so that the offering of the Gentiles may be acceptable, sanctified by the Holy Spirit. (Rom. 15:14-16)

Psalm
Psalm 21
God comes with judgment and strength

Additional Reading
Isaiah 41:14-20
God will not forget the poor of Israel

Hymn: O Lord, How Shall I Meet You, ELW 241

There are too many days when we do not seem filled with knowledge. Remind us of your grace. Help us to accept the teaching of others. Sanctify us so that we may be full of goodness.

Wednesday, December 11, 2013

Week of Advent 2

Genesis 15:1-18

God's covenant with Abram

As the sun was going down, a deep sleep fell upon Abram, and a deep and terrifying darkness descended upon him. Then the LORD said to Abram, "Know this for certain, that your offspring shall be aliens in a land that is not theirs, and shall be slaves there, and they shall be oppressed for four hundred years; but I will bring judgment on the nation that they serve, and afterward they shall come out with great possessions. As for yourself, you shall go to your ancestors in peace; you shall be buried in a good old age. And they shall come back here in the fourth generation; for the iniquity of the Amorites is not yet complete." (Gen. 15:12-16)

Psalm
Psalm 21
God comes with judgment and strength

Additional Reading
Matthew 12:33-37
A good tree bears good fruit

Hymn: Shine, Jesus, Shine, ELW 671

God who speaks from the darkness, you are full of promises that we don't fully understand. Help us to know that the terrifying darkness can contain great plans. Help us to trust that our enslavement will end.

Thursday, December 12, 2013

Week of Advent 2

Psalm 146:5-10
God lifts up those bowed down

Happy are those whose help is the God of Jacob,
    whose hope is in the LORD their God,
who made heaven and earth,
    the sea, and all that is in them;
who keeps faith forever;
    who executes justice for the oppressed;
    who gives food to the hungry.

The LORD sets the prisoners free;
    the LORD opens the eyes of the blind.
The LORD lifts up those who are bowed down;
    the LORD loves the righteous.
The LORD watches over the strangers;
    he upholds the orphan and the widow,
    but the way of the wicked he brings to ruin. (Ps. 146:5-9)

Additional Readings

Ruth 1:6-18
Ruth's fidelity toward Naomi and her people

2 Peter 3:1-10
The promise of the Lord's coming

Hymn: Praise the Almighty! ELW 877

Dear God, this Advent season is full of reminders of the vision that you have for your creation. Help us to stay faithful to your vision and to expand in justice and mercy. Watch us and lift us up.

Friday, December 13, 2013

Week of Advent 2

Lucy, martyr, died 304

2 Peter 3:11-18

Prepare for the Lord's coming

Therefore, beloved, while you are waiting for these things, strive to
be found by him at peace, without spot or blemish; and regard the
patience of our Lord as salvation. So also our beloved brother Paul
wrote to you according to the wisdom given him, speaking of this
as he does in all his letters. There are some things in them hard to
understand, which the ignorant and unstable twist to their own
destruction, as they do the other scriptures. You therefore, beloved,
since you are forewarned, beware that you are not carried away with
the error of the lawless and lose your own stability. But grow in the
grace and knowledge of our Lord and Savior Jesus Christ. To him be
the glory both now and to the day of eternity. Amen. (2 Peter 3:14-18)

Psalm
Psalm 146:5-10
God lifts up those bowed down

Additional Reading
Ruth 4:13-17
*God's fidelity toward Ruth and her
posterity*

Hymn: Take, Oh, Take Me As I Am, ELW 814

*O God, you know how hard it is to stay untwisted and how easy to
lose stability. We stand forewarned; help us to refrain from making
mistakes. Help us grow in grace and knowledge.*

Saturday, December 14, 2013

Week of Advent 2

John of the Cross, renewer of the church, died 1591

1 Samuel 2:1-8

Hannah sings in praise of God's fidelity

Hannah prayed and said,
"My heart exults in the LORD;
  my strength is exalted in my God.
My mouth derides my enemies,
  because I rejoice in my victory.

"There is no Holy One like the LORD,
  no one besides you;
  there is no Rock like our God.

"He raises up the poor from the dust;
  he lifts the needy from the ash heap,
to make them sit with princes
  and inherit a seat of honor.
For the pillars of the earth are the LORD's,
  and on them he has set the world." (1 Sam. 2:1-2, 8)

Psalm
Psalm 146:5-10
God lifts up those bowed down

Additional Reading
Luke 3:1-18
The proclamation of John the Baptist

Hymn: My Soul Now Magnifies the Lord, ELW 573

God, in this time of watchful waiting we often grow impatient in remaining steadfast to your eternal purposes for us. Help us to remember who created this world that we inhabit. Help our hearts to exult in you.

Lighting the Advent Wreath
Use this blessing when lighting three candles.

Blessed are you, O Lord our God, ruler of the universe.
Your prophets spoke of a day when the desert would blossom
and waters would break forth in the wilderness.
Bless us as we light the candles on this wreath.
Strengthen our hearts
as we prepare for the coming of the Lord.
May he give water to all who thirst,
for he is our light and our salvation.
Blessed be God forever.

Sunday, December 15, 2013

Third Sunday of Advent

Matthew 11:2-11
The forerunner of Christ

Jesus began to speak to the crowds about John: "What did you go out into the wilderness to look at? A reed shaken by the wind? What then did you go out to see? Someone dressed in soft robes? Look, those who wear soft robes are in royal palaces. What then did you go out to see? A prophet? Yes, I tell you, and more than a prophet. This is the one about whom it is written,

'See, I am sending my messenger ahead of you,
    who will prepare your way before you.'

Truly I tell you, among those born of women no one has arisen greater than John the Baptist; yet the least in the kingdom of heaven is greater than he." (Matt. 11:7-11)

Psalm

Psalm 146:5-10
God lifts up those bowed down

Additional Readings

Isaiah 35:1-10
The desert blooms

James 5:7-10
Patience until the Lord's coming

Hymn: Prepare the Royal Highway, ELW 264

Stir up the wills of all who look to you, Lord God, and strengthen our faith in your coming, that, transformed by grace, we may walk in your way; through Jesus Christ, our Savior and Lord, who lives and reigns with you and the Holy Spirit, one God, now and forever.

Monday, December 16, 2013

Week of Advent 3

Psalm 42
Hope in God

I say to God, my rock,
    "Why have you forgotten me?
Why must I walk about mournfully
    because the enemy oppresses me?"
As with a deadly wound in my body,
    my adversaries taunt me,
while they say to me continually,
    "Where is your God?"

Why are you cast down, O my soul,
    and why are you disquieted within me?
Hope in God; for I shall again praise him,
    my help and my God. (Ps. 42:9-11)

Additional Readings
Isaiah 29:17-24
The infirm will be healed

Acts 5:12-16
Many people healed by the apostles

Hymn: In Deepest Night, ELW 699

Redeemer God, during this season of growing darkness we often feel oppressed and disquieted. Help us to remember your covenant. We know where you are. Let us ignore the worldly taunts and wounds. Restore our waning hope.

Tuesday, December 17, 2013

Week of Advent 3

O Wisdom,
proceeding from the mouth of the Most High,
pervading and permeating all creation,
mightily ordering all things:
Come and teach us the way of prudence.

Jude 17-25
Prepare for the Lord's coming

But you, beloved, must remember the predictions of the apostles of
our Lord Jesus Christ; for they said to you, "In the last time there will
be scoffers, indulging their own ungodly lusts." It is these worldly
people, devoid of the Spirit, who are causing divisions. But you,
beloved, build yourselves up on your most holy faith; pray in the Holy
Spirit; keep yourselves in the love of God; look forward to the mercy
of our Lord Jesus Christ that leads to eternal life. (Jude 17-21)

Psalm	Additional Reading
Psalm 42	Ezekiel 47:1-12
Hope in God	*The wilderness will flower*

Hymn: Shall We Gather at the River, ELW 423

O God, we cannot know the time of our reunions with you. Keep us
mindful of what's important. Strengthen our faith. Remind us of your
mercy and love and hold us steadfast in it.

392

Wednesday, December 18, 2013

Week of Advent 3

O Adonai and ruler of the house of Israel,
who appeared to Moses in the burning bush
and gave him the Law on Sinai:
Come with an outstretched arm and redeem us.

Zechariah 8:1-17
God's promise to Zion

For thus says the Lord of hosts: Just as I purposed to bring disaster upon you, when your ancestors provoked me to wrath, and I did not relent, says the Lord of hosts, so again I have purposed in these days to do good to Jerusalem and to the house of Judah; do not be afraid. These are the things that you shall do: Speak the truth to one another, render in your gates judgments that are true and make for peace, do not devise evil in your hearts against one another, and love no false oath; for all these are things that I hate, says the Lord. (Zech. 8:14-17)

Psalm
Psalm 42
Hope in God

Additional Reading
Matthew 8:14-17, 28-34
Jesus heals

Hymn: Lo! He Comes with Clouds Descending, ELW 435

O God, you know how hard it can be to speak the truth and to keep our judgments pure. Give us the peace that calms our fear. Help us cultivate behaviors pleasing to you.

Thursday, December 19, 2013

Week of Advent 3

O Root of Jesse,
standing as an ensign before the peoples,
before whom all kings are mute,
to whom the nations will do homage:
Come quickly to deliver us.

Psalm 80:1-7, 17-19
Show the light of your countenance

O LORD God of hosts,
   how long will you be angry with your people's prayers?
You have fed them with the bread of tears,
   and given them tears to drink in full measure.
You make us the scorn of our neighbors;
   our enemies laugh among themselves.

Restore us, O God of hosts;
   let your face shine, that we may be saved. (Ps. 80:4-7)

Additional Readings
2 Samuel 7:1-17
God will build you a house

Galatians 3:23-29
Children of God by Christ's coming

Hymn: Gather Us In, ELW 532

God of restoration, take away our bread of tears and remind us of the
true, life-giving bread upon which we should feast. Restore and save us
so that we may be a light to all the nations.

Friday, December 20, 2013

Week of Advent 3

Katharina von Bora Luther, renewer of the church, died 1552

O Key of David and scepter of the house of Israel,
you open and no one can close,
you close and no one can open:
Come and rescue the prisoners
who are in darkness and the shadow of death.

2 Samuel 7:18-22

David prays for God's faithfulness toward Israel

Then King David went in and sat before the LORD, and said, "Who
am I, O Lord GOD, and what is my house, that you have brought
me thus far? And yet this was a small thing in your eyes, O Lord
GOD; you have spoken also of your servant's house for a great while
to come. May this be instruction for the people, O Lord GOD! And
what more can David say to you? For you know your servant, O Lord
GOD! Because of your promise, and according to your own heart,
you have wrought all this greatness, so that your servant may know
it. Therefore you are great, O LORD God; for there is no one like you,
and there is no God besides you, according to all that we have heard
with our ears." (2 Sam. 7:18-22)

Psalm
Psalm 80:1-7, 17-19
Show the light of your countenance

Additional Reading
Galatians 4:1-7
God's Son, sent in the fullness of time

Hymn: Blessed Be the God of Israel, ELW 250

Creator God, we sometimes mistake our own power as the greatest
ones. Remind us again of how great you are. Tell us again the good
news. Unstop our ears so that we may hear your promises again.

Saturday, December 21, 2013

Week of Advent 3

O Dayspring,
splendor of light everlasting:
Come and enlighten those who sit in darkness
and in the shadow of death.

John 3:31-36
The one who comes from above

The one who comes from above is above all; the one who is of the earth belongs to the earth and speaks about earthly things. The one who comes from heaven is above all. He testifies to what he has seen and heard, yet no one accepts his testimony. Whoever has accepted his testimony has certified this, that God is true. He whom God has sent speaks the words of God, for he gives the Spirit without measure. The Father loves the Son and has placed all things in his hands. Whoever believes in the Son has eternal life; whoever disobeys the Son will not see life, but must endure God's wrath. (John 3:31-36)

Psalm
Psalm 80:1-7, 17-19
Show the light of your countenance

Additional Reading
2 Samuel 7:23-29
David reminds God of God's promise

Hymn: O God of Mercy, God of Light, ELW 714

O God, help us to hear your testimony and to believe. Remind us to keep our eyes fixed on you and not on earthly things. Remind us whose we are. Give us all good things without measure.

Lighting the Advent Wreath
Use this blessing when lighting all four candles.

Blessed are you, O Lord our God, ruler of the universe.
In your Son, Emmanuel,
you have shown us your light
and saved us from the power of sin.
Bless us as we light the candles on this wreath.
Increase our longing for your presence,
that at the celebration of your Son's birth
his Spirit might dwell anew in our midst,
for he is our light and our salvation.
Blessed be God forever.

Sunday, December 22, 2013

Fourth Sunday of Advent

O King of the nations, the ruler they long for,
the cornerstone uniting all people:
Come and save us all,
whom you formed out of clay.

Matthew 1:18-25
Our God near at hand

An angel of the Lord appeared to [Joseph] in a dream and said, "Joseph, son of David, do not be afraid to take Mary as your wife, for the child conceived in her is from the Holy Spirit. She will bear a son, and you are to name him Jesus, for he will save his people from their sins." All this took place to fulfill what had been spoken by the Lord through the prophet:

"Look, the virgin shall conceive and bear a son,
    and they shall name him Emmanuel,"
which means, "God is with us." (Matt. 1:20-23)

Psalm
Psalm 80:1-7, 17-19
Show the light of your countenance

Additional Readings
Isaiah 7:10-16
The sign of Immanuel

Romans 1:1-7
Paul's greeting to the church at Rome

Hymn: O Come, O Come, Emmanuel, ELW 257

Stir up your power, Lord Christ, and come. With your abundant grace and might, free us from the sin that hinders our faith, that eagerly we may receive your promises, for you live and reign with the Father and the Holy Spirit, one God, now and forever.

Monday, December 23, 2013

Week of Advent 4

O Emmanuel, our king and our lawgiver,
the anointed of the nations and their Savior:
Come and save us, Lord our God.

Luke 1:46b-55
My soul gives glory to God

"My soul magnifies the Lord,
    and my spirit rejoices in God my Savior,
for he has looked with favor on the lowliness of his servant.
    Surely, from now on all generations will call me blessed;
for the Mighty One has done great things for me,
    and holy is his name." (Luke 1:46b-49)

Additional Readings
2 Samuel 7:18, 23-29
Your servant will be blessed

Galatians 3:6-14
The promise of the Spirit

Hymn: My Soul Proclaims Your Greatness, ELW 251

God of hope and promise, holy is your name. Surprise us with your
grace and fill us with pure joy that comes from your very being. Let the
ordinariness of life be filled with your extraordinary presence.

CHRISTMAS

Over the centuries, various customs have developed that focus the household on welcoming the light of Christ: the daily or weekly lighting of the Advent wreath, the blessing of the lighted Christmas tree, the candlelit procession of Las Posadas, the flickering lights of the luminaria, the Christ candle at Christmas.

The Christian household not only welcomes the light of Christ at Christmas, but celebrates the presence of that light throughout the Twelve Days, from Christmas until the Epiphany, January 6. In the Christmas season, Christians welcome the light of Christ that is already with us through faith. In word and gesture, prayer and song, in the many customs of diverse cultures, Christians celebrate this life-giving Word and ask that it dwell more deeply in the rhythm of daily life.

Table Prayer for the Twelve Days of Christmas

With joy and gladness we feast upon your love, O God.
You have come among us in Jesus, your Son,
and your presence now graces this table.
May Christ dwell in us that we might bear his love to all the world,
for he is Lord forever and ever. Amen.

Blessing of the Christmas Tree

Let the heavens rejoice, and let the earth be glad;
let the sea thunder and all that is in it;
let the field be joyful and all that is therein.
Then shall all the trees of the wood shout for joy
at your coming, O LORD,
for you come to judge the earth.
You will judge the world with righteousness
and the peoples with your truth. (Ps. 96:11-13)

Be praised, O God, for the blessings around us that point to you.
Be praised, O God, for the signs of this holy season
that awaken in us wonder.
Praise for the steadfast green of this tree,
like your love, enduring all seasons.
Praise for the light that illumines our darkness,
like Christ, who brings light to the world.
Join our voices with those of the tree and of all creation,
who sing at your coming:
Glory to God in the highest, and peace to God's people on earth.
Amen.

Blessing of the Nativity Scene

*This blessing may be used when figures are added to the nativity scene
throughout the days of Christmas.*

Bless us, O God, bless us who gather around this stable.
As we celebrate Christ's birth into the world,
may we receive the Christ child into our hearts
with gratitude and song. Amen.

Tuesday, December 24, 2013

Nativity of Our Lord
Christmas Eve

Luke 2:1-14 [15-20]
God with us

But the angel said to [the shepherds], "Do not be afraid; for see—I am bringing you good news of great joy for all the people: to you is born this day in the city of David a Savior, who is the Messiah, the Lord. This will be a sign for you: you will find a child wrapped in bands of cloth and lying in a manger." And suddenly there was with the angel a multitude of the heavenly host, praising God and saying,

"Glory to God in the highest heaven,
and on earth peace among those whom he favors!" (Luke 2:10-14)

Psalm
Psalm 96
Let the earth be glad

Additional Readings
Isaiah 9:2-7
A child is born for us

Titus 2:11-14
The grace of God has appeared

Hymn: Love Has Come, ELW 292

Almighty God, you made this holy night shine with the brightness of the true Light. Grant that here on earth we may walk in the light of Jesus' presence and in the last day wake to the brightness of his glory; through your Son, Jesus Christ our Lord, who lives and reigns with you and the Holy Spirit, one God, now and forever.

Wednesday, December 25, 2013

Nativity of Our Lord
Christmas Day

John 1:1-14
The Word became flesh

In the beginning was the Word, and the Word was with God, and the Word was God. He was in the beginning with God. All things came into being through him, and without him not one thing came into being. What has come into being in him was life, and the life was the light of all people. The light shines in the darkness, and the darkness did not overcome it.

And the Word became flesh and lived among us, and we have seen his glory, the glory as of a father's only son, full of grace and truth. (John 1:1-5, 14)

Psalm

Psalm 98
The victory of our God

Additional Readings

Isaiah 52:7-10
Heralds announce God's salvation

Hebrews 1:1-4 [5-12]
God has spoken by a son

Hymn: Of the Father's Love Begotten, ELW 295

Almighty God, you gave us your only Son to take on our human nature and to illumine the world with your light. By your grace adopt us as your children and enlighten us with your Spirit, through Jesus Christ, our Redeemer and Lord, who lives and reigns with you and the Holy Spirit, one God, now and forever.

Thursday, December 26, 2013

Stephen, Deacon and Martyr

Matthew 23:34-39

Jesus laments that Jerusalem kills her prophets

[Jesus said], "Therefore I send you prophets, sages, and scribes, some of whom you will kill and crucify, and some you will flog in your synagogues and pursue from town to town, so that upon you may come all the righteous blood shed on earth, from the blood of righteous Abel to the blood of Zechariah son of Barachiah, whom you murdered between the sanctuary and the altar. Truly I tell you, all this will come upon this generation.

"Jerusalem, Jerusalem, the city that kills the prophets and stones those who are sent to it! How often have I desired to gather your children together as a hen gathers her brood under her wings, and you were not willing! See, your house is left to you, desolate. For I tell you, you will not see me again until you say, 'Blessed is the one who comes in the name of the Lord.' " (Matt. 23:34-39)

Psalm	Additional Readings	
Psalm 17:1-9, 15	2 Chronicles 24:17-22	Acts 6:8—7:2a, 51-60
I call upon you, O God	*Zechariah is stoned to death*	*Stephen is stoned to death*

Hymn: What Child Is This, ELW 296

We give you thanks, O Lord of glory, for the example of Stephen, the first martyr, who looked to heaven and prayed for his persecutors. Grant that we also may pray for our enemies and seek forgiveness for those who hurt us, through Jesus Christ, our Savior and Lord, who lives and reigns with you and the Holy Spirit, one God, now and forever.

Friday, December 27, 2013

John, Apostle and Evangelist

John 21:20-25

The beloved disciple remains with Jesus

Peter turned and saw the disciple whom Jesus loved following them; he was the one who had reclined next to Jesus at the supper and had said, "Lord, who is it that is going to betray you?" When Peter saw him, he said to Jesus, "Lord, what about him?" Jesus said to him, "If it is my will that he remain until I come, what is that to you? Follow me!" So the rumor spread in the community that this disciple would not die. Yet Jesus did not say to him that he would not die, but, "If it is my will that he remain until I come, what is that to you?"

This is the disciple who is testifying to these things and has written them, and we know that his testimony is true. But there are also many other things that Jesus did; if every one of them were written down, I suppose that the world itself could not contain the books that would be written. (John 21:20-25)

Psalm
Psalm 116:12-19
The death of faithful servants

Additional Readings
Genesis 1:1-5, 26-31
Humankind is created by God

1 John 1:1—2:2
Jesus, the word of life

Hymn: Let Our Gladness Have No End, ELW 291

Merciful God, through John the apostle and evangelist you have revealed the mysteries of your Word made flesh. Let the brightness of your light shine on your church, so that all your people, instructed in the holy gospel, may walk in the light of your truth and attain eternal life, through Jesus Christ, our Savior and Lord, who lives and reigns with you and the Holy Spirit, one God, now and forever.

Saturday, December 28, 2013

The Holy Innocents, Martyrs

Jeremiah 31:15-17
Rachel weeps for her children

Thus says the LORD:
A voice is heard in Ramah,
    lamentation and bitter weeping.
Rachel is weeping for her children;
    she refuses to be comforted for her children,
    because they are no more.
Thus says the LORD:
Keep your voice from weeping,
    and your eyes from tears;
for there is a reward for your work,

says the LORD:

    they shall come back from the land of the enemy;
there is hope for your future,

says the LORD:

    your children shall come back to their own country. (Jer. 31:15-17)

Psalm	Additional Readings	
Psalm 124	1 Peter 4:12-19	Matthew 2:13-18
We have escaped like a bird	*Continue to do good while suffering*	*Herod kills innocent children*

Hymn: Lo, How a Rose E'er Blooming, ELW 272

We remember today, O God, the slaughter of the innocent children of Bethlehem by order of King Herod. Receive into the arms of your mercy all innocent victims. By your great might frustrate the designs of evil tyrants and establish your rule of justice, love, and peace, through Jesus Christ, our Savior and Lord, who lives and reigns with you and the Holy Spirit, one God, now and forever.

Sunday, December 29, 2013

First Sunday of Christmas

Matthew 2:13-23
The slaughter of innocent children

When Herod saw that he had been tricked by the wise men, he was infuriated, and he sent and killed all the children in and around Bethlehem who were two years old or under, according to the time that he had learned from the wise men. Then was fulfilled what had been spoken through the prophet Jeremiah:

"A voice was heard in Ramah,

wailing and loud lamentation,

Rachel weeping for her children;

she refused to be consoled, because they are no more."

(Matt. 2:16-18)

Psalm

Psalm 148
God's splendor is over earth and heaven

Additional Readings

Isaiah 63:7-9
Israel saved by God's own presence

Hebrews 2:10-18
Christ frees humankind

Hymn: Let All Together Praise Our God, ELW 287

O Lord God, you know that we cannot place our trust in our own powers. As you protected the infant Jesus, so defend us and all the needy from harm and adversity, through Jesus Christ, our Savior and Lord, who lives and reigns with you and the Holy Spirit, one God, now and forever.

Monday, December 30, 2013

Week of Christmas I

Psalm 20
Answer us when we call

The LORD answer you in the day of trouble!
  The name of the God of Jacob protect you!
May he send you help from the sanctuary,
  and give you support from Zion.
May he remember all your offerings,
  and regard with favor your burnt sacrifices.

May he grant you your heart's desire,
  and fulfill all your plans. (Ps. 20:1-4)

Additional Readings
Isaiah 26:1-9   2 Corinthians 4:16-18
Trust in God forever   *The temporary and the eternal*

Hymn: Good Christian Friends, Rejoice, ELW 288

God, in these days that may be fearful or troubling for people who are lonely, help us to see the light of your presence in all our journeys. You know our heart's truest desires. We find hope in your plans. Let us meet in the intersections.

Tuesday, December 31, 2013

Week of Christmas I

1 Kings 3:5-14

God grants a discerning mind

At Gibeon the LORD appeared to Solomon in a dream by night; and God said, "Ask what I should give you." And Solomon said, "You have shown great and steadfast love to your servant my father David, because he walked before you in faithfulness, in righteousness, and in uprightness of heart toward you; and you have kept for him this great and steadfast love, and have given him a son to sit on his throne today. And now, O LORD my God, you have made your servant king in place of my father David, although I am only a little child; I do not know how to go out or come in. And your servant is in the midst of the people whom you have chosen, a great people, so numerous they cannot be numbered or counted. Give your servant therefore an understanding mind to govern your people, able to discern between good and evil; for who can govern this your great people?" (1 Kings 3:5-9)

Psalm
Psalm 20
Answer us when we call

Additional Reading
John 8:12-19
I am the light

Hymn: Peace Came to Earth, ELW 285

Steadfast God, keep us secure on the paths we must travel. Help us to walk in faithfulness, righteousness, and uprightness. Give us the wisdom to discern between good and evil. Keep us anchored to you all of our days.

Lesser Festivals and Commemorations

January 1 – Name of Jesus Every Jewish boy was circumcised and formally named on the eighth day of his life. Already in his infancy, Jesus bore the mark of a covenant that he made new through the shedding of his blood on the cross.

January 2 – Johann Konrad Wilhelm Loehe Wilhelm Loehe was a pastor in nineteenth-century Germany. From the small town of Neuendettelsau he sent pastors to North America, Australia, New Guinea, Brazil, and the Ukraine.

January 15 – Martin Luther King Jr. Martin Luther King Jr. is remembered as an American prophet of justice among races and nations. Many churches hold commemorations near Dr. King's birth date of January 15, in conjunction with the American civil holiday honoring him.

January 17 – Antony of Egypt Antony was one of the earliest Egyptian desert fathers. He became the head of a group of monks that lived in a cluster of huts and devoted themselves to communal prayer, worship, and manual labor.

January 17 – Pachomius Another of the desert fathers, Pachomius was born in Egypt about 290. He organized hermits into a religious community in which the members prayed together and held their goods in common.

January 18 – Confession of Peter; Beginning of the Week of Prayer for Christian Unity The Week of Prayer for Christian Unity is framed by two commemorations, the Confession of Peter and the Conversion of Paul. On this day the church remembers that Peter was led by God's grace to acknowledge Jesus as "the Christ, the Son of the living God" (Matt. 16:16).

January 19 – Henry When Erik, king of Sweden, determined to invade Finland for the purpose of converting the people there to Christianity, Henry went with him. Henry is recognized as the patron saint of Finland.

January 21 – Agnes Agnes was a girl of about thirteen living in Rome, who had chosen a life of service to Christ as a virgin, despite the Roman emperor Diocletian's ruling that had outlawed all Christian activity. She gave witness to her faith and was put to death as a result.

January 25 – Conversion of Paul; End of the Week of Prayer for Christian Unity As the Week of Prayer for Christian Unity comes to an end, the church remembers how a man of Tarsus named Saul, a former persecutor of the early Christian church, was led to become one of its chief preachers.

January 26 – Timothy, Titus, Silas On the two days following the celebration of the Conversion of Paul, his companions are remembered. Timothy, Titus, and Silas were missionary coworkers with Paul.

January 27 – Lydia, Dorcas, Phoebe On this day the church remembers three women who were companions in Paul's ministry.

January 28 – Thomas Aquinas Thomas Aquinas was a brilliant and creative theologian who immersed himself in the thought of Aristotle and worked to explain Christian beliefs in the philosophical culture of the day.

February 2 – Presentation of Our Lord Forty days after the birth of Christ, the church marks the day Mary and Joseph presented him in the temple in accordance with Jewish law. Simeon greeted Mary and Joseph, responding with the canticle that begins "Now, Lord, you let your servant go in peace."

February 3 – Ansgar Ansgar was a monk who led a mission to Denmark and later to Sweden. His work ran into difficulties with the rulers of the day, and he was forced to withdraw into Germany, where he served as a bishop in Hamburg.

February 5 – The Martyrs of Japan In the sixteenth century, Jesuit missionaries, followed by Franciscans, introduced the Christian faith in Japan. By 1630, Christianity was driven underground. This day commemorates the first martyrs of Japan, twenty-six missionaries and converts, who were killed by crucifixion.

February 14 – Cyril, Methodius These brothers from a noble family in Thessalonika in northeastern Greece were priests who are regarded as the founders of Slavic literature. Their work in preaching and worshiping in the language of the people is honored by Christians in both East and West.

February 18 – Martin Luther On this day, Luther died at the age of sixty-two. For a time, he was an Augustinian monk, but it is primarily for his work as a biblical scholar, translator of the Bible, reformer of the liturgy, theologian, educator, and father of German vernacular literature that he is remembered.

February 23 – Polycarp Polycarp was bishop of Smyrna and a link between the apostolic age and the church at the end of the second century. At the age of eighty-six, he was martyred for his faith.

February 25 – Elizabeth Fedde Fedde was born in Norway and trained as a deaconess. Among her notable achievements is the establishment of the Deaconess House in Brooklyn and the Deaconess House and Hospital of the Lutheran Free Church in Minneapolis.

March 1 – George Herbert Herbert was ordained a priest in 1630 and served the little parish of St. Andrew Bremerton until his death. He is best remembered, however, as a writer of poems and hymns such as "Come, My Way, My Truth, My Life" and "The King of Love My Shepherd Is."

March 2 – John Wesley, Charles Wesley The Wesleys were leaders of a revival in the Church of England. Their spiritual methods of frequent communion, fasting, and advocacy for the poor earned them the name "Methodists."

March 7 – Perpetua, Felicity In the year 202 the emperor Septimius Severus forbade conversions to Christianity. Perpetua, a noblewoman; Felicity, a slave; and other companions were all catechumens at Carthage

in North Africa, where they were imprisoned and sentenced to death.

March 10 – Harriet Tubman, Sojourner Truth Harriet Tubman helped about three hundred slaves to escape via the Underground Railroad until slavery was abolished in the United States. After slavery was abolished in New York in 1827, Sojourner Truth became deeply involved in Christianity, and in later life she was a popular speaker against slavery and for women's rights.

March 12 – Gregory the Great Gregory held political office and at another time lived as a monk, all before he was elected to the papacy. He also established a school to train church musicians; thus Gregorian chant is named in his honor.

March 17 – Patrick Patrick went to Ireland from Britain to serve as a bishop and missionary. He made his base in the north of Ireland and from there made many missionary journeys, with much success.

March 19 – Joseph The Gospel of Luke shows Joseph acting in accordance with both civil and religious law by returning to Bethlehem for the census and by presenting the child Jesus in the temple on the fortieth day after his birth.

March 21 – Thomas Cranmer Cranmer's lasting achievement is contributing to and overseeing the creation of the Book of Common Prayer, which remains (in revised form) the worship book of the Anglican Communion. He was burned at the stake under Queen Mary for his support of the Protestant Reformation.

March 22 – Jonathan Edwards Edwards was a minister in Connecticut and has been described as the greatest of the New England Puritan preachers. Edwards carried out mission work among the Housatonic Indians of Massachusetts and became president of the College of New Jersey, later to be known as Princeton University.

March 24 – Oscar Arnulfo Romero Romero is remembered for his advocacy on behalf of the poor in El Salvador, though it was not a characteristic of his early priesthood. After several years of threats to his life, Romero was assassinated while presiding at the eucharist.

March 25 – Annunciation of Our Lord Nine months before Christmas the church celebrates the annunciation. In Luke the angel

Gabriel announces to Mary that she will give birth to the Son of God, and she responds, "Here am I, the servant of the Lord."

March 29 – Hans Nielsen Hauge Hans Nielsen Hauge was a layperson who began preaching in Norway and Denmark after a mystical experience that he believed called him to share the assurance of salvation with others. At the time itinerant preaching and religious gatherings held without the supervision of a pastor were illegal, and Hauge was arrested several times.

March 31 – John Donne This priest of the Church of England is commemorated for his poetry and spiritual writing. Most of his poetry was written before his ordination and is sacred and secular, intellectual and sensuous.

April 4 – Benedict the African Although Benedict was illiterate, his fame as a confessor brought many visitors to him, and he was eventually named superior of a Franciscan community. A patron saint of African Americans, Benedict is remembered for his patience and understanding when confronted with racial prejudice and taunts.

April 6 – Albrecht Dürer, Matthias Grünewald, Lucas Cranach These great artists revealed through their work the mystery of salvation and the wonder of creation. Though Dürer remained a Roman Catholic, at his death Martin Luther wrote to a friend, "Affection bids us mourn for one who was the best." Several religious works are included in Grünwald's small surviving corpus, the most famous being the Isenheim Altarpiece. Lucas Cranach was widely known for his woodcuts, some of which illustrated the first German printing of the New Testament.

April 9 – Dietrich Bonhoeffer In 1933, and with Hitler's rise to power, Bonhoeffer became a leading spokesman for the Confessing Church, a resistance movement against the Nazis. After leading a worship service on April 8, 1945, at Schönberg prison, he was taken away to be hanged the next day.

April 10 – Mikael Agricola Agricola began a reform of the Finnish church along Lutheran lines. He translated the New Testament, the prayer book, hymns, and the mass into Finnish and through this work set the rules of orthography that are the basis of modern Finnish spelling.

April 19 – Olavus Petri, Laurentius Petri These two brothers are commemorated for their introduction of the Lutheran movement to the Church of Sweden after studying at the University of Wittenberg. Together the brothers published a complete Bible in Swedish and a revised liturgy in 1541.

April 21 – Anselm This eleventh-century Benedictine monk stands out as one of the greatest theologians between Augustine and Thomas Aquinas. He is perhaps best known for his "satisfaction" theory of atonement, where God takes on human nature in Jesus Christ in order to make the perfect payment for sin.

April 23 – Toyohiko Kagawa Toyohiko Kagawa's vocation to help the poor led him to live among them. He was arrested for his efforts to reconcile Japan and China after the Japanese attack of 1940.

April 25 – Mark Though Mark himself was not an apostle, it is likely that he was a member of one of the early Christian communities. The Gospel attributed to him is brief and direct and is considered by many to be the earliest Gospel.

April 29 – Catherine of Siena Catherine of Siena was a member of the Order of Preachers (Dominicans), and among Roman Catholics she was the first woman to receive the title Doctor of the Church. She also advised popes and any uncertain persons who told her their problems.

May 1 – Philip, James Philip and James are commemorated together because the remains of these two saints were placed in the Church of the Apostles in Rome on this day in 561.

May 2 – Athanasius At the Council of Nicea in 325 and when he himself served as bishop of Alexandria, Athanasius defended the full divinity of Christ against the Arian position held by emperors, magistrates, and theologians.

May 4 – Monica Almost everything known about Monica comes from Augustine's *Confessions*, his autobiography. Her dying wish was that her son remember her at the altar of the Lord, wherever he was.

May 8 – Julian of Norwich Julian was most likely a Benedictine nun living in an isolated cell attached to the Carrow Priory in Norwich, England. When she was about thirty years old, she reported visions that she later compiled into a book, *Sixteen Revelations of Divine Love*, which is a classic of medieval mysticism.

May 9 – Nicolaus Ludwig von Zinzendorf Drawn from an overly intellectual Lutheran faith to Pietism, at the age of twenty-two, Count Zinzendorf permitted a group of Moravians to live on his lands. Zinzendorf participated in worldwide missions emanating from this community and is also remembered for writing hymns characteristic of his Pietistic faith.

May 14 – Matthias After Christ's ascension, the apostles met in Jerusalem to choose a replacement for Judas. Though little is known about him, Matthias had traveled among the disciples from the time of Jesus' baptism until his ascension.

May 18 – Erik Erik, long considered the patron saint of Sweden, ruled there from 1150 to 1160. He is honored for efforts to bring peace to the nearby pagan kingdoms and for his crusades to spread the Christian faith in Scandinavia.

May 21 – Helena Helena was the mother of Constantine, a man who later became the Roman emperor. Helena is remembered for traveling through Palestine and building churches on the sites she believed to be where Jesus was born, where he was buried, and from which he ascended.

May 24 – Nicolaus Copernicus, Leonhard Euler Copernicus formally studied astronomy, mathematics, Greek, Plato, law, medicine, and canon law and is chiefly remembered for his work as an astronomer and his idea that the sun, not the earth, is the center of the solar system. Euler is regarded as one of the founders of the science of pure mathematics and made important contributions to mechanics, hydrodynamics, astronomy, optics, and acoustics.

May 27 – John Calvin Having embraced the views of the Reformation by his mid-twenties, John Calvin was a preacher in Geneva, was banished once, and later returned to reform the city with a rigid, theocratic discipline. Calvin is considered the father of the Reformed churches.

May 29 – Jiří Tranovský Jiří Tranovský is considered the "Luther of the Slavs" and the father of Slovak hymnody. He produced a translation of the Augsburg Confession and published his hymn collection *Cithara Sanctorum* (Lyre of the Saints), also known as the Tranoscius, which is the foundation of Slovak Lutheran hymnody.

May 31 – Visit of Mary to Elizabeth Sometime after the annunciation, Mary visited her cousin Elizabeth, who greeted Mary with the words, "Blessed are you among women," and Mary responded with her famous song, the Magnificat.

June 1 – Justin Justin was a teacher of philosophy and engaged in debates about the truth of Christian faith. Having been arrested and jailed for practicing an unauthorized religion, he refused to renounce his faith, and he and six of his students were beheaded.

June 3 – The Martyrs of Uganda King Mwanga of Uganda was angered by Christian members of the court whose first allegiance was not to him but to Christ. On this date in 1886, thirty-two young men were burned to death for refusing to renounce Christianity. Their persecution led to a much stronger Christian presence in the country.

June 3 – John XXIII Despite the expectation upon his election that the seventy-seven-year old John XXIII would be a transitional pope, he had great energy and spirit. He convened the Second Vatican Council in order to open the windows of the church. The council brought about great changes in Roman Catholic worship and ecumenical relationships.

June 5 – Boniface Boniface led large numbers of Benedictine monks and nuns in establishing churches, schools, and seminaries. Boniface was preparing a group for confirmation on the eve of Pentecost when he and others were killed by a band of pagans.

June 7 – Seattle The city of Seattle was named after Noah Seattle against his wishes. After Chief Seattle became a Roman Catholic, he began the practice of morning and evening prayer in the tribe, a practice that continued after his death.

June 9 – Columba, Aidan, Bede These three monks from the British Isles were pillars among those who kept alive the light of learning and devotion during the Middle Ages. Columba founded three monasteries, including one on the island of Iona, off the coast of Scotland. Aidan, who helped bring Christianity to the Northumbria area of England, was known for his pastoral style and ability to stir people to charity and good works. Bede was a Bible translator and scripture scholar who wrote a history of the English church and was the first historian to date events *anno Domini* (A.D.), the "year of our Lord."

413

June 11 – Barnabas Though he was not among the Twelve mentioned in the Gospels, the book of Acts gives Barnabas the title of apostle. When Paul came to Jerusalem after his conversion, Barnabas took him in over the fears of the other apostles who doubted Paul's discipleship.

June 14 – Basil the Great, Gregory of Nyssa, Gregory of Nazianzus, Macrina The three men in this group are known as the Cappadocian fathers; all three explored the mystery of the Holy Trinity. Basil's Longer Rule and Shorter Rule for monastic life are the basis for Eastern monasticism to this day, and express a preference for communal monastic life over that of hermits. Gregory of Nazianzus defended Orthodox trinitarian and christological doctrine, and his preaching won over the city of Constantinople. Gregory of Nyssa is remembered as a writer on spiritual life and the contemplation of God in worship and sacraments. Macrina was the older sister of Basil and Gregory of Nyssa, and her teaching was influential within the early church.

June 21 – Onesimos Nesib Onesimos, an Ethiopian, was captured by slave traders and taken from his homeland to Eritrea, where he was bought, freed, and educated by Swedish missionaries. He translated the Bible into Oromo and returned to his homeland to preach the gospel there.

June 24 – John the Baptist The birth of John the Baptist is celebrated exactly six months before Christmas Eve. For Christians in the Northern Hemisphere, these two dates are deeply symbolic, since John said that he must decrease as Jesus increased. John was born as the days are longest and then steadily decrease, while Jesus was born as the days are shortest and then steadily increase.

June 25 – Presentation of the Augsburg Confession On this day in 1530 the German and Latin editions of the Augsburg Confession were presented to Emperor Charles of the Holy Roman Empire. The Augsburg Confession was written by Philipp Melanchthon and endorsed by Martin Luther and consists of a brief summary of points in which the reformers saw their teaching as either agreeing with or differing from that of the Roman Catholic Church of the time.

June 25 – Philipp Melanchthon Though he died on April 19, Philipp Melanchthon is commemorated today because of his connection with the Augsburg Confession.

Colleague and coreformer with Martin Luther, Melanchthon was a brilliant scholar, known as "the teacher of Germany."

June 27 – Cyril Remembered as an outstanding theologian, Cyril defended the orthodox teachings about the person of Christ against Nestorius, who was at that time bishop of Constantinople. Eventually it was decided that Cyril's interpretation, that Christ's person included both divine and human natures, was correct.

June 28 – Irenaeus Irenaeus believed that only Matthew, Mark, Luke, and John were trustworthy Gospels. As a result of his battles with the Gnostics, he was one of the first to speak of the church as "catholic," meaning that congregations did not exist by themselves, but were linked to one another throughout the whole church.

June 29 – Peter, Paul One of the things that unites Peter and Paul is the tradition that says they were martyred together on this date in A.D. 67 or 68. What unites them even more closely is their common confession of Jesus Christ.

July 1 – Catherine Winkworth, John Mason Neale Many of the most beloved hymns in the English language are the work of these gifted poets. Catherine Winkworth devoted herself to the translation of German hymns into English, while John Mason Neale specialized in translating many ancient Latin and Greek hymns.

July 3 – Thomas Alongside the doubt for which Thomas is famous, the Gospel according to John shows Thomas moving from doubt to deep faith. Thomas makes one of the strongest confessions of faith in the New Testament, "My Lord and my God!" (John 20:28).

July 6 – Jan Hus Jan Hus was a Bohemian priest who spoke against abuses in the church of his day in many of the same ways Luther would a century later. The followers of Jan Hus became known as the Czech Brethren and later became the Moravian Church.

July 11 – Benedict of Nursia Benedict is known as the father of Western monasticism. Benedict encourages a generous spirit of hospitality. Visitors to Benedictine communities are to be welcomed as Christ himself.

July 12 – Nathan Söderblom In 1930 this Swedish theologian, ecumenist, and social activist received the Nobel Prize for peace.

Söderblom organized the Universal Christian Council on Life and Work, which was one of the organizations that in 1948 came together to form the World Council of Churches.

July 17 – Bartolomé de Las Casas Bartolomé de Las Casas was a Spanish priest and a missionary in the Western Hemisphere. Throughout the Caribbean and Central America, he worked to stop the enslavement of native people, to halt the brutal treatment of women by military forces, and to promote laws that humanized the process of colonization.

July 22 – Mary Magdalene The Gospels report Mary Magdalene was one of the women of Galilee who followed Jesus. As the first person to whom the risen Lord appeared, she returned to the disciples with the news and has been called "the apostle to the apostles" for her proclamation of the resurrection.

July 23 – Birgitta of Sweden Birgitta's devotional commitments led her to give to the poor and needy all that she owned while she began to live a more ascetic life. She founded an order of monks and nuns, the Order of the Holy Savior (Birgittines), whose superior was a woman.

July 25 – James James was one of the sons of Zebedee and is counted as one of the twelve disciples. James was the first of the Twelve to suffer martyrdom and is the only apostle whose martyrdom is recorded in scripture.

July 28 – Johann Sebastian Bach, Heinrich Schütz, George Frederick Handel These three composers did much to enrich the worship life of the church. Johann Sebastian Bach drew on the Lutheran tradition of hymnody and wrote about two hundred cantatas, including at least two for each Sunday and festival day in the Lutheran calendar of his day. George Frederick Handel was not primarily a church musician, but his great work *Messiah* is a musical proclamation of the scriptures. Heinrich Schütz wrote choral settings of biblical texts and paid special attention to ways his composition would underscore the meaning of the words.

July 29 – Mary, Martha, Lazarus of Bethany Mary and Martha are remembered for the hospitality and refreshment they offered Jesus in their home. Following the characterization drawn by Luke, Martha represents the active life, and Mary, the contemplative.

July 29 – Olaf Olaf is considered the patron saint of Norway. While at war in the Baltic and in Normandy, he became a Christian; then

he returned to Norway and declared himself king, and from then on Christianity was the dominant religion of the realm.

August 8 – Dominic Dominic believed that a stumbling block to restoring heretics to the church was the wealth of clergy, so he formed an itinerant religious order, the Order of Preachers (Dominicans), who lived in poverty, studied philosophy and theology, and preached against heresy.

August 10 – Lawrence Lawrence was one of seven deacons of the congregation at Rome and, like the deacons appointed in Acts, was responsible for financial matters in the church and for the care of the poor.

August 11 – Clare At age eighteen, Clare of Assisi heard Francis preach a sermon. With Francis's help she and a growing number of companions established a women's Franciscan community called the Order of Poor Ladies, or Poor Clares.

August 13 – Florence Nightingale, Clara Maass Nightingale led a group of thirty-eight nurses to serve in the Crimean War, where they worked in appalling conditions. She returned to London as a hero and there resumed her work for hospital reform. Clara Maass was born in New Jersey and served as a nurse in the Spanish-American War, where she encountered the horrors of yellow fever. Later responding to a call for subjects in research on yellow fever, Maass contracted the disease and died.

August 14 – Maximilian Kolbe, Kaj Munk Confined in Auschwitz, Father Kolbe was a Franciscan priest who gave generously of his meager resources and finally volunteered to be starved to death in place of another man who was a husband and father. Kaj Munk, a Danish Lutheran pastor and playwright, was an outspoken critic of the Nazis. His plays frequently highlighted the eventual victory of the Christian faith despite the church's weak and ineffective witness.

August 15 – Mary, Mother of Our Lord The honor paid to Mary as mother of our Lord goes back to biblical times, when Mary herself sang "From now on all generations will call me blessed" (Luke 1:48). Mary's song speaks of reversals in the reign of God: the mighty are cast down, the lowly are lifted up, the hungry are fed, and the rich are sent away empty-handed.

August 20 – Bernard of Clairvaux Bernard was a Cistercian monk who became an abbot of great spiritual depth. Through

415

translation his several devotional writings and hymns are still read and sung today.

August 24 – Bartholomew Bartholomew is mentioned as one of Jesus' disciples in Matthew, Mark, and Luke. Except for his name on these lists of the Twelve, little is known.

August 28 – Augustine As an adult Augustine came to see Christianity as a religion appropriate for a philosopher. Augustine was baptized by Ambrose at the Easter Vigil in 387, was made bishop of Hippo in 396, and was one of the greatest theologians of the Western church.

August 28 – Moses the Black A man of great strength and rough character, Moses the Black was converted to Christian faith toward the close of the fourth century. The change in his heart and life had a profound impact on his native Ethiopia.

September 2 – Nikolai Frederik Severin Grundtvig Grundtvig was a prominent Danish theologian of the nineteenth century. From his university days he was convinced that poetry spoke to the human spirit better than prose, and he wrote more than a thousand hymns.

September 9 – Peter Claver Peter Claver was born into Spanish nobility and was persuaded to become a Jesuit missionary. He served in Cartagena (in what is now Colombia) by teaching and caring for the slaves.

September 13 – John Chrysostom John was a priest in Antioch and an outstanding preacher. His eloquence earned him the nickname "Chrysostom" ("golden mouth"), but he also preached against corruption among the royal court, whereupon the empress sent him into exile.

September 14 – Holy Cross Day The celebration of Holy Cross Day commemorates the dedication of the Church of the Resurrection in 335 on the location believed to have been where Christ was buried.

September 16 – Cyprian During Cyprian's time as bishop, many people had denied the faith under duress. In contrast to some who held the belief that the church should not receive these people back, Cyprian believed they ought to be welcomed into full communion after a period of penance.

September 17 – Hildegard of Bingen Hildegard lived virtually her entire life in convents yet was widely influential. She advised and reproved kings and popes, wrote poems and hymns, and produced treatises in medicine, theology, and natural history.

September 18 – Dag Hammarskjöld Dag Hammarskjöld was a Swedish diplomat and humanitarian who served as secretary general of the United Nations. The depth of Hammarskjöld's Christian faith was unknown until his private journal, *Markings*, was published following his death.

September 21 – Matthew Matthew was a tax collector, an occupation that was distrusted, since tax collectors were frequently dishonest and worked as agents for the Roman occupying government; yet it was these outcasts to whom Jesus showed his love. Since the second century, tradition has attributed the First Gospel to him.

September 29 – Michael and All Angels The scriptures speak of angels who worship God in heaven, and in both testaments angels are God's messengers on earth. Michael is an angel whose name appears in Daniel as the heavenly being who leads the faithful dead to God's throne on the day of resurrection, while in the book of Revelation, Michael fights in a cosmic battle against Satan.

September 30 – Jerome Jerome translated the scriptures into the Latin that was spoken and written by the majority of people in his day. His translation is known as the Vulgate, which comes from the Latin word for "common."

October 4 – Francis of Assisi Francis renounced wealth and future inheritance and devoted himself to serving the poor. Since Francis had a spirit of gratitude for all of God's creation, this commemoration has been a traditional time to bless pets and animals, creatures Francis called his brothers and sisters.

October 4 – Theodor Fliedner Fliedner's work was instrumental in the revival of the ministry of deaconesses among Lutherans. Fliedner's deaconess motherhouse in Kaiserswerth, Germany, inspired Lutherans all over the world to commission deaconesses to serve in parishes, schools, prisons, and hospitals.

October 6 – William Tyndale Tyndale's plan to translate the scriptures into English met opposition from Henry VIII. Though Tyndale completed work on the New Testament in 1525 and worked on a portion of the Old Testament, he was tried for heresy and burned at the stake.

October 7 – Henry Melchior Muhlenberg Muhlenberg was prominent in setting the course for Lutheranism in the United States by helping Lutheran churches make the transition from the state churches of Europe to independent churches of America. Among other things, he established the first Lutheran synod in America and developed an American Lutheran liturgy.

October 15 – Teresa of Ávila Teresa of Ávila (also known as Teresa de Jesús) chose the life of a Carmelite nun after reading the letters of Jerome. Teresa's writings on devotional life are widely read by members of various denominations.

October 17 – Ignatius Ignatius was the second bishop of Antioch in Syria. When his own martyrdom approached, he wrote in one of his letters, "I prefer death in Christ Jesus to power over the farthest limits of the earth. . . . Do not stand in the way of my birth to real life."

October 18 – Luke Luke, as author of both Luke and Acts, was careful to place the events of Jesus' life in both their social and religious contexts. Some of the most loved parables and canticles are found only in this Gospel.

October 23 – James of Jerusalem James is described in the New Testament as the brother of Jesus, and the secular historian Josephus called James the brother of Jesus, "the so-called Christ." Little is known about James, but Josephus reported that the Pharisees respected James for his piety and observance of the law.

October 26 – Philipp Nicolai, Johann Heermann, Paul Gerhardt These three outstanding hymnwriters all worked in Germany in the seventeenth century during times of war and plague. Philipp Nicolai's hymns "Wake, Awake, for Night Is Flying" and "O Morning Star, How Fair and Bright!" were included in a series of meditations he wrote to comfort his parishioners during the plague. The style of Johann Heermann's hymns (including "Ah, Holy Jesus") moved away from the more objective style of Reformation hymnody toward expressing the emotions of faith. Paul Gerhardt, whom some have called the greatest of Lutheran hymnwriters, lost a preaching position at St. Nicholas's Church in Berlin because he refused to sign a document stating he would not make theological arguments in his sermons.

October 28 – Simon, Jude Little is known about Simon and Jude. In New Testament lists of the apostles, Simon the "zealot" or Cananaean is mentioned, but he is never mentioned apart from these lists. Jude, sometimes called Thaddeus, is also mentioned in lists of the Twelve.

October 31 – Reformation Day By the end of the seventeenth century, many Lutheran churches celebrated a festival commemorating Martin Luther's posting of the Ninety-five Theses, a summary of abuses in the church of his time. At the heart of the reform movement was the gospel, the good news that it is by grace through faith that we are justified and set free.

November 1 – All Saints Day The custom of commemorating all of the saints of the church on a single day goes back at least to the third century. All Saints Day celebrates the baptized people of God, living and dead, who make up the body of Christ.

November 3 – Martín de Porres Martín was a lay brother in the Order of Preachers (Dominicans) and engaged in many charitable works. He is recognized as an advocate for Christian charity and interracial justice.

November 7 – John Christian Frederick Heyer, Bartholomaeus Ziegenbalg, Ludwig Nommensen Heyer was the first missionary sent out by American Lutherans, and he became a missionary in the Andhra region of India. Ziegenbalg was a missionary to the Tamils of Tranquebar on the southeast coast of India. Nommensen worked among the Batak people, who had previously not seen Christian missionaries.

November 11 – Martin of Tours In 371 Martin was elected bishop of Tours. As bishop he developed a reputation for intervening on behalf of prisoners and heretics who had been sentenced to death.

November 11 – Søren Aabye Kierkegaard Kierkegaard, a nineteenth-century Danish theologian whose writings reflect his Lutheran heritage, was the founder of modern existentialism. Kierkegaard's work attacked the established church of his day—its complacency, its tendency to intellectualize faith, and its desire to be accepted by polite society.

November 17 – Elizabeth of Hungary This Hungarian princess gave away large sums of money, including her dowry, for relief of the poor and sick. She founded hospitals, cared for

392 orphans, and used the royal food supplies to feed the hungry.

November 23 – Clement Clement is best remembered for a letter he wrote to the Corinthian congregation still having difficulty with divisions in spite of Paul's canonical letters. Clement's letter is also a witness to early understandings of church government and the way each office in the church works for the good of the whole.

November 23 – Miguel Agustín Pro Miguel Agustín Pro grew up among oppression in Mexico and worked on behalf of the poor and homeless. Miguel and his two brothers were arrested, falsely accused of throwing a bomb at the car of a government official, and executed by a firing squad.

November 24 – Justus Falckner, Jehu Jones, William Passavant Not only was Falckner the first Lutheran pastor to be ordained in North America, but he published a catechism that was the first Lutheran book published on the continent. Jones was the Lutheran Church's first African American pastor and carried out missionary work in Philadelphia, which led to the formation there of the first African American Lutheran congregation (St. Paul's). William Passavant helped to establish hospitals and orphanages in a number of cities and was the first to introduce deaconesses to the work of hospitals in the United States.

November 25 – Isaac Watts Watts wrote about six hundred hymns, many of them in a two-year period beginning when he was twenty years old. When criticized for writing hymns not taken from scripture, he responded that if we can pray prayers that are not from scripture but written by us, then surely we can sing hymns that we have made up ourselves.

November 30 – Andrew Andrew was the first of the Twelve. As a part of his calling, he brought other people, including Simon Peter, to meet Jesus.

December 3 – Francis Xavier Francis Xavier became a missionary to India, Southeast Asia, Japan, and the Philippines. Together with Ignatius Loyola and five others, Francis formed the Society of Jesus (Jesuits).

December 4 – John of Damascus John left a career in finance and government to become a monk in an abbey near Jerusalem. He wrote many hymns as well as theological works, including *The Fount of Wisdom*, a work

that touches on philosophy, heresy, and the orthodox faith.

December 6 – Nicholas Nicholas was a bishop in what is now Turkey. Legends that surround Nicholas tell of his love for God and neighbor, especially the poor.

December 7 – Ambrose Ambrose was baptized, ordained, and consecrated a bishop all on the same day. While bishop he gave away his wealth and lived in simplicity.

December 13 – Lucy Lucy was a young Christian of Sicily who was martyred during the persecutions under Emperor Diocletian. Her celebration became particularly important in Sweden and Norway, perhaps because the feast of Lucia (whose name means "light") originally fell on the shortest day of the year.

December 14 – John of the Cross John was a monk of the Carmelite religious order who met Teresa of Ávila when she was working to reform the Carmelite Order and return it to a stricter observance of its rules. His writings, like Teresa's, reflect a deep interest in mystical thought and meditation.

December 20 – Katharina von Bora Luther Katharina took vows as a nun, but around age twenty-four she and several other nuns who were influenced by the writings of Martin Luther left the convent. When she later became Luther's wife, she proved herself a gifted household manager and became a trusted partner.

December 26 – Stephen Stephen, a deacon and the first martyr of the church, was one of those seven upon whom the apostles laid hands after they had been chosen to serve widows and others in need. Later, Stephen's preaching angered the temple authorities, and they ordered him to be put to death by stoning.

December 27 – John John, the son of Zebedee, was a fisherman and one of the Twelve. Tradition has attributed authorship of the Gospel and the three epistles bearing his name to the apostle John.

December 28 – The Holy Innocents The infant martyrs commemorated on this day were the children of Bethlehem, two years old and younger, who were killed by Herod, who worried that his reign was threatened by the birth of a new king named Jesus.

Anniversary of Baptism (abbreviated)

This order is intended for use in the home. It may be adapted for use in another context, such as a Christian education setting. When used in the home, a parent or sponsor may be the leader. A more expanded version of this order appears in Evangelical Lutheran Worship Pastoral Care *(pp. 128–135).*

A bowl of water may be placed in the midst of those who are present.

GATHERING

A baptismal hymn or acclamation (see Evangelical Lutheran Worship *#209– 217, 442–459) may be sung.*

The sign of the cross may be made by all in remembrance of their baptism as the leader begins.

In the name of the Father, and of the + Son, and of the Holy Spirit.
Amen.

The candle received at baptism or another candle may be used. As it is lighted, the leader may say:

Jesus said, I am the light of the world.
Whoever follows me will have the light of life.

READING

One or more scripture readings follow. Those present may share in reading.

A reading from Mark: People were bringing little children to Jesus in order that he might touch them; and the disciples spoke sternly to them. But when Jesus saw this, he was indignant and said, "Let the little children come to me; do not stop them; for it is to such as these that the kingdom of God belongs." And he took them up in his arms, laid his hands on them, and blessed them. *(Mark 10:13-14, 16)*

A reading from Second Corinthians: If anyone is in Christ, there is a new creation: everything old has passed away; see, everything has become new! *(2 Corinthians 5:17)*

A reading from First John: Beloved, let us love one another, because love is from God; everyone who loves is born of God and knows God. *(1 John 4:7)*

*Those present may share experiences related to baptism and their lives as baptized children of God. A portion of the Small Catechism (*Evangelical Lutheran Worship, *pp. 1160–1167) may be read as part of this conversation.*

A baptismal hymn or acclamation may be sung.

BAPTISMAL REMEMBRANCE
A parent or sponsor may trace a cross on the forehead of the person celebrating a baptismal anniversary. Water from a bowl placed in the midst of those present may be used. These or similar words may be said.

Name, when you were baptized, you were marked with the cross of Christ forever.
Remember your baptism with thanksgiving and joy.

PRAYERS
Prayers may include the following or other appropriate prayers. Others who are present may place a hand on the head or shoulder of the one who is celebrating the anniversary.

Let us pray.
Gracious God, we thank you for the new life you give us through holy baptism. Especially, we ask you to bless *name* on the anniversary of *her/his* baptism. Continue to strengthen *name* with the Holy Spirit, and increase in *her/him* your gifts of grace: the spirit of wisdom and understanding, the spirit of counsel and might, the spirit of knowledge and the fear of the Lord, the spirit of joy in your presence; through Jesus Christ, our Savior and Lord.
Amen.

Other prayers may be added. Those present may offer petitions and thanksgivings.

The prayers may conclude with the Lord's Prayer.

Our Father in heaven,
   hallowed be your name, your kingdom come,
   your will be done, on earth as in heaven.
Give us today our daily bread.
Forgive us our sins
   as we forgive those who sin against us.
Save us from the time of trial and deliver us from evil.
For the kingdom, the power, and the glory are yours,
   now and forever. Amen.

BLESSING
The order may conclude with this or another suitable blessing.

Almighty God, who gives us a new birth by water and the Holy Spirit and forgives us all our sins, strengthen us in all goodness and by the power of the Holy Spirit keep us in eternal life through Jesus Christ our Lord.
Amen.

The greeting of peace may be shared by all.

Other suggested readings for this service:
John 3:1-8: *Born again from above*
Romans 6:3-11: *Raised with Christ in baptism*
Galatians 3:26-28: *All are one in Christ*
Ephesians 4:1-6: *There is one body and one Spirit*
Colossians 1:11-13: *Claimed by Christ, heirs of light*
1 Peter 2:2-3: *Long for spiritual food*
1 Peter 2:9: *Chosen in baptism to tell about God*
Revelation 22:1-2: *The river of the water of life*

Prayers during Sickness and for Other Occasions

One who is sick or injured
O God of power and love, be present with *name*, that *her/his* weakness may be overcome and *her/his* strength restored; and that, *her/his* health being renewed, *she/he* may bless your holy name; through Jesus Christ, our Savior and Lord.

This prayer may be recited by a child, repeating brief phrases after the caregiver.
Gentle Jesus, stay beside me through this day [night]. Take away my pain. Keep me safe. Help me when I'm afraid. Make my body strong again and my heart glad. Thank you for your love that surrounds me.

Before a medical procedure or surgery
Almighty God, our heavenly Father, graciously protect *name* in *her/his* surgery. Fill *her/his* heart with confidence that, though *she/he* may be anxious, *she/he* may put *her/his* trust in you; through Jesus Christ our Lord.

After a medical procedure or surgery
Almighty and gracious God, we give you thanks that you have protected *name* during surgery. Enable *her/him* to trust in your goodness, to find comfort in your abiding presence, and to praise your holy name; through Jesus Christ our Lord.

Difficult choices regarding treatment
Lord Jesus, in the night before your suffering and death, you struggled with all you were about to encounter. Be with *name* [and *her/his* family] in this anxious moment as they face difficult choices about medical treatment, especially those that may involve suffering and pain. Through it all, Lord Jesus, be a strong companion and guide along the way, for your love's sake.

Grieving loss

God of all grace, we give you thanks because by his death our Savior Jesus Christ destroyed the power of death and by his resurrection he opened the kingdom of heaven to all believers. Make us certain that because he lives we shall live also, and that neither death nor life, nor things present nor things to come, will be able to separate us from your love in Christ Jesus our Lord, who lives and reigns with you and the Holy Spirit, one God, now and forever.

Mental illness

Mighty God, in Jesus Christ you deal with forces that trouble our minds and set us against ourselves. Give peace to those who are cast down, beset by anxiety, or torn by inner conflict. By your great might, drive from us the powers that shake confidence and shatter love. Bring us into the light of your truth, and give us your strong assurance that we are your beloved children in Jesus Christ our Lord.

Addiction, recovery

O Lord, mercifully regard your servant *name*, who is bound with the chains of addiction. Give *her/him* strength, that *she/he* may be freed from fear and guilt and be restored in you to the liberty of the children of God, now and forever.

Caregivers and others who support the sick

God, our refuge and strength, our present help in time of trouble, care for those who tend the needs of *name*. Strengthen them in body and spirit. Refresh them when weary; console them when anxious; comfort them in grief; and hearten them in discouragement. Be with us all, and give us peace at all times and in every way; through Christ our peace.

Restoration of health

O Lord, your compassions never fail and your mercies are new every morning. We give you thanks for giving our *sister/brother [name]* both relief from pain and hope of health renewed. Continue in *her/him* the good work you have begun; that *she/he*, daily increasing in bodily strength and rejoicing in your goodness, may so order *her/his* life and conduct that *she/he* may always think and do those things that please you; through Jesus Christ our Lord.

From *Evangelical Lutheran Worship Pastoral Care*, pp. 169–197

Waking Prayers

We give thanks to you, heavenly Father,
through Jesus Christ your dear Son,
that you have protected us through the night
from all harm and danger.
We ask that you would also protect us today
from sin and all evil,
so that our life and actions may please you.
Into your hands we commend ourselves:
our bodies, our souls, and all that is ours.
Let your holy angels be with us,
so that the wicked foe may have no power over us.
Amen.

Luther's morning prayer

Jesus, bright morning star,
show us your mercy.
(*See Revelation 22:16*)

Upon waking, one may make the sign of the cross and say:
In the name of the Father,
and of the Son,
and of the Holy Spirit. Amen.

or
The Sacred Three be over me,
the blessing of the Trinity.

A Simplified Form for Morning Prayer

OPENING

O Lord, open my lips,
and my mouth shall proclaim your praise.
Glory to the Father, and to the Son,
and to the Holy Spirit:
as it was in the beginning, is now,
and will be forever. Amen.
The alleluia is omitted during Lent.
[Alleluia.]

PSALMODY

The psalmody may begin with Psalm 63, Psalm 67, Psalm 95, Psalm 100, or another psalm appropriate for morning. Psalms provided in this book for each week may be used instead of or in addition to the psalms mentioned.

A time of silence follows.

A hymn may follow (see the suggested hymn for each day).

READINGS

One or more readings for each day may be selected from those provided in this book. The reading of scripture may be followed by silence for reflection.

The reflection may conclude with these or similar words.
Long ago God spoke to our ancestors
in many and various ways by the prophets,
but in these last days God has spoken to us by the Son.

GOSPEL CANTICLE

The song of Zechariah may be sung or said.

Blessed are you, Lord, the God of Israel,
you have come to your people and set them free.
You have raised up for us a mighty Savior,
born of the house of your servant David.
Through your holy prophets, you promised of old
to save us from our enemies,
from the hands of all who hate us,
to show mercy to our forebears,
and to remember your holy covenant.
This was the oath you swore to our father Abraham:
to set us free from the hands of our enemies,
free to worship you without fear,
holy and righteous before you, all the days of our life.
And you, child, shall be called the prophet of the Most High,
for you will go before the Lord to prepare the way,
to give God's people knowledge of salvation
by the forgiveness of their sins.
In the tender compassion of our God
the dawn from on high shall break upon us,
to shine on those who dwell in darkness and the shadow of death,
and to guide our feet into the way of peace.

PRAYERS

Various intercessions may be spoken at this time. The prayer provided in this book for each day may also be used.

The following prayer is especially appropriate for morning.
Almighty and everlasting God,
you have brought us in safety to this new day.
Preserve us with your mighty power,
that we may not fall into sin
nor be overcome in adversity.

In all we do, direct us to the fulfilling of your purpose;
through Jesus Christ our Lord.
Amen.

THE LORD'S PRAYER

Our Father in heaven,
  hallowed be your name,
  your kingdom come,
  your will be done, on earth as in heaven.
Give us today our daily bread.
Forgive us our sins
  as we forgive those who sin against us.
Save us from the time of trial
  and deliver us from evil.
For the kingdom, the power, and the glory are yours,
  now and forever. Amen.

BLESSING

Let us bless the Lord.
Thanks be to God.

Almighty God,
the Father, + the Son, and the Holy Spirit,
bless and preserve us.
Amen.

Additional materials for daily prayer are available in Evangelical Lutheran
Worship *(pp. 295–331) and may supplement this simple order.*

A Simplified Form for Evening Prayer

OPENING

Jesus Christ is the light of the world,
the light no darkness can overcome.
Stay with us, Lord, for it is evening,
and the day is almost over.
Let your light scatter the darkness
and illumine your church.

PSALMODY

The psalmody may begin with Psalm 141, Psalm 121, or another psalm appropriate for evening. Psalms provided in this book for each week may be used instead of or in addition to the psalms mentioned.

A time of silence follows.

A hymn may follow (see the suggested hymn for each day).

READINGS

One or more readings for each day may be selected from those provided in this book. The reading of scripture may be followed by silence for reflection.

The reflection may conclude with these or similar words.

Jesus said, I am the light of the world.
Whoever follows me will never walk in darkness.

GOSPEL CANTICLE

The song of Mary may be sung or said.

My soul proclaims the greatness of the Lord,
my spirit rejoices in God my Savior,
for you, Lord, have looked with favor on your lowly servant.
From this day all generations will call me blessed:
you, the Almighty, have done great things for me,
and holy is your name.
You have mercy on those who fear you,
from generation to generation.
You have shown strength with your arm
and scattered the proud in their conceit,
casting down the mighty from their thrones
and lifting up the lowly.
You have filled the hungry with good things
and sent the rich away empty.
You have come to the aid of your servant Israel,
to remember the promise of mercy,
the promise made to our forebears,
to Abraham and his children forever.

PRAYERS

Various intercessions may be spoken at this time. The prayer provided in this book for each day may also be used.

The following prayer is especially appropriate for evening.
We give thanks to you, heavenly Father,
through Jesus Christ your dear Son,
that you have graciously protected us today.
We ask you to forgive us all our sins, where we have done wrong,
and graciously to protect us tonight.
For into your hands we commend ourselves:
our bodies, our souls, and all that is ours.

Let your holy angels be with us,
so that the wicked foe may have no power over us.
Amen.

THE LORD'S PRAYER

Our Father in heaven,
 hallowed be your name,
 your kingdom come,
 your will be done, on earth as in heaven.
Give us today our daily bread.
Forgive us our sins
 as we forgive those who sin against us.
Save us from the time of trial
 and deliver us from evil.
For the kingdom, the power, and the glory are yours,
 now and forever. Amen.

BLESSING

Let us bless the Lord.
Thanks be to God.

The peace of God,
which surpasses all understanding,
keep our hearts and our minds in Christ Jesus.
Amen.

Additional materials for daily prayer are available in Evangelical Lutheran
Worship *(pp. 295–331) and may supplement this simple order.*

At Bedtime

Gracious God, we give you thanks for the day, especially for the good we were permitted to give and to receive; the day is now past and we commit it to you. We entrust to you the night; we rest securely, for you are our help, and you neither slumber nor sleep; through Jesus Christ our Lord. Amen.

Night Prayers with Children

Now I lay me down to sleep,
I pray the Lord my soul to keep.
God's love stay with me through the night
and keep me safe till morning light.

Lord, keep us safe this night,
secure from all our fears.
May angels guard us while we sleep,
till morning light appears.

A parent or caregiver may trace the cross on the child's forehead or heart and say one of these blessings:
God the Father, Son, and Holy Spirit watch over you.

May God protect you through the night.

May the Lord Jesus keep you in his love.

Suggestions for guiding your reflection on each day's scripture texts

God's word for me this day is:

God's word will shape my day by:

I will share God's word with others through:

My prayers today will include:
- The church universal, its ministry, and the mission of the gospel
- The well-being of creation
- Peace and justice in the world, the nations and those in authority, the community
- The poor, oppressed, sick, bereaved, lonely
- All who suffer in body, mind, or spirit
- Special concerns

CPSIA information can be obtained at www.ICGtesting.com
Printed in the USA
BVOW012030261212

309166BV00002B/2/P